First Edition

undressed

Gem Dentith

© 2025 Gem Dentith

All rights reserved. No part of this publication may be reproduced, distributed, or transmitted in any form or by any means, including photocopying, recording, or other electronic or mechanical methods, without the prior written permission of the publisher, except in the case of brief quotations embodied in critical reviews and certain other noncommercial uses permitted by copyright law.

ISBN: 978-1-5262-1051-7 (hardcover)
ISBN: 978-1-5262-1050-0 (paperback)
ISBN: 978-1-0369-6866-3 (kindle)

For enquiries regarding permissions, please contact:
Email: gem@gemdentith.com

Disclaimer
The views, thoughts, and opinions expressed in this book are solely those of the author. This book is intended for informational, educational and inspirational purposes only. It does not constitute professional, legal, medical, or psychological advice. Gem Dentith disclaim any liability for any errors, omissions, or consequences arising from the use or interpretation of the content. Readers should seek appropriate guidance where necessary.

Dedication

To my beloved sisters, mother, nieces, nan, aunts, friends, and darling daughters. To the many people I have wanted to tell how powerful you are, but couldn't find the words during our interactions. Here are the words I wanted to say.

And to you, my love. You may never read this, but it was written with you in the undertow. In the quiet between sentences. In the spaces we never reached with words. Some stories teach through presence. Others through absence. You were both. And some part of me always knew that we were undressing, even when we didn't know how.

CONTENTS

Foreword By Lee Holden

Author's Foreword

Prologue

Letter to the Reader

How to Read This Book

Introduction

Part One: undress

    1. The Seduction

    2. Happiness Whore Habit

    3. Quick Fix Lie

    4. Branded of Worth

    5. Stripping the Roles

    6. The Body Doesn't Lie

    7. Undressing Survival

    8. Turning Inward

Part Two: awaken

9. Penthouse of Perception
10. Getting Turned On
11. Jewelled
12. The Threshold
13. Being Naked
14. Surrender to Flow
15. Sacred Self-Care

Part Three: align

16. Embodiment
17. Purpose
18. The Map
19. Living Document
20. Aligned Action
21. Living Undressed
22. 2:50 A.M.

Stay in Touch

About the Author

Undressed

A full-body awakening. A sacred stripping of everything that you were never meant to wear.

It begins subtly, a button slips free without you noticing, a seam splits, and a collar that once felt crisp becomes a chokehold. Until one day, the fabric of your survival self-pools at your feet. Representing a life that no longer belongs to you.

The roles. The rules. The rewards no longer fit. But this is not a collapse. Not even slightly. You're unlayering and returning to your original essence.

Through raw storytelling, soul-deep truths, and a three-phase method that fuses nervous system mastery with energetic alignment, these pages guide you back to the self beneath the performance. Back to the woman who never needed to perfect herself to be loved. To the one who never had to carry it all to be worthy.

These pages will undress you. Peeling back patterns and stories until only the real remains: magnetic, aligned, and alive.

Underneath what the world told you that you had to be, there is a version of you who speaks without performing, stands without defending, and lives without pretending. *That* woman? She sparkles with unprecedented power.

This is living undressed.

FOREWORD

by Lee Holden

Qi Gong Master & Author of Slow and 7 Minutes of Magic

There are moments when the soul decides it's time to wake up. Sometimes that awakening arrives gently, through quiet intuition. Other times, it appears suddenly through collapse: burnout, grief, or the realization that the life you've built no longer fits the person you've become.

Gem shares her awakening with unflinching honesty, a journey familiar to anyone who has questioned, "Is this all there is?" or whispered, "I cannot keep living this way."

What makes these pages different is the energetic depth. Not mindset or motivation, but energy itself. How it moves through your body, gets stuck in patterns, and how to shift it so your outer life aligns with your inner truth.

Gem is a rare kind of guide. She doesn't teach from a pedestal. She teaches from lived experience. She has walked through the fires of burnout, spiritual disconnection, and societal pressure, and emerged with a method that is both soulful and grounded.

The Undressed Method: a framework for remembering who you truly are. Through her three-part arc of Undress, Awaken, and Align, you'll be invited to shed what no longer serves, reconnect with your essential self, and begin living in alignment with your purpose.

Read these pages slowly. Let them move through you. Let

them open something ancient within you that's ready to return.

Because, as Gem so clearly reminds us, something within you has always known the way home.

AUTHOR'S FOREWORD

A Letter From The Undressed Self

I once honestly believed that something was wrong with me. On paper, I had everything: career, accomplishments, family, and a reputation for being the one who always managed to hold it together. Behind the scenes, though, I was slowly unravelling.

After years of striving, I burned out physically, emotionally, and spiritually. The question haunted me: 'Why is life so hard when I've done everything right?'

I had been chasing fool's gold: status, validation, and success, believing that if I achieved more, looked perfect, held it together, I'd finally feel safe and whole. Instead, I felt emptier.

So I started writing. Not to create a book, but to make sense of the pain. And as words poured out, something else also emerged. A thread. A truth. A whisper: *You're not broken. You're undressing.*

I've always had a gift for seeing patterns across systems, behaviors, relationships, and energy. I used to apply it to corporate structures. But when I turned that lens inward, I found the deepest pattern of all: the one I'd been living unconsciously, and the one I was ready to rewrite.

My body broke before my mind caught up and admitted

the truth. This wasn't failure; it was the body's wisdom. The body knew first that I was out of alignment with my path. It is the oracle that had to protest, so loudly that there was an unignorable call back to my path.

I didn't want to write another polished self-help book. I wanted the real deal. The messy, magical, inconvenient truth of waking inside a life that no longer fits.

These pages are my reclamation. The framework that found me in my unravelling and asked me to make me whole again. I was training to be a coach, delving into yoga and energy work, learning from multiple paths, but something was still missing. There was no integration point. No map.

What you're reading now is the map. A sacred arc through three energetic stages: **Undress** (unlayering what no longer serves), **Awaken** (excavating the jewels hidden within), and **Align** (embodying that truth in the world). The Undressed Method ®.

I offer these pages as a reflection of what's possible when you stop chasing for your worth and start excavating your true brilliance. Of what happens when you take off the world's expectations and return to the original self of who you really are.

If you've been performing for scraps of love, chasing validation, or holding it all together while quietly falling apart, these pages are also your excavation.

May my words hold you through the unravelling and remind you that your truth was never lost, only buried.

With all my heart, undressing beside you.

Gem

PROLOGUE

The Collapse That Undressed Me

There was nothing at all unusual about that morning. I dropped off my seven-year-old at the childminder's, five months pregnant, wrapped in my black thigh-length military-cut wool coat. I was going through the motions, preparing for another day of high-pressure government meetings and stakeholder management, which meant firefighting and navigating politics with a poised smile and an overloaded calendar. I had done this hundreds of times. Suit up. Show up. Deliver. Except that morning, something inside me had missed the memo.

That morning was crisp with autumn light, and everything looked as it always did: busy commuters dashing for trains, loud tannoy announcements, and bored-looking ticket sales staff. I boarded the train with my usual calm. Laptop bag in hand, coat buttoned, and my schedule running through my mind. But as the carriage rolled forward, I sensed, instinctively, that something wasn't right. It started with a sharp wave of nausea. Heat was climbing the back of my neck, flooding my face until my skin flushed as though sunburned. My breath became shallow, while sweat gathered beneath my shirt, clammy against my skin.

I gripped the pole. Two more stops to Blackfriars, I told myself, repeating it like a quiet mantra, as if the words alone could steady me. My mind scrambled to rationalise what was going on with me, I thought it could be pregnancy hormones or maybe the vitamins I'd downed in a rush before leaving. I was running through my morning routine, looking for any clues that might explain a cause.

Feeling intensely hot, I peeled off my coat in a panic, but now my vision started to blur. It was at this point that instinct pivoted me from denial that anything was wrong to moving into survival mode, knowing I was not just about me; I had to protect my unborn child. And as someone who had once served on the frontline of the emergency services, I knew this moment well, just never from the inside.

As my vision started to close in, I threw my body sideways to protect my baby bump from hitting a seat at the front of the carriage to save myself from collapsing onto the floor. Then everything went black. Complete nothingness, as though the world itself had been switched off.

I'm not sure how long I was out for, but somewhere in my mind, the sounds of train doors beeping snapped me back into waking consciousness and shot me bolt right. I was drenched in sweat and disoriented, but I managed to get out onto the platform, trying to look normal, but my heart was racing, my legs felt like they were trembling, and my mind was totally blank. Not in a peaceful way. It was gone.

That morning, I stood on the platform, and I froze. Unsure if I should attempt the office, unsure if I should call my partner, unsure what this meant going forward. I froze because I didn't want to admit the truth that pushing on isn't strength. This is survival. And it's killing me.

We imagine burnout as a dramatic breakdown, a cry for help. But sometimes burnout just whispers to you. Hiding behind competence and wearing the face of "I'm fine." It shows up as color-coded calendars, unread messages, chest-deep resentment, and endless to-do lists.

At the time, I was leading change communications for a major central government technology transformation. High-stakes and politically sensitive, I was the bridge between bureaucracy and humanity, fielding directors, pacifying stakeholders, solving conflicts, running messaging strategies, and being the calm one in every storm. At the same time, I was carrying a child, navigating the fragile beginnings of a new relationship, and living in a body whose nervous system was permanently locked in fight-or-flight, jammed into survival mode as if the off-switch no longer existed.

The truth is, there was no space for me. There hadn't been for years. Or so I'd thought. People relied on me, and my role was to hold it all together. I had become fluent in the language of performance, delivering at the expense of my own well-being. I had trained myself to ignore the whispers of fatigue, the signals of depletion, and the desire to rest. That is, until my body decided it was done being ignored. *If you won't stop, I will.*

As I stood on that platform, trembling and stunned, a strange kind of awareness cut through the fog. Not the spiritual kind. The sarcastic kind. Britney Spears started playing in my head, "Oops, I did it again." I actually laughed. Not because it was funny, but because it was ridiculous. I had done it again. I had pushed too far. Ignored the signals and kept moving when life had been begging me to pause.

There's a kind of dark humor that arrives when you finally see how far you've wandered from yourself. It isn't pretty, and it isn't polite. It's the laugh that bursts out at a funeral, the one that makes no sense to anyone else, but in your bones feels like truth. That laugh was the first honest breath I'd taken in months.

That morning wasn't a failure. It wasn't some dramatic collapse. It was a tearing, the moment the illusion ripped clean apart, and with it the performance I'd been clinging to. What rushed in wasn't fear, but honesty. A raw, undeniable honesty that left no place to hide.

You may not have fainted on a train, but I know you've had

your own version of collapse. A moment where your body or your life whispered, *'this is not it.'* You might be having it right now. And if you are, good. It means you're ready.

Welcome to Undressed.

LETTER TO THE READER

You don't need another self-help book. You've tried all the courses, coaches, breathwork, and plant medicine journeys. You've optimized, journaled, surrendered, healed, and hustled, but despite it all, that quiet ache remains. And it's an emptiness that your biggest achievements can't fill.

Welcome. This path isn't about trying to become better, though you will become better. This is about becoming real. You've just been building on the wrong blueprint. One that never came in your size.

I want this book to be a mirror for you, the woman who looks fine (more than fine), but feels fragmented. Take it as your permission slip to stop striving and start making your way home. It's not about adding more but unlayering what was never for you in the first place.

Inside these pages, you'll find stories, teachings, and practices designed to help you excavate the jewels within: your worth, your clarity, your love, your power, and your purpose.

Read slowly. Let the words and energy land in your body. Notice what stirs, what softens, and what stings.

This will be a journey to remember.

HOW TO READ THIS BOOK

I wrote this book for the whole of you. There's a theory for the conceptual mind that loves to analyze. You'll find exercises for the creative mind. And most importantly, there are invitations for your body, breath, nervous system, and your deep inner knowing within these pages, too.

These invitations will arrive as questions, meditations, awareness prompts, and truth triggers. Each is designed to bring you back to yourself. Not to teach you anything you don't know, but to help you remember what you've always felt beneath the noise.

To Deepen Your Experience:

- Download the Undressed Playbook, where you will find all the deep inner work exercises and audio meditations that accompany this book.

Go to **https://www.gemdentith.com/playbook** to download your free companion guide.

Who This Book Is For

The high-functioning, soft-hearted women who look like they've got it all together. The ones who've achieved, created, and contributed, yet still sense a subtle emptiness. You may be a driven professional, an exhausted homemaker, an entrepreneur, or someone with influence and freedom, but beneath it all, you're tired of striving, and your soul is tired.

You've tried it all: courses, healers, retreats, plant medicine, nervous system hacks. Yet you still know that something's missing.

If you've been chasing something in the world, believing it will finally make you enough, these pages are for you.

The magic comes through realization, through insight, and remembrance.

It took me more than twenty years of relentless seeking to realize what I now share with you. That journey has ended for me. My nervous system is softer, my joy is deeper, and my truth is louder. I finally stopped searching and started being.

How to Navigate This Journey

Undressed is a rebirth manual at its core, a full deconstruction and reconstruction of the self.

The only requirements here are an open, curious mind and a heart willing to receive.

It builds in three distinct phases:

Undress – strip away the masks, roles, and survival habits.
Awaken – reconnect with your inner self, excavate
 and activate your inner jewels.
Align – live your life in congruence with that truth, walking your life assignment every day.

Embracing Realizations: A Deeper Way to Learn

Most of us were taught to learn by memorizing, striving, and comparing. But there is another kind of learning that goes much deeper. It happens when something shifts in your awareness and in your body, not just your brain. When you truly see something new, your entire perspective rearranges itself.

That kind of learning, the kind that reshapes you from the inside out, can't be handed down like a textbook or memorised like a manual. It isn't something another voice can drill into you. It only arrives when your own sight clears, when the fog lifts, and you finally see what was there all along.

These pages are an invitation into that kind of learning. An insight, inner sight, and a remembering that comes unquestionably inside your mind and is alive inside your own body.

What Success Will Look Like

On the other side of this journey, you'll stop wasting time, energy, and money chasing the next big thing. You'll stop outsourcing your wholeness to a future version of you who always seems just out of reach. Instead, you'll begin living from a deeper place. A quiet, steady knowing that your original self came here with a purpose, and you're finally ready to honor your assignment.

You'll remember that the life you once thought was only available to other people, the spacious, magnetic, aligned kind of life, is yours too.

You don't have to quit your job, change partners, renounce all pleasure, or meditate for eight hours a day. You don't need to numb your longings or bypass your desires. You simply need to stop coping and come home to yourself.

When you shift, everything shifts.

Your health transforms. You release the stress-fueled habits and begin working *with* your body instead of against it. Energy rises. Sleep deepens, and your nervous system softens.

Your relationships evolve. You attract deeper, safer connections and let go of what drains you. Love becomes rooted in truth instead of transaction.

Your work becomes an extension of your natural design. No more dreading Monday mornings. You begin to lead, create, and contribute in ways that light you up and serve something greater.

INTRODUCTION

"What if your true self isn't waiting to be improved, but undressed?"
— Your Higher Self

When I was little, I was always doing one of three things. I was either on a stage, prancing around the living room, desperate to entertain and express myself. Naked, with my mum constantly reminding me, "Gemma, put some clothes on!" Or I was staring at my mum's Swarovski crystals, utterly mesmerized by their beauty. Once, when I was five, I even stole one and took it to school. I would talk to it, convinced it held a secret kind of power.

I didn't know it then, but those three things: (authentic expression, nakedness, and crystals) were the prophecy of my life. Hints of the work I was born to do, but I didn't yet have the language to understand it.

Now, don't worry, I'm not suggesting we should all wander through life stark naked, wearing nothing but our family jewels and a Swarovski crystal or two. What I am saying is: remember that freedom? The freedom of childhood. The freedom of bare skin against grass, of laughter spilling out without asking permission, of twirling in your own strange costumes without caring who was watching. The freedom to be alive, unfiltered, and to feel utterly held by life itself.

As a child, I believed it was the crystals that held the magic, tiny prisms catching the light, treasures I thought could keep me safe. I clutched them like talismans, convinced they were the source. But as a woman, I discovered the truth: the jewels were always inside me. My real power was never in the diamonds I could hold, but in the essence I only needed to remember.

Like most women, I forgot. Instead, I learned to cover up, perform for applause, and trade naked power for approval. I people-pleased, shrank, climbed higher, and felt emptier with each and every push.

By my early thirties, I was burned out. Totally exhausted, completely disconnected from myself and the wonders of life, and surviving on caffeine. I was chasing everything I thought would finally make me feel whole, but it was just fake promises, leaving me emptier than a relationship built on potential that never becomes reality. Just a story you once told yourself about them in your head.

I made it my quest to undress the illusions. I had to undress the perfectionism, the endless certificates I collected as if another qualification might finally make me enough, and one of the other things that always bit hard was the pedestals I put my partners on. I had to undress the identities and the "maybe life will get better, they'll change, or perhaps I just need to be more" statements that had kept me trapped for so long. I had to undress the belief that without looking like I'd just walked out of a photoshoot, without the men, without the certificates, without the external stamps of approval, I wasn't enough.

But in that stripping back, I rediscovered what I'd always known instinctively as a child: that real power is found when you are naked and unattached. Power that doesn't come from letters after your name or papers on your wall. Power that is unadorned and already mine. The jewels I'd been searching for in my mum's crystal cabinet were inside me the whole time. And they are inside you, too.

A New Soul Is Born

It's 2:50 a.m., and cries echo through the delivery ward. A

new baby girl has just entered the world. Her parents exhale, relief giving way to joy, as they lock eyes and share silent words. First come the instinctive thoughts: is she breathing, is she healthy? Then the bigger one slips in quietly, almost too big to hold: Who will she become?

This is how it all begins.

You arrive pure. Bare and Unburdened. A perfect presence wrapped in soft skin, where you're more soul than self. There you are, wrapped lovingly in your parents' arms, with no expectations. No worldly identity yet. Just the being.

But life doesn't leave you undressed for long. Slowly and silently, you begin to absorb the world around you. Innocently at first, it's the beliefs of your parents. Then, the tone in a teacher's voice. The unspoken rules of what makes you lovable or not. You learn to smile on cue, strive for approval, and perform for safety.

By the time you're six or seven, you're no longer just you. You've already started becoming someone else's version of who you're meant to be. This is when the rules slip in, quietly at first: be good, be clever, be what makes them smile. You learn how to shape-shift and how to read a room before you even know how to spell the words. You learn how to bend yourself to be loved, to succeed, to survive. You get praised for fitting in, for carrying the weight of expectation, and so you keep doing it.

And somewhere in the middle of all that pleasing and proving, you lose touch with the still, sacred knowing that once lived inside your skin jacket. That raw, wordless essence that didn't need to perform to be worthy. You forget its hum and begin chasing worth outside yourself, always searching, never finding, always believing the next teacher's gold star will finally make you safe and whole.

Fast forward. You're grown now. You think you've made it. You've built a life: you have the career, the partner, maybe even children. And from the outside, it looks full and enviable. The boxes from your list are ticked, and you could say, the picture is complete.

But inside, something else stirs. A whisper that won't leave you alone. A heaviness that settles in your chest at night when the house is finally quiet. A weariness that no holiday or promotion seems to shake. And underneath it all, a secret sense of disconnection; not from your job or your family but from yourself, and the very current of life itself. It's as if you've been swimming hard to keep afloat, of all everyone's needs, but you no longer feel the river carrying you.

At this stage of life, you might be performing well, but you know you're not present. The lights are on, but the real you is not home.

And no wonder. We're not just wearing heavy layers. We're dragging clunky and overstuffed suitcases full of old attachments and stories behind us, with who we're supposed to be. Suitcases crammed with striving and shame, with over-functioning and self-abandonment, with identities we never consciously chose but somehow agreed to carry. And all the while, our original self is somewhere underneath it all, covered over by these accumulated stories and survival strategies, left gasping for air. Waiting for the moment you finally set the luggage down, and remember who you are without it.

The Dance of the Selves

One of my first realizations was that life is experienced as a dance. Not a straight line, not a fixed path, but a rhythm. The constant movement of remembering we are a soul, then forgetting we are a soul. Back and forth, in and out, like stepping onto the floor and losing yourself in the music, only to stumble and find you are counting steps again.

At times, it can feel as though there are two of you, and I don't mean in a clinical sense, but in that quiet inner tug-of-war between your true self and the version of you the world expects you to be. There is the you who is weighed down by fear, exhaustion, and striving, the dressed self. And there is the you that is light, clear, and connected, the undressed self. But in truth, there is only one you, expressed in different ways depending on whether your soul is shining through or being covered over.

The dressed self is the one you probably know most intimately. It is the self that suffers, a condition known to be universal across cultures and timelines. The way I have come to understand it is this: suffering arises when your soul is buried beneath too many layers.

Imagine putting on outfit after outfit, jacket over jacket, each one stitched from other people's expectations, until the weight of them bends your spine over and the heat inside makes it hard to breathe. That is what suffering is. I'd like to reframe suffering as a sign. A symptom, or a signal that you are carrying too many layers. That you have forgotten the freedom of being undressed.

The dressed self isn't inherently "bad," and the undressed self isn't inherently "good." Both create ripples. One brings ripples of fear, depletion, and disconnection. The other brings ripples of clarity, vitality, and peace. What I know to be true is that the quality of your life, your health, fulfillment, relationships, and peace depend on which self you choose to live from most of the time.

Once you see clearly that there are two expressions within you, two paths to choose, you realize you're not bound to the self that suffers. You can choose to walk a path of presence, peace, and profound self-remembrance at any time, and that's exactly what I intend to guide you to do.

The true dance of life is the journey from the survival self to the universal Self. It's not linear, and no one can walk it for you. But one day, if the weight of suffering becomes too heavy, you'll feel the sacred tug that you need to find your way back to the more expansive expression of you.

If you're lucky, that tug may already have arrived. It might have come through heartbreak, illness, collapse, or in a quiet breakdown that no one else has witnessed but you. Or it may arrive like lightning in a sudden clarity that can't be ignored. Either way, these moments are invitations. Nudges from the universe to begin undressing all that was never really you.

When you do, you'll unfasten the stories, patterns, and identities that have kept your true self hidden until you're standing naked once more, not in the helpless, newborn nakedness of your first breath, but in the grounded, magnetic, aligned nakedness of a woman who has fully landed in herself.

This is the sacred transition of the selves. We're going to strip away the false, reclaim the brilliance of who you are, and embody your most connected, purpose-led, limitless self.

Then, even when you forget (which you will), you'll always know how to return.

The Transformation: Who You Become When You Undress

If you're anything like I was, you've been surviving in stilettos, succeeding in overdrive, and smiling through pressure for so long that it's started to feel like that's just how it needs to be if you want to succeed. But when you've outperformed and over-delivered on expectations at some point, you arrive at a place where you know that something deeply essential must be missing.

But what if more success was never what you needed? What if it were simply less of what you're not? And what if the doorway has always been through subtraction? Because less is not emptiness. Less is more spacious. Less is where your soul can finally be known.

Undressed isn't an improvement plan. It's your return. Back to the woman beneath the roles, the body beneath the performance, and to the breath behind the chase.

But what happens when you finally take it all off?

Your Mind Becomes Free

You stop identifying with the noise and the busyness. The storylines lose their grip. The static softens. Where there was once spiraling, there's clarity. Where there was performance, there was peace.

Your Emotions Stabilize

You realize you've been 'feeling your thinking,' not the truth. Your emotions don't flood you anymore; instead, they flow through you. You become a woman who can feel deeply without collapsing and who can respond wisely rather than react. You become the woman who still feels, expresses, holds spaces for others, but no longer outsources her worth to others, and whose heart is capable of staying soft, open, and ready to receive what she deserves.

You Begin Living

The chase ends. You stop managing life like it's a living room you constantly need to rearrange, hoping it will finally feel right. You realize your outer world was never the cause of your experience. It's always been the reflection of your inner world. So you don't wait for the right time or the right person anymore, and you don't try to fix them or wait for permission. You become a fully expressed, aligned version of you, living with clarity and true expression.

You Reconnect With the Real You

You stop hiding behind the curated version of yourself and drop the filters. You drop the pressure and the exhausting need to impress, too. And suddenly, there you are. Familiar, fierce, and finally free.

You Feel Connected to Something Greater

You remember what was always true: that you were never meant to do this alone. You reconnect to something larger than you. You don't soften because you're weak. You soften because you're safe and you trust life again.

Your Health Improves

Your body finally exhales. Your nervous system resets, and your digestion returns to normal. Your hormones harmonize, and your sleep deepens. You stop outsourcing vitality and you start generating it from within yourself. And you don't punish your body anymore. Instead, you partner with it.

What It Really Means to Be Undressed

Being undressed is less about removing fabric and more about removing distortion. To be undressed is to return to the place where everything in you says, *Here I am, let's go.*

It's the moment your mind stops spinning, your energy stops scattering, and your mission stops waiting; you're no longer performing for belonging, proving your worth, or pretending to be 'fine.' You're not asking for permission.

You're not interested in adrenaline, the temporary high of a peak moment, or the dopamine hit of one more achievement. You drop into the quiet, sovereign power of knowing who you are and finally living like you're worth it.

To be undressed is to strip the static, the distortion, and everything that blocks the clear signal of who you really are, so you can hear your real self again and tune back into the original frequency of your soul. This includes the timelines you didn't choose and the roles that robbed your radiance. You undress not to reveal your body, but to reclaim your essence. When a woman stops shape-shifting, self-surveilling, and starts self-honoring, her presence sharpens. Her 'Yes' becomes sacred, and her 'No' becomes a holy boundary. She no longer moves under pressure. She moves from a quiet inner power. And her energy doesn't scream attention; it is felt.

This isn't only a change in how you conceptually see yourself; it's a deep, cellular one. You know who you are, what you want, and what you're here for. And most importantly, what you're no longer available for. This is because you're too busy living your purpose. When you're living undressed, you're not just in alignment. You *are* the alignment. Magnetic, grounded, and guided by something deeper than logic.

When you're undressed, your entire life starts to orbit the center of who you actually are, instead of who you've been performing to be. Your relationships. Your revenue. Your rest. They all recalibrate.

You stop outsourcing your worth. You stop chasing wholeness. You stop asking the world to mirror back what only you can claim.

You become unbound. No longer tethered to titles or timelines that don't reflect your truth. You become unedited. No longer dimming the very power that makes you magnetic. You become unstoppable. Not because the world gets easier, but because you're no longer in your own way.

You're not only a better version of you, you are the real you. Fully expressed. Fully turned on. Fully present.

You feel in your bones that it's safe to simply be you. To drop the performance and to stop trying to be everything to everyone else, and finally become everything to yourself.

PART ONE:
UNDRESS
UNDRESS
UNDRESS
UNDRESS

The Striptease

Chapter 1:
The Seduction
When Life Whispers 'This Isn't It'

In the seductive pursuit of happiness, we become ensnared by the illusions of external validation and material gain. We're enticed by society's promises that success, wealth, and acclaim will bring us the fulfillment we seek. Yet, in our relentless chase, we risk losing sight of our true essence. We must awaken to the seduction, step back from the intoxicating allure, and rediscover that the path to lasting happiness lies not in the external world, but in the depths of our own being. Only then can we free ourselves from the grip of the seduction and embark on a journey towards authentic joy and inner fulfillment.

— Deepak Chopra

Every high-achieving woman eventually meets this moment: the applause fades, the to-do list is complete, and the mirror reflects someone who's ticked every box. Except the one that matters. The one that asks if she's truly living on purpose.

If she were to take an honest inventory of her life, you would see that the accolades have been earned. Life has been built, and the dreams have been achieved. *And yet, beneath it all, there's a quiet knowing as something in her whispers: I'm made for more.*

This moment rarely arrives in the middle of a crisis. It lands in the silence after success. When the house is bought, the job title is achieved, and the love is secured. And the feeling sets in that what you've built isn't quite the end. A quiet voice insists: No. *This isn't it. This isn't me anymore. This isn't the life I came here to live.*

Somehow, no matter how beautiful or valuable, nothing you see on the outside reflects the you inside. You are much more powerful than you know. The you hidden from sight, the you that you secretly know yourself to be. And no matter how much you try to silence that whisper, it doesn't go away. It just gets louder. And eventually, if you don't move towards expansion and keep yourself small as a way of keeping with the status quo and resisting the very change that life wants you to take, it shows up as resistance, stress, or even complete collapse.

That inner knowing that you are made for more sets you off on a search. *If not this, then what?* But the lack of clarity creates a low hum of dissatisfaction, a tension that never quite lets you rest. At first, it begins innocently with a hunger to grow, evolve, and become someone bigger than your past. But over time, that drive morphs into a quiet, relentless addiction.

You start to perform and over-function. You strive not from joy, but from fear of staying still. Not the fear of being unworthy, but the fear of leaving your true potential untapped. The fear of dying with your music still inside you, that's what drives you, and it's not wrong; it's the universe also saying that it wants you to expand, but you miss that message, and instead of moving with the aligned clarity of where you are going, you move frantically in different directions without focus. And that's the seduction's trap: believing your brilliance will be found in doing more, when in truth the doing only distracts you. You've been chasing sparkles without substance. The whisper you keep hearing is the reminder that you're mining in the wrong cave.

The clarity you long for will never come from busyness. It comes when you undress first, when you strip back the noise, the masks and distractions, and align with your true nature. Only then can your potential finally shine and your energy be directed as it was always meant to.

The Decision I Made at Fourteen

At fourteen, I started to see the world very differently. While others seemed content with what they had, I felt a rising frustration. Why were they surrendering to a life that looked so small? Watching people settle stirred something fierce in me. I didn't want to accept a life I hadn't consciously chosen. I wanted out.

What I didn't realize then was that the true escape would not come from leaving, but from unlearning everything I thought would make me happy.

With no mentors, no roadmap, and only the attention of men who wanted something else entirely, I anchored into the only thing I could control: my work ethic. I got up at six in the morning that summer to start a job at a downtown café. Fourteen years old. Living on a council estate. Raised by a single mother. I had already decided: as much as I loved my mother, what she had done for me and my three sisters, I would not be the girl who got pregnant at sixteen and queued for a housing allowance. I saw the suffering that came with this way of life. I was determined; I made an oath to myself, for the sake of my children and my children's children, I was going to rewrite the script.

There was a fire in me. Raw, relentless, and deeply inconvenient to the expectations around me. I was not content being another system statistic. I knew my mother was made for more. I saw it in her and the others around her; all I could see was potential, but I was confused as to why they couldn't see it in themselves. I believed the world didn't need more rule-followers; it needed people who could rise beyond their postcode, their upbringing, and their limitations. And while I adored my family, who were sharp, funny, and warm, they hadn't broken free from the hand life had dealt them. But I decided I would.

Every raised eyebrow and every "just settle down" comment only added fuel to the furnace. I used it all. I was determined to win. Exams, solo sports, jobs; I stayed in forward motion. Always improving. Never still.

Self-improvement became my religion. At first, it seemed noble. Hard work, ambition, and achievement. But beneath it was a hollow truth I couldn't shake: I believed *more* would make me happy. More money. More qualifications. More validation. More beauty. More of everything. But no matter how much more I got, nothing filled the void.

That quiet discontent became my baseline. And this is the seed of what I now call the Happiness Whore Habit.

For me, it showed up as an obsession with being better, looking better, and achieving more.

My biggest fear was being trapped in a life where I had to rely on the state to feed my kids. Where I'm from, benefits weren't taboo. They were a rite of passage. But I knew deep down that was not going to be my story. I made a vow within myself, and I kept it.

For the next two decades, I threw myself into performance, perfection, and professional polish.

I chased external approval like it was oxygen. If I looked the part, played the part, lived in the right area, and said the right things, then maybe, just maybe, I would finally feel like I mattered. I never let anyone look down their nose at me. Their excrement didn't smell any sweeter than mine.

In my twenties, validation became my drug of choice, and I craved it most from the one person who had never given it to me: my dad. The silent ache of his absence echoed in every milestone. Maybe if I achieved enough, he would notice. Maybe he would say, "Gemma, I'm proud of you." He never did. So I just kept climbing.

Eventually, I became addicted to the high of achievement. My life became a carousel of deadlines, wins, and the constant hustle to prove my worth. But beneath the curated perfection was a growing disconnection from my body, my truth, and myself.

The World Hands Us a Ladder

We live in a world that rewards performance. It praises the polished image and crowns those who deliver more than is humanly sustainable, and where achievement becomes the currency for self-worth.

Striving isn't the enemy. But when striving becomes your identity, it steals from the very self you're striving for.

At first, success feels intoxicating. The promotion. The new apartment. The praise. You feel seen, wanted, and enough. But that feeling is fleeting, so you chase it again. And again. And again. Before long, you're running on fumes, chasing a finish line that keeps moving.

Now, for a moment, just pause here and ask yourself, where in your own life have you chased money, love, titles, or approval, only to feel emptier after the high faded?

Real fulfillment comes when your outer life reflects your inner brilliance.

And you can't buy or build your way into that kind of alignment. You have to strip for it.

Society feeds this illusion that more equals better. But the more you chase what's not aligned, the further you drift from yourself. And the further you drift from yourself, the louder the emptiness becomes.

The world hands us a ladder and says, "Climb this, and you'll be happy." So we do. But what happens when we reach the top and realize it was the wrong ladder all along? That we've exhausted ourselves in pursuit of a life that doesn't actually feed our souls at all?

When you're chasing the image of success, the postcode, the title, the shiny exterior, it's rarely because you're satisfied. It's usually because you're quietly discontent, like being at a garden party with a leaking tap dripping behind someone's shoulder. You can't focus on the person because your attention is locked on what's not right: that distracting dripping tap behind them. That constant low-grade hum of dissatisfaction keeps you distracted and, moving, tricking you into thinking more of something will fix it.

If you're climbing the wrong ladder, it doesn't matter how high you go. You're still going in the wrong direction.

When you're on the wrong path, the destination doesn't exist. There's no finish line where happiness waits. I promise that you won't find a pot of gold at the end of the rainbow, just another rainbow to climb.

The present is the only place where true bliss and joy exist. So if you're not enjoying the now, it's time to ask why. Often, the answer is internal: your thinking, your mindset, your state. An attachment to a thought, story, outcome, or situation or person is disturbing your peace, and until you examine that, no amount of external success will ever be enough.

The Pivot

You've been seeking happiness the wrong way. You've future-batted it. Pushed it out three, five, ten years. *When the business is built, when the body is toned, when the family is thriving, then I'll be happy.* But it never arrives. Because you're not designed to feel happy "one day." You're meant to experience joy now.

So what do you do? You go inward. You strip away the noise and return to the qualities of your natural state. You reconnect with your real self, the one beneath the striving, the proving, the pretending. And once you do, everything else becomes clearer. You start putting your energy into people, projects, and places that align with your true essence.

This inner journey isn't a detour. It's the most practical recalibration you can take. Think of it as a pit stop or a systems check. You wouldn't drive an F1 car through a championship race without stopping to change tires and refuel. Why do you keep running your life without pausing to ask, 'Am I still on the right track?'

Ask yourself:

- What truly matters to me?
- What does success look like if I'm in line with my deeper design, not society's?
- Am I building a life that's actually mine?

Because if your current life doesn't make you want to jump out of bed in the morning, something's off. That's your litmus test.

The good news: getting back to your true self is easier

than you think. Your natural baseline is joy. Not the fleeting dopamine of achievement, but the grounded, consistent joy of being in alignment with your truth. Once you remove what's blocking that: old wounds, outdated beliefs, subconscious habits, then you'll tap into a fire that's always been there.

That is when you'll discover your true gifts. Your purpose. Your actual path. And it will feel so clear and alive, you'll stop asking whether you're on the right track because you'll *know*.

For me, the hunger to achieve was never really about goals. It was about filling the void. A void I now recognize as childhood grief and shame. The kind that comes from growing up without a father figure. That silent ache shaped me. I used overachievement to prove I was worthy of love, attention, and approval.

But eventually, I got tired of the chase. I let go of the need to impress him, myself, or the world. I began to soften. To question. To rediscover who I really was. And as I did, the flame within me that was once dimmed by busyness came roaring back.

I didn't stop striving, but my fuel changed. No longer powered by fear or proving, I became lit from within. Purpose replaced pressure. Alignment replaced addiction.

As Dolly Parton said, "If you don't like the road you're walking, start paving another one." That's exactly what I did. And now, I invite you to do the same.

My mess led to my method. My burnout became my blueprint. And in writing these pages, I'm not just sharing what I learned. I'm living it.

You don't have to write a book or speak on stages. But you do have to decide that your life is worth living fully.

Are you ready?

Meet the Happiness Whore

Let me clarify a term you'll become familiar with as you journey through these pages.

Throughout, you're going to see Happiness Whore appear again and again. Don't let your prudish side get the better of you. This isn't a label for an X-rated profession, or the insult you hurled at the girl your boyfriend cheated on you with.

No, my love, this is a name I gave myself. And by the end of this chapter, you might just realize it's one that's been living inside of you, too.

You might wonder why I use the word "whore" instead of something softer like "Happiness Hustle." I chose that word with intention. Because what I saw in myself, and in so many others, was a kind of promiscuity with paths, pleasures, and pursuits.

A whore gives themselves away in exchange for something superficial. And that's what this pattern looks like, too. Chasing happiness through one quick hit after another, jumping from project to project, relationship to relationship, and trend to trend, without ever touching your own depth.

It's not about sex but distraction. It's about giving your energy away in the hope of being paid back with fulfillment. But that transaction never works.

I know it's provocative, but I use it with purpose. This is the term I give to anyone who treats happiness like a finish line. The ones who believe that once they get the body, the title, the man, the house, the number in the bank, then they'll finally feel whole. But "there" never really comes. It's a mirage. It moves every time you get close.

But, my love. This isn't a personal flaw. It's a cultural pattern and a psychological loop. Painful, yes, but absolutely breakable.

A Happiness Whore can be anyone. It's not about gender. I use "she" because I wrote these pages for the woman I used to be, and for the woman I know still lives in many of you.

She's magnetic, ambitious, beautiful, accomplished, and never satisfied. She says things like, "I'll be happy when..." with the same casual certainty she says, "I'll just grab a latte." She chases a better quality of life like it's a trophy that proves that she mattered. That she was good enough. That she counted for something.

She's not proud of how hard she pushes. She's just never been taught another way. And she's not greedy, but hungry. Starving for meaning, wholeness, love that feels like safety, and a life that feels as good as it looks.

She's outwardly thriving but inwardly aching. She's accomplished but is always chasing. She's relentless in her pursuit of "more" and believes that more success, more beauty, more perfection will somehow make her feel enough.

This woman? This archetype? This energy? I know her. I lived her.

Happiness Whores are intelligent, driven, deeply capable women who are fueled by an unconscious belief that the next thing will finally bring them peace. She's not trying to be superior or more deserving than others. She's just running on an outdated operating system that says doing equals worth, perfection equals love, and busyness equals value.

In her world, slowing down feels dangerous. Standing still feels like failure. So she keeps going. She sacrifices rest, softness, even joy, for the hit of external validation. She'll go to war with herself and others for the dream she's chasing. Not because she's selfish, but because she's scared.

The search for contentment becomes her full-time job. And in that pursuit, she becomes promiscuous, not with people, but with paths. She jumps from idea to idea, coach to coach, dream to dream, hoping one of them will finally stick and bring her home to herself.

She wants it all: the Vogue-worthy lifestyle, the fulfilling relationship, the glowing skin, the spiritual awakening, the wealth, the accolades, the family, the friends, the figure, the feminine softness, and masculine power all wrapped in a curated feed and a sense of purpose.

She wants it all because, deep down, she believes that if she gets it all, she will finally feel safe. That she will finally feel like she matters.

What she doesn't realize is that she can have it all, but not like this. The problem isn't the dream. The problem is the way she's going about getting it. She's running at life from the outside in, hoping the next shiny achievement will fix the ache inside. But it never does, and it never will.

Because here's the thing, wholeness doesn't come from performing harder, safety doesn't come from another certificate, title, or partner. And love doesn't arrive when you've finally perfected the body.

The real way, and in fact the only way, is to flip the order. And to build from the inside out.

When you're rooted in your truth, awakened to your aliveness, and aligned with something greater, everything you thought you had to hustle for begins to arrive differently. That's when "having it all" stops being a chase and starts being a conscious, realistic choice.

The Anatomy of a Happiness Whore

Let's break this down even further, so you can really get a sense of how a Happiness Whore operates.

Consumerism is the foundation of the Western world. If you like shopping, marketers will love you. As a Happiness Whore, you'll have a strong inclination toward buying new things to enhance your lifestyle or image. Anything to show the world, "You're worth it." That said, placing value on acquisition doesn't always mean luxury. You might just as easily choose simple items that still feed your perception of what it means to be happy. Such as those crystal bowls that are now gathering dust on your shelf, well, at least they look pretty.

Comparison trap. We know it as comparisonitis. We've all been there on Instagram, measuring our success, wardrobe, and self-worth against what others in our industry, friendship group, or age bracket are doing or wearing.

Attention-seeking. What if you're the one posting for attention? Seeking likes, approval, applause, without delivering real value? Every post quietly (or loudly) screams, "Please validate me." Unless you're selling a product or service, every like is just another penny in your self-worth piggy bank.

Chasing highs. This concept came from a friend who confessed he's always seeking the next dopamine hit, a quick pleasure that comes from experience. It could be the high you get from a wild night out, alcohol, drugs, extreme sports, a hedonistic experience, or even the post-ice bath buzz. Chasing the high is a clear sign of Happiness Whore tendencies, constantly trying to shift your baseline state from low to high. And when you can't shift it, you feel like you're dying inside.

Transactional relationships. In more extreme expressions, you might be someone who prioritizes what you can gain from a relationship over the connection itself. In this space, relationships become transactional; a means to an end. Something that's not focused on connection, but a strategy disguised as intimacy.

A Happiness Whore is someone who becomes promiscuous on the path to finding happiness. When you're operating from this place, life becomes something to manipulate rather than something to meet. You're no longer living. You're leveraging. A life of getting, over a life of giving. You become that person who is endlessly busy, convinced that inner contentment is just one external win away.

If you're reading these pages, chances are high that you've been living in this energy, or love someone who is. You may not even realize it. But if you zoom out and look at your life objectively, the traces are there.

The Addiction to Having

The desire for a high-quality life, happiness, and success is not wrong. It's a deeply natural drive. Humans are wired for growth, evolution, and expansion.

The problem isn't in wanting more. It's in why you want it, and how much of your true self you're willing to sacrifice to get there.

The Oxford Dictionary defines a "whore" as someone who will do anything to get a particular thing. When that "thing" is happiness, take a close look at your behaviors. You might find yourself constantly moving from one goal, one purchase, one dream to another, never feeling quite satisfied, always hoping the next thing will finally be it.

But if happiness is always placed outside of you, tied to

achievement, possession, or approval, you'll only ever experience it in flashes. Because once you finally get IT (whatever "it" is), the initial hit wears off, leaving you empty and restless, again.

We rarely pause to ask: Why is this satisfaction so fleeting? Instead, we double down. We fill the emptiness up with new distractions, new people, and new plans. Until one day, after many expensive lessons and unfulfilling wins, you realize that even with the house, the partner, the brand-new life, a part of you still feels missing.

And that is where change begins.

Because at some point, in a quiet moment of self-reflection, you'll see it. No perfect relationship, no luxury purchase, no ten-thousand-dollar mastermind is going to deliver the lasting happiness you crave.

But even then, the habit of seeking stays deeply embedded in your subconscious.

You may do nothing with that awareness at first. You may just observe it. You'll notice the urges. The quiet restlessness inside. That gnawing emptiness in the pit of your stomach, the one that demands to be soothed. It will whisper, *buy something, text him, drink, scroll, run.* Anything to relieve the ache.

And you'll feel it. There will be the impulse, a sense of urgency, and a force that rises inside you that needs you to act. You can't stay still. You're pulled toward whatever will pacify the discomfort. And off you go, chasing the next thing.

Eventually, the truth hits. You realize nothing outside of you was ever the answer. Like me, though, most of you will need to exhaust yourself before you reach this point. And now you're exhausted. You're done with your old ways.

And the real work can then begin

The Universal Human Program

Forget the term Happiness Whore for a moment and zoom out to the bigger picture. At our core, every human being is wired the same way. We move toward what we believe will comfort us, satisfy us, and make us happy. And we move away from what we believe will cause discomfort, dissatisfaction, or pain.

Watch five people around you today, and you'll see it clearly. A micro-lean toward what feels good. A subtle flinch away from what feels bad. This operating system of seeking pleasure and avoiding pain is hardwired into our biology and psychology.

When I started noticing my own Happiness Whore patterns, I saw how dualistic they were. I was chasing highs and avoiding lows. Craving what I thought would bring happiness, and resisting anything that might bring perceived suffering. And it wasn't just me. Everyone was moving like magnets, pulled toward comfort and repelled by discomfort.

It made me ask: Is this it? Is life just an endless cycle of craving and avoiding? Or are we missing something?

One thing became crystal clear: the drive for happiness is universal. Not a luxury of the privileged, nor a spiritual side quest. It's the default human program. Ask anyone in the world why they want something and, underneath it all, the answer collapses into the same thing: *because I think it will make me happy.*

But what people really mean is this: *because I think it will make me free, and then I'll finally be at peace.*

We say we're chasing happiness, but we're not. We're

chasing the conditions we believe will allow happiness. The salary, the body, the partner, the lifestyle, the brand, the house, the reputation. We tell ourselves that once those are in place, then we'll be free to exhale. Free to rest. Free to feel whole.

But the deeper truth: beneath all the striving, what we're hungry for is not another achievement. It's freedom.

Not the motivational-poster kind of freedom. Not the political kind of freedom. Most of us already have physical freedom. We can travel, date, work, eat, move, and buy.

What we're starving for is psychological freedom.

Because while our bodies are free to roam, our minds are trapped. Trapped in attachments to the thoughts of comparison. Trapped in the feelings of shame. Trapped in the fear of being ordinary. Trapped in the belief that we're only lovable if we're improving, impressing, or indispensable.

Psychological freedom is the absence of internal war. When your nervous system is no longer hijacked by your history. When you can sit in stillness without guilt. When your worth is no longer tethered to your output. When mental freedom and peace become your baseline, not a prize you earn.

And when that happens, happiness doesn't have to be chased. It rises on its own.

The Lack Belief That Drives Everything

Consider the woman who books another cosmetic tweak, only to wake up still disliking her reflection. The man who collects designer watches, not for time but for status. The overachiever who compulsively signs up for yet another certification course, because learning gives her a temporary high and a reprieve from her chronic restlessness.

What's really happening here?

We choose what we choose and chase what we chase because we're trying to feel more than what we currently do. But that drive is fueled by a belief most people won't admit out loud: *I am not enough as I am.*

Somewhere in your personal history, maybe as a child, maybe as a teen, maybe last year, a seed of lack was planted. And now it has grown roots in your psyche, whispering that you're somehow less than. Less attractive. Less intelligent. Less worthy. Less lovable.

Wanting more is the fruit of that seed. The belief behind it? *I am nothing without it.*

It's not the desire itself that's the problem. It's the craving energy that comes from an internalised idea that you're fundamentally not enough. That belief, buried deep in your subconscious, is what sends you sprinting toward the next goal, relationship, project, or purchase.

It's also what exhausts you. Over time, these self-doubts become a war. And they are being fought inside your own head.

Two Roads

So you have two roads.

The first one is the one you're familiar with: you keep going as you are. You keep chasing. You keep dressing your pain in designer labels and diplomas, hoping they will one day finally fill the void. You keep proving and performing. You keep accumulating shiny things that temporarily distract you from the gnawing ache inside.

Or you take the second road.

On this road, you take a long pause from who you've been; you stop. You turn inward. You locate the attachments to the old stories and the pain that these cause you. And you begin to heal them, not through hustle but through seeing the truth about them.

These pages are here for that second path. To guide you back to the place inside you that is already whole, already worthy, and already free.

But you can't do that if you're still outsourcing your peace and freedom to things that live outside of you.

The dis-ease you feel doesn't come from the world. It comes from within. So no matter how many handbags you buy, titles you earn, or partners you attract, nothing out there can fix the ache in here.

And trying to make it work that way only strengthens the illusion that you're broken, behind, or are not designed to be ok as you are. The thing is, you're not broken, and you are already designed to have these experiences. You're simply responding to a system that taught you to seek externally what was always meant to rise from within

The Illusion Breaks

The first rite of passage: to fully recognize that your feelings of lack cannot be resolved by external means. Not in the long-term and not deeply enough to satisfy you.

You must confront the belief that you're not enough and stop trying to soothe it with stuff.

Let's get naked and honest. You've probably already tried a million ways to distract yourself from that inner ache of suppressed aliveness, misalignment, and unexpressed truth. Most of us have. You might have reached for another Biscoff biscuit, texted an ex for some validation, or drowned yourself in success theatre: car, house, spouse, abs, and accolades.

On the outside, it looks like you're thriving. On paper, you're impressive. But if you're still quietly suffering, still craving, still numbing, still holding your truth deep inside you, still burned out, then you're not living. You're performing survival.

And nobody tells you about that game: it doesn't end. You never arrive. The chase for more is infinite. So you push harder toward a fantasy that doesn't even exist, an idea of fulfillment that lives only in your head. And when that striving doesn't deliver, it doesn't just disappoint you. It devastates you.

You crash. You spiral. You question your worth. You become vulnerable to despair, to addiction, and to the subtle numbness that feels safer than facing, owning, and expressing your truth.

Because when you're running away from yourself, the self you know yourself to be, rather than running to yourself, expressing that self every day, you need something to quieten that voice of truth, and sometimes, if you're honest, alcohol looks like relief. So does overworking. So does overachieving. So does scrolling. But none of them resolve it. They just dull the signal. And eventually, even that stops working.

What's left is fatigue, broken relationships, frayed health, financial debt, and still, the ache of knowing: this life, it isn't it.

That's why learning to live your truth is an inside job. It always was.

Nothing external can truly satisfy the internal discontent born from an inner knowing you're living a lie. At best, those things offer a hit of relief. A dopamine rush or a momentary exhale.

But they don't free you. They don't shift your center back to alignment.

The First Step: Awareness

So how do we begin to rise out of this illusion?

The first step in breaking the trance of the promiscuous Happiness Whore is self-awareness. Real, rooted, razor-sharp self-awareness. The kind that turns the light on in the parts of you you've been afraid to meet. The kind that sees through the coping strategies and gently asks, *What are you really trying to avoid?*

Like a staircase, awareness has many levels. And the first rung is noticing. Noticing your thoughts. Noticing the compulsions that drive your behavior. Noticing the emotional cues your body gives you every time you chase or numb.

Start there. That noticing will give you access to a deeper intelligence, one that was never dependent on more to begin with.

Because when you stop trying to outrun yourself, you can finally hear the truth beneath it.

You've Been Seduced

You've just met The Seduction. And maybe, for the first time, you're seeing it for what it is: an illusion. A myth. A beautifully branded illusion designed to keep you hungry, hustling, and hooked.

Like most high-functioning women, you've probably spent years chasing the promise that more equals happiness. More stuff. More success. More likes. More love. But the inconvenient truth is, the more you gather, the further you are from your true self and the emptier you feel. The chase never satisfies you. It just seduces you into staying and doing it again.

But here's the good news. You're off it now.

This chapter was your first taste of something radically different. A new way of looking at your constant struggles. One that doesn't ask you to add more, but to undress. To peel back the identities you didn't even realize you were wearing: all the roles, the rules, and the reflexes that told you who to be and how to win.

In the chapters ahead, we'll shine a light on your happiness-seeking patterns, the ones that have been running silently in the background of your life, shaping your choices, moods, and energy. You'll begin to recognize them not as flaws but as protective strategies. Brilliant, once-necessary survival strategies that now deserve to be retired.

This first step, *self-awareness,* isn't small. It's everything. It's how you reclaim your power. It's how you disarm the beliefs that have been quietly dictating your behavior for decades. And it's how you begin to return to the only thing that ever truly mattered: your truth.

So take a breath. Not a performance breath. A real one. The kind that softens your heart, relaxes your body, and reminds you that you're not here to prove. You're here to remember.

You've seen the seduction. Now it's time to understand the specific habits that keep you trapped in the chase.

Chapter 2 is where we strip those bare, so you can finally stop performing for happiness and start living from it.

Chapter 2:

Happiness Whore Habit

Shadow Play of Desire, Avoidance, and Control

The moment you know how your suffering came to be, you are already on the path of release from it.

— Samyutta Nikaya

You can spend a lifetime believing that you're chasing happiness when really, you're caught in a shadow play. The unseen dance of desire, avoidance, and control can sneak up on you with such expert stealth that it can fool you into believing that you're on the exact path you want to be on. In actual fact, though, these hidden patterns are pulling you in a thousand different directions, keeping you busy, brilliant, and exhausted, all while keeping you further from the place where the real, aligned life you crave, where you and true joy live.

These are the habits beneath the habits. The patterns pulling the strings when you think you're in charge. Welcome to the underworld of your behaviors: seductive, relentless, and invisible until you shine a light on them.

In this chapter, we'll undress the compulsive pursuit of happiness. The endless chase for a feeling that always seems just out of reach. The habits we adopt, believing that one day we'll finally arrive at our own version of nirvana. All in the hope that one day we'll wake up and think, *ah, I made it. I'm happy now.* But these are the shadow behaviors that drive high-functioning humans into burnout, bitterness, and a thousand fleeting highs that never last.

My Realization

I remember the exact moment it hit me. I had just dropped my eldest off at school, reached for my AirPods in the baby bag, and set off on my ritual. A brisk morning walk with my newborn and A Course In Miracles whispering truth in my ears.

Out of nowhere, I muttered, "Damn."

Because suddenly I saw it. I had been chasing. Chasing achievements, chasing validation, and chasing the quick high of external wins, believing they would finally add up to lasting happiness. No one had told me the truth yet. That real joy doesn't come from what you achieve, get, or gain. It rises from who you are when you stop running from yourself.

But I couldn't stop running. Not with the voice that lived in my head.

Enter Karen

My inner heckler. Constant. Critical. And conniving. I named her Karen after a woman from my childhood who always had a prickly word ready for me. Maybe you've got a Karen too. She's the voice that tells you you're not thin enough, not smart enough, not spiritual enough, not successful enough. Not 'whatever the case may be' enough. She doesn't whisper to you, though. She narrates your life loudly, never stopping.

The problem isn't that these voices exist. The problem is that we listen to and believe them.

So let me ask you, when did you first start believing you weren't enough? Who told you that? Those "not enough" thoughts become coded into your operating system like a virus. They run silently in the background, dictating every choice you make. They drive you into the arms of anything that promises relief. Achievements, shopping sprees, yoga classes, green juices, men, mantras, and even spiritual practice.

But the Happiness Whore isn't a villain, far from it. She's just a woman stuck in survival mode.

The Inner Workings of a Happiness Whore

We already described a Happiness Whore in detail in Chapter 1, so in this chapter, we're going to bring her to life a little so you can really get a sense of her.

She is magnetic, ambitious, and, on first meetings, very impressive. But her nervous system is shot, and she will outwork anyone in the room if she believes it will earn her the one feeling she has been chasing since girlhood. Safety. Safety to be herself. And accepted, no cherished for it. Feeling she's enough now, and her nervous system can finally exhale.

Picture her at a masquerade ball. Dressed to kill. Sequins, silk, the perfect mask. She moves through the room dazzling, collecting glances, sipping pleasures like cocktails. But she never takes the mask off. She never stops to feel what is real. She mistakes the performance for connection, the chase for meaning, the attention for love. She is always on stage, but never at home within herself.

What she doesn't realize is that she is chasing a mirage. Real pleasure does not demand a costume. It does not require a script. It rises from stillness, from the body, from the truth you stop long enough to feel. But she has forgotten how to be still.

Her instincts have been replaced with overthinking. Her inner rhythm was replaced with restlessness. The very mind that makes her so powerful, able to create, build, and solve problems, has become her cage. Her thoughts, instead of tools, have become traps. And what once made her magnificent now keeps her stuck.

So she keeps on running. Striving. Performing. Trying to outpace a feeling she can't name and never quite manages to escape.

She runs from mask to mask, high to high, and bed to bed. Mistaking the performance for the pleasure. Mistaking the costume for the cure. And the cruelest part of all? She could stop at any moment. She could drop the mask, strip bare, and finally meet herself. But the party is seductive, the chase is addictive, and the emptiness is disguised as ecstasy. Until she remembers, she will keep dancing for an audience who never really knows her.

And that is her shadow. The masquerade without end. The relentless seduction of the high, keeping her spinning, smiling, surviving, while her true self waits behind the mask. Meanwhile, the thing she has been aching for (freedom to express, peace, joy, enoughness) has been quietly waiting inside her. But she is too busy entertaining to notice.

Chasing the High, Dodging the Truth

A Happiness Whore's desires and her dislikes are cut from the same cloth. If you are relentlessly chasing what you want, there is usually a matching pattern right behind it. You are also avoiding what you do not want.

It is a subtle but powerful tug of war. A nervous system dance, if you like. Forwards and toward the high. Backwards away from the discomfort. This is how the mind is wired. At any given moment, you are either moving toward pleasure or away from pain. It's the default setting. The human operating system.

If you are someone who is always striving for more (goals, healing, meaning, money, or anything at all), it is likely because you believe that happiness lives in the arrival. In the acquisition. On the other side of your effort. It's the reward.

And if you are someone who avoids difficult conversations, sidesteps discomfort, or numbs out at the first sign of friction, it is likely that you believe discomfort is dangerous and threatens the fragile peace you are desperately trying to protect.

Before anything else, just realise you are not broken. You are human. It is a tendency deeply ingrained in all of us. And you are not alone. Almost everyone is moving in one of these two directions at any given moment. This pattern lives in all of us. You are not an exception. You are an example.

Look closely at your own behavior, and you will see it playing out in your life. The impulse to reach for whatever feels good or you perceive to feel good, and the urge to run away from whatever feels or you perceive to be threatening. Sometimes it is obvious. Other times, it is disguised in busyness, in productivity, in false positivity. Aversion does not always look like fear. Sometimes it looks like over-functioning.

It is the impulse to escape. The urge to leave your hometown, quit your job, end a relationship, or avoid certain people who stir something uncomfortable in you. That something is the thing that is healed in you, that you are resisting to look at and feel, so it keeps on running the show and you. It is that tightening in your chest when a situation feels threatening, unpleasant, or just off. Without thinking, you move away, believing that distance will solve the problem.

And yes, aversion can certainly be useful. It keeps you from staying in toxic relationships, dead-end jobs, or literal danger. If your house were on fire, you wouldn't just sit there debating whether or not you should leave. But there is a difference between survival and avoidance. Between wisdom and escapism. When aversion becomes chronic, it shapeshifts into avoidance. That is when it becomes seductive, addictive, normalized, and frankly, dangerous.

You start ghosting the conversations that matter. You scroll past the hard truths. You replace healing with shopping, awareness with affirmations, and presence with performance. You call it alignment, but really, you are just avoiding yourself.

Desire pulls. Aversion pushes. Together, they form a loop. A cycle that never lets you land. You are either reaching or retreating. Never arriving.

I know this cycle intimately because I lived inside it for years. As a self-proclaimed Happiness Whore, I spent a decade promising myself that the next goal, the next relationship, the next breakthrough would finally bring me peace. And sure, I manifested the hell out of my life. I had the success, the acclaim, the shiny things. From the outside, I looked like the poster girl for having it all.

But on the inside? I was restless. Disconnected. Quietly exhausted and still searching. Still stuck in a cycle of wanting more while avoiding what truly needed my attention. Me.

We didn't get it wrong. We just missed a piece.

This is not about shaming the pursuit itself. It is about noticing the pattern. Are you chasing something, or are you running from something? What are you not willing to feel, and what are you doing instead?

See it clearly. Not to judge, but to reclaim the power you have been outsourcing to the chase or to the escape. Because the truth is simple, happiness is not found in the hunt or the avoidance. It lives in the courage to be with what is.

The Game You Didn't Know You Were Playing

Happiness is an inner game; it truly is. And if you want to win this game, you first have to know that you're even playing. Most people don't. They're too busy reacting, chasing, dodging, and performing under invisible rules. They sprint after the promise of peace, dodge discomfort like it's the plague, and call it "living." But really? They're competing in a game they never consciously agreed to.

Your mind has been at it far longer than you realize. Running the board. Making the moves. Quietly shaping your path without your permission. It knows how to nudge you towards what feels good, pull you away from what doesn't. It's efficient, yes. But efficiency isn't the same as truth. Just because your mind is steering doesn't mean it's taking you where your deeper nature (the deeper intelligence in you) longs to go.

Thoughts are like clouds. Shapeshifting by the second, forming and dissolving in an endless loop. Some drift by without consequence. Others gather into emotional storms that alter your entire internal climate without warning. One thought can change the texture of your entire day, your breath, your body, even the way you hold someone you love. Like wind carving the sky, your thoughts shape everything.

And the part most of us miss is this. We believe we're in control. We walk through life assuming our choices are intentional, our living is conscious. But zoom out for a moment. Look closer. If you do, you'll see the truth. Most of us aren't steering the ship at all. We're just reacting to a current we don't understand. Sprinting towards what we think will deliver joy. Dodging what we assume will bring pain. Either way, we're moving. But we're not free.

And here's why. Thoughts, especially the ones that repeat a thousand times (the ones charged with heavy emotion), don't just disappear. They etch themselves into you. They hardwire. They sink into the deepest creases of the mind, laying down tracks like railway lines. Automatic, predictable, efficient. Your fears, your cravings, your compulsions filed neatly into the subconscious, like a well-oiled machine, running on cue.

Some of these patterns keep you alive. They remind you how to cross the street, type your password, and brush your teeth. But others? Others are prisons dressed up as preferences. They keep you looping. Overthinking, overdoing, overcompensating. You chase the high, dodge the silence, micromanage your life to avoid sitting in the quiet hum of your own being. You hunt happiness like prey. And still, you never arrive. You never get 'there.'

Here's the holy fuck twist, though. You don't need to run. Happiness isn't waiting at some mythical finish line. Peace isn't hiding on the far side of your next breakthrough. They're not out there, dangling like medals. They're here. Steady. Quiet. Already inside you. They've been with you all along. But you've been so busy playing the game, you never stopped long enough to notice.

Thought Loops and Mind Traps: The Architecture of Your Inner Reality

Do you ever stop to think about your thoughts? Most of us don't. We stay in go mode: living, reacting, doing, and never pausing to question the script running our day. But I want to invite you into a moment of radical awareness. Right now, if you dare, pull out a notebook and write down everything that's swirling in your head. No editing. No spiritual filters. Just raw, uncut thought stream. Three full pages. Let the pen bleed it all out.

You might begin with, I don't know what to write. This is stupid. I'm bored. Then suddenly it shifts to, I need to get oat milk. Why did she not text me back? My boss is a dick. Before long, you're ranting about your boyfriend not asking about your day, or how it grates when people don't say thank you properly. It doesn't matter what comes out. What matters is that it does.

The first step is realizing that this narrative is always at work inside of you. You are always thinking. Constantly. In loops. In layers. In loud, messy monologues. But until you see it on paper, you won't realize how incessant it is.

Now for the next step.

When you do think about your thoughts, what do you actually do with them?

Most people don't engage with the thought itself. They skip straight to the content. They latch onto what they're thinking about (my partner, my weight, my future, my to-do list) instead of recognizing that these are thoughts, not facts. Then they categorize them. Good. Bad. Positive. Negative. Spiritual. Petty. Productive. Shameful.

If you're a self-aware overachiever (hello), you might go one level deeper. You observe your thoughts like a well-meaning researcher, trying to detect the pattern beneath the chaos. This is metacognition. Thinking about thinking. The ability to witness your mind in motion.

It sounds evolved. And it is, to a degree. But even metacognition can become a trap. Because it still keeps you focused on the content rather than its nature. You might notice you always catastrophize, or replay awkward conversations like a Netflix rerun, or compulsively label every thought you have. But when you do this, you're still tangled in the story.

It's like realizing your playlist is full of sad songs, and deciding to add happy ones, without ever questioning who gave you the playlist in the first place.

Here's what you rarely stop to consider when you're in this space. Everything in your mind is a thought. Everything. Your entire inner reality is composed of mental content. Stories, opinions, fears, daydreams, agendas. Most of it isn't conscious. But it's there, running the show.

If you're absorbed in your thoughts, you're not paying attention to the nature of thought itself. You're just watching the movie on the screen of your mind, reacting to whatever is playing.

Maybe it's a memory of perfectly poached eggs on warm toast. Maybe it's a fantasy about your next beach holiday or a mental loop obsessing over someone else's opinion of you. Either way, your attention is hooked, not on the projector, but on the projection. You're fixated on the thing, not the mechanism behind it.

And here's the kicker. When you're caught in content, you react. A thought pops up, stirs emotion, and boom. You're off. Into the spiral. Into the storm. And the craziest part is that none of it is actually happening in real life. It's all just a story that's playing out in your head.

But here's the shift that most people never come even close to making. Instead of analyzing what you're thinking, what if you questioned what thought even is?

Where does it even come from? Why does it feel so believable? And more importantly, are you actually the one choosing it?

This is where the game really begins to unravel. When you stop focusing on what you're thinking and start observing the nature of thought itself, you stop being the puppet. You stop getting dragged by every emotional surge or mental projection your mind throws at you. You begin to see your mind for what it is. A thought-producing machine. Beautiful, yes. But temporary. Random. Frequently unreliable and not always trustworthy.

Let's make it real. Imagine you've been invited to speak at an event, something you've always wanted to do. At first, you say yes. You see yourself on that stage, confident, delivering your message to a captivated audience. But then a single thought creeps in, seemingly out of nowhere. What if I forget my words? Suddenly, that thought has a physical effect. Your chest tightens. Your palms sweat. More thoughts pile on. What if I embarrass myself? What if I make a fool of myself? Before long, your brain is running an entire horror movie where you're stammering under bright lights while everyone in the audience silently judges you.

The result? You back out, telling yourself, I'm just not ready yet. But what actually happened?

You had a thought. You believed it. And you let it dictate your reality. But the reality wasn't the public speaking event. It was the movie your mind made about it. That scene never happened. It wasn't real. Your body just responded as if it were.

This is how the mind works. It's a thought-producing machine. Constant, unfiltered, and non-stop. And just because a thought arises, it doesn't mean it's true, or that it's worth believing.

Trying to swap negative thoughts for positive ones might feel like the solution. 'I'll just tell myself I can do it.' And maybe you will. But that's still playing within the same operating system. You're still taking the thought seriously. You're just choosing a shinier one.

The real shift happens when you stop assigning truth to *any* of it. When you realize that thoughts are just thoughts, not facts, not commands, and not prophecies, they're like passing clouds. Some heavy and ominous. Some are bright and harmless. But none of them is you.

Your mind generates thoughts as naturally as your lungs breathe air. Some are insightful. Some are absurd. Some are echoes of your childhood. Some are echoes of your mother's anxiety. Some are just nonsense. But when you stop attaching to them, when you can truly watch a thought float by without grabbing onto it, you stop being controlled by them.

Here's where it gets interesting. Emotions and bodily sensations are often just thoughts in disguise. Your body is a memory bank. It holds stored emotional data from childhood, heartbreak, trauma, and rejection, sometimes from yesterday, sometimes from decades ago. These memories don't always come to mind as clear thoughts. They show up as moods, as tension, and as unshakable dread you can't quite explain.

Ever had a day where you just felt off, but you couldn't figure out why?

That's because what you're feeling isn't always from the present. It's an old mental thought code. And it's running in the background of your nervous system like a looping track you didn't press play on.

The first step to breaking the spell isn't to go digging for every belief you've ever had. It's way simpler than that.

It's just slowing down and noticing how your system works.

We tend to assume that what we think is fact. We just assume that what we feel is, of course, the truth. But that's the illusion. We don't feel the world. We feel our thoughts about the world. And that subtle distinction changes everything.

You don't have a thinking problem. You have an attachment problem. You've been attaching to your thoughts as if they are the truth, when really they are just the inner weather of the moment.

That's all feelings are. Your thoughts, felt in your body.

This is how the system is designed. You feel what you think. That's how human technology works. The problem isn't that you're broken at all. The problem is that you have a brilliant mind, but no one taught you how that mind operates.

Once you see the mechanics, you'll stop personalizing the story and drowning in the narrative and simply start recognizing the pattern instead.

And when you observe your own mental patterns with neutrality, without needing to fix or fear them, you begin to see how you've been caught in the Happiness Whore trap without even realizing it.

The Cycle That Keeps You Stuck in Survival Mode

We've talked about the chase for pleasure and the avoidance of pain, but there's another sneaky behavior that too often slips under the radar, too. Control. That need to grip onto, to stabilize, and to keep everything 'just so.' And here's what I noticed in myself, again and again. When I wasn't running toward something shiny or bolting away from discomfort, I was clinging on for dear life to whatever felt safe, familiar, or survivable.

A person. A job. A lifestyle or identity that no longer fit me, yet I didn't know who I was without it, so it felt like I needed it to survive. Because in a way, at this level of being, I did.

This is what I call The Cycle of Survival. A triad of shadow behaviours. A high-functioning, emotionally draining merry-go-round of chasing, avoiding, and controlling that keeps you moving but never arriving. It keeps you busy but disconnected. It keeps you almost happy, but never quite at peace.

And the worst part is that most people live their entire lives stuck in this loop, and they never even realize it. They chase freedom and peace, search for ease, and try to soothe that inner ache with external band-aids. They try more yoga. More money. A cleaner house, a better partner, and a "higher-vibe" morning routine. They busy themselves by always searching for peace in the wrong places, mistaking their internal feelings for a problem, rather than a symptom of disconnection, and therefore trying to silence them with external fixes. But the ache was never out there. It was you, disconnected from you.

To break free, you have to see the pattern for what it is. Not as if there's something wrong with you, or that there's something missing, but a survival pattern. A loop that was never designed to make you happy, only an attempt to keep you safe. These are what I call Happiness Whore Habits. The habitual ways we try to find joy, safety, or worth in things, people, and circumstances outside of ourselves, but ironically, they are the very things that keep us separate from it.

There are three main ways the Happiness Whore cycle plays out.

1. The Chase for More

This is every high-achiever's drug of choice. The next launch. The next milestone. The next breakthrough. If you're always chasing the next thing, you're probably living under the illusion that happiness lives in the future and that it's always just one promotion, one detox, or one lover away.

You tell yourself, Once I get that house, that body, that success, that recognition, then I'll finally be happy. But the high never lasts. Because as soon as you "get there," your nervous system doesn't feel safe and is already scanning for the next thing.

Here's how this might look. You sign up for your third online course this month. You order £400 worth of skincare promising youth. You spend another Sunday watching manifestation reels while filling a new vision board, all while still feeling restless, while wondering, "Why hasn't it worked yet?"

2. Running from Discomfort

Now, if you're not chasing, you're probably running. Avoidance is just desire flipped inside out. Instead of moving towards what you think will bring you happiness, you move away from anything that might stir discomfort or awaken a feeling you've stuffed down deep inside you.

That hard conversation? Avoided like a pro. That old wound? Buried under mountains of glitter. That inner nudge asking you to slow down and feel? Muted with productivity or wine.

It might feel like self-protection and self-preservation in the moment, but in the long term, what this does is create emotional numbness and prolongs the disconnection from your true self and the life you're meant to be living.

Here's one way this can appear. You ghost people who

trigger you. You "keep the peace" by silencing your truth. You mindlessly scroll until your thumbs ache to distract you from taking corrective action. You eat, clean, exercise, or work yourself into the ground. Anything to avoid sitting in the now to face what you need to face in order to feel, heal, grow, and realign.

3. The Illusion of Control

And then there's control, the most deceptive of them all. When you're not chasing or running, you're gripping. Holding on to routines, roles, and relationships with white-knuckled intensity, terrified that if you loosen your grip, it will all fall apart.

But control is a false sense of safety, not the reality of it. You can't control everything. But that doesn't stop you from trying.

How does this likely look? You over-plan every detail of your week, down to the minute. You micromanage your partner, your kids, your team, believing that if everyone just listened, you could finally breathe. You repeat rituals obsessively, thinking this keeps you grounded, when really, you're just avoiding the chaos you feel inside.

These patterns don't make you weak. They make you human. But they are still the habits that keep you locked in the Cycle of Survival and separate from your true self.

And until you see the pattern clearly, you can't rewrite it.

So I dare you to ask yourself.

Are you ready to see? Which of these has been running your life lately?

What are you chasing, avoiding, or gripping onto?

And what would happen if you let go, just a little?

Brief Introduction to My Happiness Whore Habits

"Hello," I said, "my name is Gem." I was introducing myself to my new university lecturer, a short man with a thick South African accent and a beaming smile. I was the classic front-row student. Eager, studious, always asking questions. At the time, I had convinced myself that learning was the key to happiness, and as long as I was absorbing knowledge, I felt motivated, excited, and safe.

This was my first happiness-seeking habit. Consuming knowledge like an addict looking for the next fix. Whenever I felt the slightest hint of sadness or restlessness, I would sign up for another course, attend another workshop, or buy yet another self-help book. Literature, business, science, religion, wealth, and creation. You name it, I studied it, convinced that if I just learned enough, I would unlock the secret to happiness. But no matter how many seminars I attended, how many time-management strategies I mastered, or how many diplomas I framed, the feeling never lasted. The excitement of learning something new would fade, and before long, I would be on the hunt for the next life-changing course.

Then there was retail therapy, another happiness-seeking habit. If I wasn't feeding my mind, I was feeding my wardrobe. New clothes, shoes, and handbags. Each purchase gave me a brief high, a momentary sense of satisfaction. But just like the books and courses, the thrill wore off fast, leaving me with nothing but a pile of receipts and a nagging feeling that I needed more.

And the last habit? Avoidance. I was a professional conflict dodger, a master at sidestepping tough conversations and pretending everything was fine. If a relationship felt tense, I would smile through it and convince myself I wasn't upset. If work became stressful, I would focus on pleasing others rather than expressing my own needs. At the time, I thought avoiding conflict meant preserving happiness, but all it really did was suffocate me, trapping me in relationships and situations that drained me instead of fulfilling me.

I didn't realize it then, but real happiness wasn't in the things I was chasing. It wasn't in books, shopping bags, or conflict-free interactions. True joy, the kind that lasts, doesn't come from external rewards. It comes from living authentically, in alignment with who you really are.

We've been sold the idea that happiness is something to earn, find, or buy. That it's out there somewhere waiting for us. But here's the truth. Happiness isn't something you get. It's something you become.

And that is where Happiness Whore Habits come in.

These habits aren't just behaviors that you repeat. They are deeply wired thought patterns, a cluster of automatic responses that have become so ingrained in your subconscious you don't even realize they are running the show. Like muscle memory, they shape all your actions, decisions, and emotions without much conscious thought. They are the invisible drivers behind all the pursuing, withdrawing, and controlling that have been keeping you stuck in an endless cycle of repeated heartbreaks, setbacks, and addictions.

By reading this book, you may be realizing for the very first time in your life that you have been innocently searching for happiness outside yourself. You have been relying on external people, things, and achievements to fill a void that external sources can never truly fill. Most people never wake up to this. They continue through life, chasing after more, without ever understanding why they feel the way they do.

But now, you have a choice.

How These Patterns Shape Your Life

When these patterns of chasing, avoiding, and controlling take hold, they don't just influence your mood. They become the silent architects of your entire life. They shape how you think. Everything you choose. And who you believe you are.

You convince yourself that the next course, the next purchase, the next conflict-free day will finally bring you peace. Just one more breakthrough. One more dopamine hit. One more thing off the to-do list. But somehow, you always find yourself back at square one. Restless. Unsatisfied and wondering why, for you, a contented life never really lands.

Maybe you are on the other end of the spectrum, constantly sidestepping discomfort. Avoiding the hard conversations. Numbing out the emotions. You scroll, overwork, people-please, or binge something - anything. Netflix. Snacks. Self-help content. It all counts. You will do anything but feel what is actually there.

Or perhaps, without even realizing it, you are clinging. To people, roles, routines, and the way things should be. You hold on tight because letting go feels so unsafe. But the truth is, the tighter you grip, the more life resists your control.

The common thread among all these patterns is a void. A silent ache beneath the noise of doing. And no amount of chasing, avoiding, or gripping will ever fill it, because what's missing isn't out there. It's you. And you can't find yourself *out there,* or in someone else, or in a thing.

And unless you step back and see the cycle for what it is, it will keep running the show.

Identifying Your Survival Style: The Happiness Whore Habits

Before you can break free, you have to see the patterns that have been running you, so let's recap. These patterns, which I call Happiness Whore Habits, are not random. They're learned survival strategies, and you've reached a level of mastery with them. They once kept you safe, but now you've outgrown them, and they're keeping you stuck in the Cycle of Survival.

They usually show up in three ways.

Desire behaviors, where you're always chasing the next high, believing happiness is always "out there."

Avoidance behaviors, where you're always keeping things light, calm, or numbed so you never have to feel the chaos beneath the surface.

Control behaviors, which often come with neediness, gripping, and believing that if you can just control everything, you'll finally feel safe.

For women like you and me, these patterns show up in two clusters. Cluster A is how they look in everyday life. Overachieving, people-pleasing, shopping for identity, filling your calendar. Cluster B is how they look once you're "on the path." Chasing healers, forcing rituals, preaching good vibes only, spiritual bypassing. Same survival, just dressed up differently.

Now, pause. Allow yourself to be radically honest with yourself. Which ones feel most familiar? Where are you still outsourcing your true worth?

The full checklist and three "Undressing Survival" practices are waiting for you inside the Undressed Playbook at https://www.gemdentith.com/playbook

That's where you'll take these insights deeper and actually begin stripping the patterns away.

Explore the Playbook, and when you are ready, move into the next section. I want to make it clear that we are not here to shame these behaviors. We are just seeking to understand them here. Because once you see your patterns clearly, you can start choosing differently. And then you can start living undressed.

If this chapter has stirred something in you, I want you to know that you are not alone. Most of us are caught, to varying degrees, in the loops of desire, avoidance, or control. These are the psychic mechanics of survival. Brilliantly seductive but entirely incapable of delivering lasting peace.

So, complete these self-inquiry exercises before turning the page. Not from urgency. Not from self-improvement, but from a deep devotion to truth. You are not here to be fixed. There's no need, because you are by design perfectly whole, perfectly divine. You are here to remember who you were before these patterns convinced you to shrink, to shape-shift, or to seek.

You will soon notice something else, too. Most people, unless they are aware that these survival layers exist, are caught in this cycle, to some extent. This is not a personal flaw. It is a collective trance. But now that you have seen it, the illusion is already beginning to break.

Because at some point, whether it is the dream job, the perfect partner, or the polished body, everything you have been clinging to will dissolve. Change is inevitable.

And then the question becomes: Will you just keep chasing,

avoiding, clinging? Or will you finally break the cycle for good, and finally ask yourself, "Who am I really?"

Some people begin to feel really low and sad after realizing the way a certain habit, belief, or event has been playing out in a story in their life for so long, without them even realizing it. It is as if they have been blindly going through the motions of living on autopilot. But whatever your experience and reflections are from this exercise, just sit with them and reflect on how this understanding can inform your future choices and actions.

Remember, these exercises are not designed to judge how you have been living your life or the many ways in which you may have been coping with your beliefs and traumas. You are learning about yourself and discovering what's been going on within you. By gaining more clarity on the invisible beliefs that have been driving your behaviors, you can make the invisible visible, which is the first step toward making more conscious decisions and aligning your actions with your authentic self.

Meet three women. Pippa, Shakti, and Hope. I've given them different names to protect their identities. They are a group of friends who met at school and, fifteen years later, decided to meet up for a school reunion-themed lunch. Allow me to introduce each person and see if you can identify their happiness-seeking habits.

Meet Pippa. Management Today's Under 40s has voted her as "one to watch." She is a career woman in her thirties. Pippa is unmarried, has no children, drives a top-of-the-range sports car, and owns a stylish penthouse apartment in a desirable part of town. She works in the city, indulges in long and expensive lunches, and enjoys lavish cocktails with friends after work. Her only commitment is her cat, Yogi. Pippa attended a private school, is well-educated with multiple qualifications, and is currently pursuing her second

PhD. She has many high-profile friends and is popular with the opposite sex. Pippa takes pride in her appearance and has undergone enhancements such as breast augmentation and regular Botox injections. Every year, she treats herself to expensive vacations, basking in the sun while savoring local cuisine. Pippa is also a fan of extended detox and de-stress retreats. Despite her seemingly glamorous lifestyle, she secretly wishes she had Shakti's life.

Next, we have Shakti. She is a happily married mother of two who works part-time as a self-employed nutritionist from home. Shakti fills her days with juggling her children's homeschooling and client appointments. She is a member of a local yoga studio and makes time for a few hot yoga sessions each week, for herself. Shakti strongly believes in the adage "you are what you eat" and ensures her family gets superfood nutrition. They also enjoy traditional family walks in the countryside on weekends. Shakti meticulously measures out food quantities, strictly adheres to organic and homegrown produce, and operates on a well-structured schedule. She bans technology devices for her children and does not allow sugar in their household. Shakti firmly believes that discipline and control are key to maintaining her family's strict routine.

Finally, we have Hope, a single parent raising one child. Hope is currently unemployed but striving to create a better life for herself and her child. She often feels stuck and sorry for herself, attributing her misfortunes to her parents, ex-partners, and society. Despite her financial struggles and living in a rundown house, Hope is never short of admirers because of her attractiveness, and she is aware of it. She falls in love quickly and clings to them as if they are her rescuer, her knight in shining armor who will rescue her from her difficult circumstances. Hope finds solace in her evening glass of wine, which sometimes turns into a bottle. She believes it helps her unwind and maintain balance in her life.

Unbeknownst to each other, all three characters regularly visit their doctors to get medication for anxiety or depression. Pippa seeks medication for confidence and self-esteem issues, as well as her quest to find the right partner. Shakti has a long-term eating disorder that she manages through various coping mechanisms rather than seeking professional help. Hope experiences bouts of frustration and depression, struggling to regulate her emotions daily.

During their lunch reunion, the topic of happiness arises, prompting Pippa to reveal that she has been taking medication for the past five years. This leads each character to confess their level of dissatisfaction and unhappiness, as well as the various attempts they have made to ease their persistent, empty feelings.

Now, which character do you think is exhibiting happiness-seeking behaviors? All of them are. Pippa strives to be perceived as the cool kid in the group, regularly attending Ayahuasca, Kambo, Yoga, and Detox Retreats. She also takes part in a weekly ecstatic dance class, where her soul dances to the music. She received the opportunity to attend a leadership coaching program through her work.

Shakti has explored various methods, including counseling, cognitive behavioral therapy, diet pills, Neuro-Linguistic Programming, hypnosis, Chinese herbs, homeopathy, acupuncture, Kabbalah, Ayurveda, and mindfulness. She quickly moves through these different solutions in her quest for happiness.

Hope's approach to dealing with life involves exercise but also relies on numbing aids such as drugs and alcohol. She has sought guidance from clairvoyants, palm readers, and mediums to gain insight into whether her life will improve in the future.

These characters are all very similar. They all feel unsatisfied with themselves and employ different tactics of distraction, avoidance, control, or numbing, all seeking a solution to their unhappiness problem. They are also unaware of another way to live because this book wasn't written in time for them, and their world didn't show them how to find what they are each looking for. Healing, contentment, inner peace, and alignment.

Before we close this chapter, I want to invite you into a brief, powerful pause. A simple meditation. Not to fix anything. Not to transcend your current life. But to drop beneath it. To remember, more viscerally, that you can access a sense of peace, softness, and contentment right here, right now. Not when the job is done. Not when the relationship is healed. Not when the chaos stops swirling. But in this very breath. At this moment. No matter what's happening around you. Because true peace was never out there, it's always been here. Beneath the noise, beneath the chase, beneath the armor.

For the audio version of the meditation, "Undressing into the Space Beneath It All", visit https://www.gemdentith.com/playbook

Allow me to share a short story of when I witnessed inner calm and peace emerge, even in the most desperate of situations.

During my time as a trainee ambulance grade one paramedic, I often encountered individuals with mental illnesses who, in the midst of mania, rage, or deep depression, would transition, sometimes briefly, into moments of calm and connection. In those fleeting moments, it was as if they'd stepped into a state of clarity, even exceeding what we might call "normal" mental health. I'm not suggesting that mental health conditions aren't real or significant. They absolutely are. But I noticed something profound. When I engaged with these individuals and asked them about their past passions, hobbies, or things they loved, they would light up. Their faces would soften, their eyes would brighten, and their words would flow with a sense of purpose.

Then, there would be a pause. We'd sit together in silence, and it was in that silence that I often noticed a kind of glow around them, an unmistakable shift in their energy. It would compel me to ask, "How are you feeling right now?" And almost without fail, they'd reply with one word. "Content."

But as our time together came to an end, and the weight of their current reality crept back in, that glow, that sense of peace and connection, would retreat, like a heavy cloud rolling in and obscuring the sun. The thing I had been speaking to, the clarity and light I had glimpsed, seemed to disappear from them completely.

This repeated observation taught me something invaluable. Even those grappling with significant mental health challenges can experience moments of connection, calm, and contentment. These moments, however brief, revealed a deeper truth to me. That beneath the layers of pain, turmoil, and thought, there exists a space of clarity and healing. In those cracks, where the swirling thoughts momentarily quietened, I saw something unbroken, something whole.

It was through these experiences that I began to understand that happiness and contentment exist not in our circumstances, but in the spaces in between our thoughts. This insight motivated me to explore practices that could offer people an inner refuge from the relentless chattering of their minds and the continually changing conditions of their lives.

There were moments in my practice when I'd witness people, people in pain, people in chaos, suddenly touch something still. Not because their life got better. But because they did. They came home to themselves, if only for a few breaths.

That's what this next meditation is for. Not to change your life, but to help you remember that peace isn't something you chase. It's something you return to. Something you choose.

Undressed Realizations

By now, you are hopefully beginning to see it. That the relentless chase for happiness, the high-achieving hustle, the perfectly curated life, the next big hit of approval, is not where your joy lives. And it never was.

The Happiness Whore is not just a shadow. She is a habit. A persona you picked up to survive in a world that told you worth had to be earned. Even now, she dresses your longing in designer distractions. But no matter how fast you run, you cannot outrun yourself. Luckily, you don't need to, because you were never broken. Just buried.

What if your happiness habit is only a symptom? A symptom of a world that taught you to chase love instead of resting in it. To prove your value instead of embodying your truth. To seek pleasure in the future instead of dropping into peace here and now.

This chapter didn't ask you to stop wanting beautiful things. It asked you to stop believing they would complete you. And that distinction? That is where your freedom begins.

Mirror Moments

Pause here and ask yourself a few questions.

What am I most afraid would happen if I stopped chasing happiness?

Who would I be without the performance of having it all together?

Can I remember a moment, recent or past, when I felt deep, quiet contentment without needing to earn it? What did that feel like in my body?

What layer of fabric am I willing to loosen now?

Embodied Practice

For the next seven days, see if you can begin to notice whenever you reach for a fix. It might be an impulse purchase. A scroll for validation. Or a loop of perfectionism.

Pause long enough to ask. What feeling am I trying to buy, prove, or outrun right now?

Then, instead of feeding the chase, feed your deeper knowing. Replace one external hit with an internal ritual:

A bath.

A barefoot walk.

A breathwork moment.

Ten minutes of stillness.

Let this be your new form of devotion.

Final Undressing Thought

When your inner Happiness Whore shows up again, as she will, don't shame her. She was just trying to help. She thought that chasing was the only way to stay safe. So thank her for her well-meaning intentions. And then let her have a rest.

You don't need to 'become happier.' You need to become less distracted from the happiness already inside you.

Let this be the moment that you finally choose to stop outsourcing your peace. Let this be the chapter where you start coming home.

Turn the page, my love. We are about to go deeper.

Chapter 3:
Quick Fix Lie

You're trying to solve a problem without addressing the thinking that created it.

As to methods, there may be a million and then some, but principles are few. The man who grasps principles can successfully select his own methods. The man who tries methods, ignoring principles, is sure to have trouble.

— Harrington Emerson

At 5 AM, the soft hymn of birdsong outside my bedroom window acted as my daily summons. I opened my eyes, eight hours of sleep behind me, a copper water vessel within arm's reach, carefully filled the night before with exactly 250ml of spring water, because that was what the protocol said. I sipped slowly, said a silent prayer of gratitude, and padded into the living room where my yoga mat lay, loyal and waiting.

On paper, I was the embodiment of wellness. I chanted Sanskrit invocations. I dropped into ninety minutes of full-body flow. I twisted myself into advanced postures that once seemed impossible. I followed it with drills, because progress demanded strength. Then came pranayama. Then meditation. Then visualization. Then, I had a detox tea in a crystal glass mug while I reviewed my goals and set intentions for the day. And all of this before the rest of the house had even begun to stir.

Afterwards, I shape-shifted into mum, consultant, fixer. My day consisting of client calls, transformation plans, deadlines and a few unexpected curveballs, here and there. After work, a high-intensity gym class. After dinner, yin yoga, parasympathetic breathing, meditation round two, and visualization round three. Then, finally, 8 hours of uninterrupted sleep.

It looked like a dream life, and for a while, I believed it was. I was doing all the things. The ones the self-help books promised would bring peace. The ones the wellness coaches sold in their courses. The ones that seemed to work for everybody else on Instagram. I thought I was healing.

But the truth?

My routine was a regimen. A self-improvement job I did not remember applying for. Relentless, rigid, and quietly fueled by fear. Because if I stopped, even for a day, what might catch up with me?

And this is the sneaky thing about quick fixes. They often look like they are working. Yoga gave me a high. Meditation brought temporary calm. Ticking off my goals made me feel capable, even in control. But the effects wore off. The stillness did not stick. The affirmations lost their magic. The high of high performance, whether in wellness or work, always came with a crash.

I had swapped one obsession for another. I used to chase qualifications; now I chase nervous system regulation. I used to collect jewelry; now I collect techniques. But the chase was the same. Yes, the shape of it had changed, but the energy hadn't.

This is where most high-functioning women get stuck. We are so good at managing the surface that we completely miss the root. We think we are healing, but in truth, we are just upgrading our coping mechanisms. We become high-achieving healers. Disciplined, devotional, but still disconnected.

I was still holding on to the same broken story. That if I just did enough, achieved enough, healed enough, I would finally feel okay.

But no method, no matter how ancient, structured, or sacred, can fix what is not broken.

Because here is the real medicine. Methods are tools. But the truth is the transformation. And until you return to the truth of who you are underneath all the practices, you will always feel like something is missing.

The Inner Problem

So, what is this inner problem we keep trying to fix from the outside?

For me, it was this. A deep, almost invisible belief that I was incomplete. That something was missing that I needed something else (a soulmate, a certificate, a next-level morning ritual, a shiny milestone) to finally feel whole. To finally feel enough. At one level, I was right: there was something missing, me.

It didn't matter that the method was sacred or scientific. If I were still using it to patch the illusion of a void I did not yet understand, I was abandoning myself. Again.

This wiring often starts early. Maybe you were the high achiever because love came through applause. Maybe you learned to look the part so no one questioned your value. Or maybe, like me, you became so good at performing that even your healing became a performance.

Whatever the origin, the message was clear. You, as you are, won't cut it.

And so we hustle for wholeness. We micromanage our mornings. We vision-board our way to self-worth. We think if we can just control enough, achieve enough, evolve fast enough, we will finally silence that quiet hum. The one that tells us, 'no, that's not quite it, not yet."

But here is the real trap. If you don't pause long enough to address the core issue driving all of this striving, the cycle can't end. It just changes clothes. When one method stops working, you grab the next. When one affirmation fades, you write a new one. When the yoga doesn't land anymore, you book a different kind of retreat.

And underneath it all, the whisper remains. Maybe the next thing will fix me. This is not healing. It is a spiritual hustle dressed up as growth.

Tools vs. Principles

This is where so many of us get beautifully, heartbreakingly lost.

We become curators and collectors of methods. Yoga flows. Breathwork tracks. Detox rituals. Journaling prompts. All in the belief that the right technique will finally deliver us, to us, we have been promised. We master morning routines like devotionals. We drink the tea. We whisper the affirmations. We do the damn work.

But we miss the point.

Because tools are not the truth. Tools are temporary. Principles are what liberate you, which guide you back to you.

Think of it this way. If you do not understand the deeper design of how your inner world actually works (how thoughts shape feelings, how emotions drive behaviors, how your beliefs create your lived experience), then no method, no matter how sacred or science-backed, can hold you when life gets real.

Trying to fix your life with just methods is like slapping duct tape on a leaking pipe. It might stop the drip today, but what happens when the pressure builds up again tomorrow?

For a while, that was exactly what I was doing in my own life. I used yoga like a bandage. Meditation as a mask. Detox teas as a distraction. Visualization exercises as a way to fantasize about a future and dissociate from the life I had. And who can blame me? They gave me the hits of calm that I wanted at the time. But that calm was conditional. It depended on my discipline, my energy, and my ability to keep doing everything. The moment I missed a step, skipped a session, or felt human, the discomfort came roaring back. And with it, the same silent belief. 'You're still not there yet.' And the truth is, I wasn't. How could I be, if I were still avoiding claiming the life that was meant for me? That is the thing with methods. They only work while you are working them. The second you let go, though, you are back in the ache. Back in the scroll. And back on the search.

Because methods are external solutions for an internal wound of disconnection from your true self.

Until you address the real problem, no technique will ever be enough, because you're treating the symptom, not the cause.

I'm not intending to strip away your tools here. But I do want to help you stop worshipping them. You don't need more practice. You just need to understand the principle behind why you are practicing in the first place and what it is you are actually trying to get from it.

And when you do? Everything changes. Not because you finally found the magic method, but because you stopped looking for one.

The Problem with Quick Fixes

The issue with quick fixes isn't the tools, techniques, or practices themselves. Yoga, meditation, detox teas, and breathwork. Even the latest somatic craze or sacred cacao ceremony. They all have their place. The problem is how we use them. If you're relying on them to "fix" you or find you, you may be missing the deeper lesson. You're not broken, you are hidden. You're just buried under layers of 'not you.'

True transformation doesn't come from doing more. It comes from realizing more. From recognizing the invisible architecture of your experience. The inner code that's been running your system without your conscious consent.

Without this understanding, every method becomes a temporary patch like pressing a sticky plaster over a wound while ignoring the infection festering beneath. It might cover things up for a while. It might even look like it's working. But eventually, it seeps through. Because the core wound, which is purely a covering over of your true nature, was never addressed.

This is what we've been sold. The illusion that healing is a checklist. That peace comes at the end of a perfectly curated ritual. That if you can just find the right morning routine, mantra, or mentor, that ache inside you will finally dissolve. But in reality, healing isn't a pill. And you're not a project. You don't need more methods. You need more clarity.

When you begin to understand the true nature of human experience (that is, how thoughts, feelings, sensations, and beliefs shape your world), you'll realize that the tools you've been clinging to aren't always necessary, and there's freedom in that. Not because tools are bad, but because they stop being a crutch. I still use tools with my clients, not to make them dependent, but to offer them a glimpse of what's possible and to stabilize their nervous system while we upgrade the software beneath.

Because that's what's really going on here, most practices aren't connecting you back to you; they are giving you a temporary taste of your innate qualities: peace, contentment, and joy. They're simply giving you micro-reboots to get you back to your factory settings. The problem? You've been rebooting so often, you haven't realized it's time for an upgrade. An upgrade to your true identity, and with that, the mind. An elevation in perception. A clearing of the shadow patterns that keep glitching your system.

As we move through this book, I'll guide you beneath the surface, toward the principles and the energy that powers the practices. So you can choose the ones that nourish you, not the ones you feel pressured to perform. You'll understand why the shortcuts you've been relying on never truly work and why stepping away from the chase is the portal to lasting transformation.

Moving Beyond The Quick Fix Mentality

With hundreds of tools and techniques fighting for your attention and your purse strings, it's easy to get swept up in the temptations of the self-help and personal development world. Today's coaches and wellness influencers are using the same psychological tactics as global advertisers. They feed your fears. Tease your desires. Package transformation into a six-week promise. Become a millionaire. Become your best self. Become someone else entirely.

The problem isn't that these coaches don't have value. Many

do. The issue is that their techniques are often diluted to appeal to the survival ego-based self. So even if their work has depth, the delivery is surface-level. A sliver of gold dust stretched thin across a thousand desperate souls. And when the method doesn't work for you, you're left thinking you are the problem, when in fact the approach was never designed to dissolve your old identity and realign you to your divine path.

This is why discernment is your next spiritual practice and why it's vital that you wake up.

Only by pausing and reflecting on your patterns, your habits of reaching, rushing, and consuming, can you start to see exactly how completely you've been seduced by performance in spiritual clothing. Break the trance, and you break the cycle. And in doing so, you open the gateway to true self-healing, self-discovery, and eventually, self-mastery.

So before you jump into another course, another coach, another shiny healing modality, stop and ask yourself. What are the fundamental principles behind this? Every path from art to astrology, from psychology to somatics, is built on principles. And when you understand those principles, you gain the power to assess whether a tool is right for you, whether it aligns with your truth, or whether it's just another escape dressed up as expansion.

Don't get me wrong. Tools can be powerful allies. But without first grasping the principles that shape your experience, you'll always be looking outside yourself for answers. You'll keep chasing the next spiritual fad, wondering why nothing sticks, and missing the deeper invitation. To live from truth, not just seek it.

Understanding these principles isn't just helpful; it's essential. It's foundational. It's about stopping outsourcing your power, and finally embodying your truth so you can start choosing with clarity.

Why You Need to Understand the Principles Before Chasing the Next Fad

Intelligently choosing a healing modality at the right time in your life is invaluable. But if you haven't first understood the principles that are shaping your inner world, even the most promising wellness trend will eventually lose its shine. You'll be left with a stack of techniques, a lighter bank balance, and an unfed soul. It's not failure, though. It's just misalignment, and that can absolutely be fixed.

The truth is, you can only integrate what your system is truly ready for. And without a clear grasp of the energetic and psychological principles behind healing, you're likely to fall into a loop of temporary highs, fleeting breakthroughs, and endless chasing. Let's look at why.

The Superficial Application Trap

When you don't understand the deeper mechanics of how healing actually works, every tool becomes a checkbox. You meditate, journal, repeat mantras, not because they anchor you, but because everyone on Instagram said they should. The practice becomes performative. Hollow. Something you do for five days before abandoning it, wondering why it didn't change your life. You consume techniques instead of integrating truth. You move on quickly, not because you've outgrown the practice, but because it never truly brought you back to you.

The Outsourcing of Personal Truth

Without a solid internal compass, you'll end up borrowing everyone else's (or just someone else's) map. Influencers can become gurus, and coaches can become gods. Authors become your answer to everything. But in truth, their terrain is not your terrain. Their pain is not your pain. What worked for them may not meet you where you specifically and uniquely are. The issue is that if you don't question why you're doing something, you hand over your power and start mistaking imitation for transformation. But when you understand the universal principles of human experience, you begin to filter methods through the lens of your own truth. You stop outsourcing wisdom and start trusting your own inner voice.

The Lack of Depth and Real Change

Most techniques, no matter how ancient, modern, or magical, can only take you as deep as your level of understanding allows. If you're skimming the surface, you'll keep swimming in the shallow end of your potential. And even the best modality, in the hands of someone who is not integrated, becomes a blunt instrument. The sad reality? Many practitioners are selling depth they haven't yet lived. You'll feel it. You'll sense something missing because the technique without embodiment is just performance in disguise. Principles, on the other hand, invite you into intimacy with yourself. They're what allow real, anchored change to happen, not because someone told you to, but because something clicked in you so deeply, it couldn't not change.

The Inconsistency Problem: Chasing the Next High

We live in a world addicted to immediacy. One that markets miracles in minutes and promises 10X returns on your inner peace by next Tuesday. But deep transformation is rarely that convenient. It requires stillness. Integration. The courage to sit in discomfort instead of dancing away from it. Now, don't get me wrong. Quantum shifts are real. You can experience an embodied realization so profound it changes your trajectory forever. But if you don't understand why it landed, or how to hold it, that breakthrough will fade. Without integration, even your most sacred "aha" moments become stories you tell, not truths you live.

So before you pour your energy, money, or heart into yet another modality, pause, ask yourself. Do I understand the principle behind this? Because if you don't, you may just be spiritual window-shopping, mistaking novelty for nourishment.

Understanding Principles = Freedom from the Chase + Freedom to Choose

The self-help world is bloated. Overflowing. Saturated with tools, techniques, and shiny new modalities that promise to change your life in three steps or less. Some of them do work, momentarily. But only when paired with deep understanding. Only when you are no longer trying to fix yourself, but instead trying to excrement yourself. That is the shift. That is the reframe.

Because if you do not grasp the deeper design of your lived experience (how your thoughts shape your feelings, how your emotions drive your behaviors, how your beliefs create your reality), you will always be chasing. Always hungry. Always hoping the next thing will finally be it.

So the real question is not, What is the next thing I can try?

The real question is, why do I believe I need this tool in the first place?

What fear, doubt, or void am I trying to fill?

And is this tool helping me see more clearly, or is it just keeping me distracted?

Once you start asking better questions, the game changes, and you stop being a passive consumer of self-improvement, endlessly swiping for salvation. You become a conscious participant in your own transformation. You lead. You choose. You decide.

The truth is that most tools and techniques are scaffolding. Helpful for a time. Necessary forever? No. There are thousands of options out there, but very few people teach the universal truths that underlie them all. These truths do not belong to any guru. They are not bound to any lineage. You know them in your bones when you hear them spoken.

And here is where this book will take you. In Part Two, we will go deeper into those universal naked truths. The core energies that have always been here, waiting for you. The ones that free you from the chase and give you back your choice.

Once you live from these truths, not just in your head, but in your body, your breath, and your cells, everything changes.

Why? Because truths are the real medicine. They do not fix you. They free you. And when you start living from this deeper awareness, you may find that the thing you were reaching for (the meditation, the retreat, the nervous system hack) is no longer required. Not because the tool was wrong, but because the root system it was trying to stabilize has now grown strong on its own.

Without this level of awareness, every technique becomes another dopamine hit. Like the buzz of ordering a new pair of designer boots. Temporarily exciting, never enough. A plaster on a wound that lives much deeper.

And this is what I want you to remember. When you understand the truths, you get to choose your method, if you still need one at all.

Yes, tools can soothe. Yes, techniques can help. But without the depth to hold them, they become distractions dressed as devotion.

Awareness without understanding is just intellectual noise in your head, and healing without naked truth is just more performance dressed up as healing.

Awareness of Your Problem is Not Enough to Change

My clients often ask if awareness is enough. "If I'm aware of the problem, doesn't that mean I'm already halfway to fixing it?" To which I often reply, "How many people do you know are aware they're overweight, trapped in addiction, or cheating on their partners, and still keep doing it?" No comment needed.

Awareness alone is not transformation. It is not even the starting line. It is just the flag that signals you might be ready to start the race.

At the time of writing this chapter, I had been working as a change management consultant since 2014. And if all it took was awareness and if simply knowing that a company needed to change were enough to cause that change, my job would have been redundant. Or blissfully easy. But we both know it is not.

Yes, awareness is important. Crucial, even. It is often the first breath of change. But then comes the grit. The commitment to change. Knowing how to change. And finally, the hardest part. The daily act of changing.

What I have witnessed again and again is this. If you want to change anything (your habits, your health, your relationship with yourself or others), then your current experience needs to be unsatisfying enough to create desire. You do not have to be in a full-blown crisis, although, let's be honest, most of my clients are in some version of breakdown or reckoning by the time we work together. For others, life might look good from the outside, but there is a gnawing sense that something more is possible. Not more in the hustle sense. More as in truer. Deeper. Cleaner. The wisdom in you starts whispering. This isn't it.

To initiate real change, you need to be pulled. Not just by pain, but by purpose. Not just by discomfort, but by the vision of who you could become if you stopped betraying your own aliveness. You need to be moved not only by what isn't working, but by the impact you could make if you got your shit together emotionally, mentally, and spiritually.

Whether you are seeking change because of chronic low-grade dissatisfaction or because you are teetering on the edge of collapse, your "why" matters, if you have been carrying around an unnamed ache your whole adult life and have spent hundreds, maybe thousands, trying to fix it, then of course you are going to be tempted by anything that offers a glimmer of relief. We all are.

But that is the danger. When you are hungry enough, everything looks like food.

Traditionally, after awareness and desire comes knowledge. Training and skill development. In organizations, this is how change is managed. Through planned transitions and strategic behaviors. But personal change? That is a different beast.

In your own life, you do not just need someone else's roadmap. You need to build an inner compass that lets you walk your own. Adopting someone else's beliefs might get you short-term results, but they will not set you free. True change happens when you see the truth for yourself. No convincing necessary. The truth becomes self-evident, and in that moment, you cannot unsee it.

That is how I work with people. Not by handing them a list

of affirmations or hacks. But by facilitating realizations. The kind that hits you in your bones and rewrites how you see life itself. I call them mind experiments. They let you witness, in real time, how your thoughts create your emotional landscape, how your beliefs shape your nervous system, how your worldview filters every experience.

When the insight is real, really real, change does not feel hard. It feels inevitable. Like a switch flipped. Like, "Oh, that's why I was doing that. That no longer makes sense." And suddenly, a habit that has defined your entire adult life, such as overthinking, people-pleasing, or self-sabotaging, just stops.

Because here is the thing. Behavior always follows feeling. And feeling always follows thought. So when the thought shifts, when the mechanism behind the experience is seen clearly, the downstream pattern dissolves. It is not magic. It's just how the system works, but it does feel miraculous when you feel the shift.

Turning Your Attention Inwards

For a little while, I am going to ask you to do something radical. I want you to stop all the healing work. Not forever. Just for now. Pause the podcasts. Put down the self-help book you were planning to read after this one. Step back from the endless scroll of tools, techniques, and five-step fixes that promise to change your life if you just try harder.

Instead, I want you to do something you might not have done in a long time, if ever.

Turn your attention inward.

Not in the way that loops you into rumination. In the way that lets you witness, quietly, curiously, and without judgment. I am not asking you to solve anything or figure anything out.

I am asking you to observe the inner workings of your mind. Not as a philosopher, but as an explorer. As the only person who can truly access what is going on in there.

Throughout this book, I will guide you to temporarily shift your gaze away from the external world. Away from your list of problems, your obsession with solving them, and the mental gymnastics you have been performing to try to get "there," wherever there is. Instead, I will invite you to focus on the only place where real transformation happens. Within.

Why? Because when you begin to observe the mechanics of your mind: how it generates thoughts, how it builds beliefs, how it fuels emotion and reaction, you stop being the puppet and start seeing the strings.

When you witness your patterns in real time, something wild happens. The illusion begins to crack. The thoughts that once felt so convincing begin to lose their grip. You start to see clearly, not just conceptually, but viscerally, that what you are experiencing right now is not the objective truth. It is a projection, built from layers of thought that are constantly moving, shifting, and being filtered through your own invisible system.

Here is the thing no one told you in school, in therapy, or even in your last breathwork class. When you deeply understand that everything you are experiencing is being created from the inside out, not the outside in, you stop being at the mercy of your circumstances. You start becoming the creator of your experience.

That is when power returns. That is when wholeness begins.

This is not about detachment or bypassing. It is not about ignoring what is hard or pretending your trauma does not exist. It is about reclaiming authorship. About becoming someone who no longer gets seduced by every passing thought or consumed by every emotional storm.

When you learn to spot the invisible, internal machinery behind your reactions, your inner critic, your fear, your craving, you become your own guru. You no longer need to ask Instagram, a chatbot, or your therapist what to do. You know. Because you have seen the truth for yourself, and once that happens, you cannot unsee it.

What Creates True Change? Becoming Aware

We have talked about awareness, about spotting the issue. But let us get honest. What does becoming aware actually mean?

I teach awareness at many different levels. At its most basic, it starts like this. You bring something into your conscious mind. That is it. You notice. You name it. You see it clearly, without judging or resisting. And from there, you have a choice.

Even if it is a split-second decision, awareness gives you a moment of pause. A flash of spaciousness, where a window of time opens. And in that moment, you can either follow the old groove, the conditioned pattern, or you can choose differently. This, in its simplest form, is awareness of your current way of being. And it is the first step toward true change.

But let us go deeper.

When you begin to see, not just think but see, that your experience of life is created from the inside out, moment by moment, it changes everything. Even if it looks like the outside world is pulling the strings. When you realize this through direct experience, your entire relationship with your thoughts, people, and problems begins to shift. And when your understanding shifts, your world shifts with it.

You stop reacting from the surface and you start witnessing the machinery beneath.

At this level of awareness, you are no longer just aware of your habits. You are aware of your mind in motion. The thoughts are forming. The beliefs are swirling. The emotions are rising. You are not just inside the storm. You are watching it with the eye. And from that place, change becomes natural. Eventually, this deeper awareness leads you to the most essential discovery. That you are not your thoughts, your habits, or even your preferences. You are awareness itself. And from this place, old mental states lose their grip. The suffering begins to unravel. Your system regulates itself in real time. Not because you have mastered a thousand techniques, but because you have returned to the truth of what you are.

This is not a theory. This is not some lovely Instagram quote about self-awareness. I lived, felt, and realized this myself. That is why I do not just give you ideas in this book. I offer you experiments and invitations. Because real transformation comes from your own aha moments, not my teachings. You need to see it, not just read it.

So let me show you what I mean.

In my late twenties, I was always running late. And when I say always, I mean Olympic-level late. I had a cute little Fiat 500, and my partner had a sleek Audi. We had an agreement. Whoever took the car with the most petrol had to fill it back up. Sounds simple, right?

Except every time I pulled into the petrol station, no matter which car I was in, I parked on the wrong side. Every time. Fiat on the left. Audi on the right. And still, I got it wrong.

Leaning out the window like a contortionist, trying to drag the nozzle across the boot, hoping I had just misjudged the length.

Then, out of frustration, I actually opened the car manual. And there it was. The little arrow next to the petrol symbol on the dashboard. That tiny arrow pointed to the side of your tank is on. It had been there all along. Both cars had it. I had just never seen it.

The truth had always been there, quietly pointing, patiently waiting. I did not need a new car. I did not need to try harder. I needed to see what was already true. Once I realized that little arrow was there to guide me, I never parked on the wrong side again. I did not have to try. I just knew.

That is the difference between reading about something and realizing it.

You do not forget a realization. You do not have to force it into your memory like a Post-it note. It lands. It sticks. It rewires your behavior effortlessly. You change not because you should, but because something finally clicks. The design of life reveals itself, and suddenly, you stop fighting it.

How to Read This Book

Reading between the lines and realizing the truth between the words.

This is not the kind of book you skim while scrolling your phone. It is a journey. A return. A reclamation. And like anything sacred, it asks something of you.

My only request is that you read this book from start to finish with an open heart and a curious mind. Even when your mind gets distracted, because it will. Even when parts feel repetitive, because some truths are worth saying twice, this book was not written to entertain your intellect. It was written to awaken something ancient within you. And sometimes, awakening takes repetition. Rhythm. Repatterning.

If you read it in the order it was designed to be read, it will work its way through you like a coded invitation. A pathway back to your higher self. A key to unlock what is already inside. Your gifts, your power, your clarity, your real purpose. This is not just reading. This is remembering.

Throughout this undressing journey, you will find stories, raw and real, offered as mirrors, not performances. You will be met with metaphors that crack illusions, and meditations that lead you beyond the noise. You will be asked not simply to absorb information, but to experience the deeper transmission underneath the words because that is where your aha lives. And those moments will be your turning points. The kind that melts lifelong patterns and returns you to the truth of who you already are.

Part One strips you bare. You will unravel the roles, identities, and masks that once kept you safe but now keep you small. It will gently strip away your performance patterns and protection strategies, helping you break up with the noise of "shoulds" and come home to silence. The place where your truth still lives.

Part Two brings the fire. This is where truth bombs drop and illusions collapse. You will realign with the universal truths that have always governed your life, even when you did not know their names. This part is your sacred remembering, where your wisdom begins to speak louder than your fear. Your awareness sharpens. Your energy recalibrates. And the compass of your life begins to point somewhere real.

Part Three is where the rubber meets the road. No more knowing without doing. No more spiritual highs with no structure. This is your sacred embodiment. You will learn how to integrate what you have realized, anchor what you have awakened, and actually live it. Out loud, in motion, through your breath, your choices, your voice, your relationships. This is not the performance of alignment. It is the transmission of it. You will fall back into the right rhythm with yourself and move through the world as the real you. No proving. No chasing. Just being. Fully. This part helps you build a life that reflects who you are, not who you were taught to be.

The best way to read this book is simple. Begin at the beginning. Move through it like a rite of passage. If you have already read every personal development book, tried every method, and seen every therapist, it's beautiful. Now let them go for now. Pause the picking and mixing. Let this book be your full-body yes until the final page. Then breathe. Let it settle. Let the magic find you.

This book is not a hack. It is a holy interruption. I am honored to walk this with you.

Let us undress.

Chapter 4:
Branded of Worth

You were born worthy, but you were taught to prove it.

Happiness, like a fleeting butterfly, dances just beyond our grasp. We chase it relentlessly, only to find it elusively slipping through our fingers. Yet, perhaps in the pursuit itself, we discover that true happiness is not a destination but a state of being. It is not found in the external world, but within the depths of our own hearts. Let go of the chase, and you may find that happiness, like a gentle breeze, softly embraces you when you least expect it.

— Dalai Lama

"This is the last pair I'll buy this season," I said, lying through my teeth, as my then-husband handed me yet another AloYoga delivery. He barely batted an eyelid. "You're up and down the garden more than a whore's drawers," he smirked, amused by my ever-expanding spiritual athleisure wardrobe.

I laughed, but inside I knew. I was not just collecting leggings. I was collecting illusions.

This was not a new obsession. It was an old addiction dressed in new fabric. Once upon a time, it was Mulberry handbags and patent Louboutins that made me feel worthy. Sophisticated. Seen. I thought they told the world who I was, a successful woman, a woman who had made it.

Eventually, I grew out of that identity. Or so I thought. I traded the stilettos for barefoot grounding and the handbags for hemp. What I did not realize was that consumerism did not die. It shapeshifted.

Now I was buying chakra-colored leggings and ethically sourced crystals. I had swapped my obsession with looking powerful for the obsession with being aligned, or at least appearing as if I had ascended my way to higher consciousness.

The designer logos changed, but the performance remained the same.

And it was not just the clothes. Shelves were groaning with self-help books, a graveyard of half-finished online courses. "This is the one," I would whisper as I clicked Buy Now. This one will fix it. This one will unlock the part of me that still felt a bit off, a bit empty, a bit not enough.

But the fix never came. And I kept paying for the promise.

Because society does not just sell us products, it sells us prescriptions. Prescriptions for a life we never consciously wrote but unconsciously signed up for. We are taught that happiness is always just one upgrade away. One program. One planner. One next-level version of ourselves.

And the spiritual space? It is not immune. It is just savvier. It does not peddle beauty or status. It peddles enlightenment.

"This is not just about looking good," it says. "This is about becoming your higher self."

And what achiever type would not want that?

But here is what I learned, on my knees, through the detours, under the glow of all those Himalayan salt lamps. The pursuit of more, even when dressed as healing or wholeness, still leaves you hungry.

Whether it is more leggings, more learning, or more lunar rituals, the chasing will not stop until you stop and ask.

What story am I still performing for? Whose script am I still playing out?

Because we think we are growing. But often, we are just costume changing. Shapeshifting from one identity to another without ever stopping to question who we were before the world told us who to become.

True transformation does not come from adding more layers. It comes from unclothing the script.

And the script? It is old. Worn. Built by a culture that thrives on your not-enoughness.

This chapter is about exposing the lie that your worth can be branded, bought, or performed, and reclaiming the deeper truth that your happiness has never lived in products, personas, or perfection. It has always lived in you.

A Misguided Common Belief Shaped by Consumer Culture

Here it is, the golden lie. The one we have all been sold, swallowed, and shaped by. The belief that happiness comes from outside of us. From the right face. The right fortune. The right filter. We have been seduced into thinking that if we just acquire enough (money, status, milestones, partnerships), we will finally feel enough.

But if that were true, would not every millionaire in Malibu be wrapped in joy? Would not the surgically perfected, designer-draped women of the world be radiating peace? We know they are not. We have read the interviews, seen the breakdowns, watched the addictions unfold behind the curated highlight reels of perfection. And yet, we keep chasing.

Because this illusion is powerful. And profitable. We do not just want things. We want what they represent. Safety, recognition, worthiness, love. We imagine that if we just had her life, his confidence, their lifestyle, we would finally exhale. Finally, stop proving. Finally feel held. But the truth is, no matter how fast you run toward the next upgrade, the further you run away from yourself, and the moment you catch it, it fades.

That handbag's glow dulls. That man starts to feel distant. That job, that opportunity, that big moment, it drains you like the last one. And what do we do? We pivot. We upgrade. We label it "evolution" and call it growth. But really, we are just swapping one chase for another. Same cycle, new costume.

The chase is addictive. And when the next hit does not deliver, the ache deepens. Self-doubt creeps in. Maybe I am the problem. Maybe I am broken. Maybe I will never feel satisfied. That is the cruelty of consumer culture. It does not just fail you. It gaslights you. It whispers, You are just one step away. Keep going. Try harder. Buy more. Fix yourself.

And like a well-intentioned woman with a vision board and a perfectly curated cart, you listen. You invest, and consume, not just in the products, but in the identities and personas they promise.

But let me say it clearly. You are already perfectly designed for your role in this lifetime, if only you'd stop believing the ads and get your safety-seeking ego out of the way. You are simply caught in a beautifully marketed lie. It is not your fault.

But it is your invitation to awaken to the lie.

The Mulberry bag alone will not align you. The AloYoga leggings will not save you. The next self-help course will not hand you your true purpose on a platter because happiness has never lived out there. It has been within you this whole time, quiet, still, unassuming, and waiting for you to listen to your next move.

The Rise of Western Consumerism

Every culture carries its own coded beliefs about what it means to be happy. In Western societies, the scales are heavily weighted toward external indicators. Wealth, status, possessions, and professional achievements. If you live in a Westernized country, chances are you have absorbed, consciously or unconsciously, the belief that happiness comes from the outside in.

But where did that idea even come from?

To trace the roots, we have to go back to the Industrial Revolution of the late 18th century. It was a time when technology flipped the script on how goods were produced. Suddenly, items were not just handcrafted luxuries for the elite. They were churned out en masse, ready for the rising middle class. Expanding transport networks meant that for the first time in history, products could travel faster than word of mouth. But with mass production came a new challenge. Mass persuasion. Enter advertising.

By the mid-20th century, just after World War II, consumerism had entered its golden era. Disposable income rose, factories boomed, and businesses seized their moment. Glossy magazine ads and slick TV jingles did not just sell products; they also shaped cultures. They sold lifestyles. The message was simple and seductive. Own more, live better.

Consumerism became the oxygen of Western economies. A thriving society was no longer defined by collective well-being, but by individual spending power. The more you bought, the more successful you appeared. And so the seed was planted. Happiness is not something you feel; it is something you buy. Every checkout became a vote for your worth.

This is how modern materialism was born. It was not just about buying things. It was about buying into a story. And before we knew it, that story had become our subconscious script.

The Cultural Machinery of Consumerism

At its core, consumerism is more than an economic system. It is a psychological script. A belief system. A cultural hypnosis that Westerners have inherited, inhaled, and internalized. It tells you that satisfaction is not something you are; it is something you buy. That success looks like a bigger house, that happiness feels like a newer watch, and that fulfilment comes with wearing designer heels while sipping a six-pound flat white with your laptop open at Soho House.

Here is the real seduction. Consumerism is not just about what you buy. It is about who you believe you are when you buy it.

In a culture obsessed with individuality, possessions become proxies for personality. The car you drive, the trainers you wear, the skincare on your bathroom shelf, all quietly broadcasting a curated identity. It is branding for your soul.

And it is a double-edged blade. On one side, you are told to express yourself. Build a unique life. Create a brand for you. On the other hand, you are pressured to conform, to match the aesthetic, to chase the milestones, to perform the illusion of having it all together. The result? We trade authenticity for acceptance. We abandon our inner truth for a version of ourselves the world might clap for. And then we wonder why we feel so goddamn exhausted, even when everything looks right.

The Role of Advertising and Media

Advertising did not just fuel the consumer machine. It became its most persuasive weapon. The moment the printing press could mass-distribute messages, marketing was born. From then on, businesses were not just selling products. They were selling stories. Stories that taught us who we should be, what we should want, and how happiness should look.

Early ads made subtle promises. A new soap would make you beautiful, a new car would make you powerful. Now the promises are more seductive and far more personal. With every scroll, your feed whispers directly to your insecurities. This serum will fix your tired eyes. This course will make you magnetic. This retreat will unlock your feminine power. It is curated precisely for you, based on your fears, your clicks, your hesitations.

Even in your downtime, the consumer story keeps playing. You watch your favorite shows to unwind, whether classics like Sex and the City, Desperate Housewives, or The Kardashians, and unknowingly download a narrative that happiness is found in status, beauty, money, and romance. We do not just admire the characters. We want to be them. And why would we not? They seem to have it all.

Here is the trick. What is presented as entertainment is often quiet indoctrination. You are not just watching a show. You are absorbing a lifestyle. And over time, the lines blur. The script becomes your own.

A System Designed to Keep You Consuming

Let us call it out clearly. The system thrives on your belief that you are incomplete.

Think about it. How many babies have you looked at and thought, Gosh, they need to be more productive, polished, or put together? None. They are perfect in their snot-smeared, half-naked, belly-giggling glory. They do not need anything to be enough. But somewhere along the way, you were taught otherwise.

That lesson was not personal. It was strategic.

Consumerism works by making you question yourself. Marketing campaigns are designed to tap into your fears and amplify your flaws. Find the pain point. Stoke the insecurity. Then offer the "solution." That was my job in my old life in PR and marketing. I was the girl behind the copywriting curtain. And it worked every time. Not because people were gullible, but because the script was everywhere, and we were too tired, too trusting, or too busy trying to be better to see through it.

But this is not about shame. This is about awakening.

You were not a fool. You were programmed. You did not fail. You were conditioned. And the real heartbreak is this. The void you were trying to fill never existed. You were whole all along. You just believed you were not. That is the con. And the moment you see it, you get to opt out.

So the next time you are about to buy that one final thing, one more crystal, one more pair of leggings, one more life-changing retreat, pause. Breathe. Ask yourself. What am I actually reaching for?

Because if happiness was never in the cart to begin with, where is it really hiding?

Consumerism's Grip on Our Inner Peace

Let's pause for a moment. Step back. Zoom out from the scroll, the shopping carts, and the mounting to-do list of your "ideal self." Because while desire is not the enemy, unchecked desire can quietly become your prison.

Materialism in itself is not bad. The beauty industry is not bad. Wanting more is not wrong. It is human to appreciate elegance, to enjoy life's comforts, and to desire experiences that light up your senses. But when the chase for "more" hijacks your peace, when it stirs your insecurities, wrecks your finances, and leaves you hollow unless you have that thing, that is when you know you are no longer in charge. The script is.

This is not just about consumption. It is about control.

And here is the kicker. We have come so far, haven't we? As women, we have inherited freedoms our grandmothers could only dream of. We can vote, learn, earn, speak, leave, and lead. We can build our own empires. And yet we are still being sold cages. Only now they are gold-plated and algorithm-approved.

Because the battle today is not for equality, it is for autonomy. It is the fight to write your own script without being labeled difficult, ungrateful, unhinged, or unfeminine. It is the right to opt out of the corporate fairytales, the Pinterest-perfect lives, the lifestyle porn served up in your feed, without being made to feel like a woman who just cannot keep up.

And in the age of tech, that pressure is not just in your workplace or living room. It is in your pocket, on your screen, and inside your subconscious. We are connected like never before, but that connection comes at a cost. Exposure without end. Targeted ads, digital influencers, sponsored posts, every square inch of your digital life is monetized. Every insecurity is a data point.

Comparison has shifted from a passing feeling into a full-blown syndrome. I call it comparativitis. The constant compulsion to measure your life against someone else's curated highlight reel. The mindless scroll becomes a ritual of self-erasure. Look at her holiday. Look at her abs. Look at her calm children and minimalist kitchen. Meanwhile, you are left wondering why the wisdom inside you feels a little louder and your fridge a little messier.

And this is no accident. The system is designed this way. The constant feed tells you that you do not measure up. You are behind. You are late. It does not say it outright (it does not have to). It drips into your nervous system in soft, seductive ways. One influencer at a time. One "must-have" at a time. One algorithmic torment is that your life, as it is, is not enough. And that is the theft of your peace.

The Impact on Women

Let's be honest. This is not just about big bad brands. Marketing machines are not villains. They are fulfilling their purpose. They sell, we buy. That is the game. And yes, in recent years, many brands have started to wake up. They are spotlighting "real" women, weaving diversity into their campaigns, and championing narratives that appear socially conscious.

But for those of us raised in the 1980s and 1990s, the imprint runs deep. We grew up marinated in images of airbrushed perfection. Women who juggled high-flying careers, pristine homes, hyper-intentional motherhood, and bodies that never bloated, aged, or broke down. They smiled with a glint of knowing. They made it look effortless. And somewhere between a Pantene ad and a Cosmo article, we internalized a dangerous belief. I should be able to do it all too.

We were sold the story that we could "have it all," but no one warned us about the cost. No one whispered about the sacrifice, the self-abandonment, or the slow erosion of joy under the weight of trying to live up to the script. The version of "all" we were sold came with silent strings, puppet strings we did not even know we had been tangled in.

And so, we contort. We strive. We chase. We are expected to be self-made and spiritually evolved. Emotionally intelligent and financially independent. We should be raising conscious kids, holding down high-powered jobs, making passionate love to our partners, building empires from our living rooms, and somehow still glowing like a twenty-seven-year-old wellness influencer with an eighteen-year-old's body and a billionaire's sleep schedule.

The result? A generation of women quietly burning. Burnout is not just a buzzword. It has become our baseline. Behind the filters, the feeds, and the flawless yoga selfies lies an epidemic of soul fatigue. Women lie awake at night wondering why they still do not feel enough, despite doing everything "right."

We exist in a loop of quiet discontent. Always reaching for the next version of ourselves. Always holding ourselves up against some glittery phantom of perfection that never really existed in the first place. We scroll and compare. We strive and criticize. We perform and pretend. And beneath it all, a single belief pulses like a low-grade fever.

I am not good enough.

That belief is like a virus. It is what feeds the Happiness Whore habit. It whispers that there is something missing, something broken that needs fixing. And so we buy, we chase, we prove. But what if there is no hole to fill?

What if the only thing keeping you from feeling whole is the belief that you are not?

From Cradle To Consumer

Your relationship with external comfort did not begin with your first credit card or your first crush. It began in the cot.

Before you could speak, before you knew what a shoe brand was, your nervous system was already wiring its patterns. Who to trust, what soothes, where safety lives. From the very beginning, we learn how to cope. And more often than not, we learn to reach outside ourselves in order to feel okay.

Watch any newborn. Their survival depends on their caregiver. Every cry, every cuddle, every bottle shapes the blueprint of their emotional world. If their needs are met with warmth and presence, the body softens. Trust forms. The infant learns, I cry, I am held. I am safe. The world is safe.

But what happens when comfort is outsourced? When the parent does not pick them up, but instead pops in a dummy, hands them a blanket, or places a soft toy by their side? The baby, clever and adaptive, makes the link. I feel better when I have this object. They do not know they are substituting presence for possession, but their body does.

And that wiring does not disappear with age. It evolves. The pacifier becomes a plush toy. The plush toy becomes a handbag. The handbag becomes a holiday. The holiday becomes a six-figure launch. It is the same loop dressed in adult clothing.

We keep reaching for the external because once it worked. Because once, it brought a little relief. Because in some small way, we really did feel better. But now the cuddle has been replaced with consumption, and the comfort feels emptier every time.

Here is the part that breaks the spell. Your patterns were built for survival. They were intelligent responses to a world that taught you to soothe through external objects, to find worth through achievement, and to get love by meeting everyone else's needs but abandoning your own. But this is not your truth. And this way of living is no longer required.

So what if, the next time you were about to buy something you didn't need, you paused and asked yourself. What am I really needing right now? Love? Presence? Rest? Reassurance? What if the thing you were reaching for was just a stand-in for the very need you have not yet been taught to meet yourself from within or speak up so that need is met through your relationships?

This is where it gets juicy. This is where the pattern is revealed, not to shame you, but to free you. Because once you see how deeply these habits were etched (from the cot to the closet), you can stop playing dress-up in someone else's identity. You can come back to your own.

Yes, buy the shoes if they amplify your truest expression of life. Yes, wear the lipstick if it turns your energy on. But do it from wholeness, not from hunger. Let your joy, not your emptiness, be the one making the choices.

Uncovering the Origin of Your Consumer Story

Most of what we believe about happiness didn't come encoded in our souls. It was drip-fed through family patterns, cultural slogans, glossy magazine covers, and the ads between Disney films. Without even realizing it, we inherited a script about what happiness looks like. Success, purchases, milestones, and appearances; we've been performing for it ever since.

But that script isn't ours. It's conditioning. And here's the thing. We fall for it every time, but every time we buy into it, we chase fool's gold. The handbags, the goals, the image. They might sparkle for a moment, but they collapse the moment you touch them, because they were never built on truth.

So what's your story? Where did you learn that happiness had to be earned, bought, or performed? And how is that story still running your life today?

Let me take you deeper. I've created a guided practice, a step-by-step exercise to trace your original programming, decode the cultural rules you absorbed, and rewrite the script you didn't know you inherited. You'll find it in the Undressed Playbook, available free at https://www.gemdentith.com/playbook

Undressed Realizations

Consumerism did not just teach us how to shop. It taught us how to seek.

It trained us to believe we were missing something and then offered endless solutions to fix the lack it created. It whispered, 'You will feel better when, and kept us hooked on the next thing, the next glow up, the next mask.

But the deeper truth is this. You were sold a survival strategy, not a path to wholeness.

This culture did not just shape your habits. It shaped your identity. And unhooking from that is not about guilt. It is about power. The power to finally stop performing. To stop patching over your soul with purchases. To come back to your body.

Back to your truth. Back to what is real.

Mirror Moments

Where in my life have I been outsourcing happiness, rather than feeling it from within?

What have I been taught I must have in order to be enough?

Can I remember a moment I felt deeply content without buying, achieving, or proving anything?

Embodied Practice

Pause Before the Purchase. Next time you feel the urge to consume, whether it is a product, a scroll, or a story, **S**top. Breathe. Ask. What part of me is hungry? And what would truly nourish her?

Choose One Day of Sacred Non-Consumption. No buying, no binge eating, binge watching, or binge shopping. Just you, your breath, your body, and the presence of the moment; perhaps just go for a walk in nature, with no phone, if it's safe to do so, and just what emerges in the stillness. This is where your truth lives.

Undress a Cultural Belief. Write down one internalized belief that no longer serves you. Burn it. Bury it. Or speak it out loud and let it go. Then choose one small act of rebellion, your way of rewriting the script.

Final Undressing Thought

You are waking up from a dream that was never yours. So the next time the world tries to sell you something to fix you, remember this.

The only thing missing was the realization that nothing was ever missing.

And now you are coming back. Back to your original self, back to what was always there beneath the layers.

Let's keep undressing.

Chapter 5:

Stripping the Roles

Slip off the costume that once kept you safe but no longer lets you grow.

The greatest illusion is to think that you are what you think you are. To discover your true essence, you must release the false identifications that bind you. Uncover who you are not, and in that sacred emptiness, the truth of your being will shine forth.

— Eckhart Tolle

It was a quiet Wednesday evening, the 11th of October 2023, around 9:49 PM. I found myself in deep reflection, contemplating the countless "work" roles I had taken on since I started earning money at the grand age of thirteen. My first job was babysitting a toddler who lived across the street. Before I had even hit sixteen, I was doing paper rounds, helping my aunty with her cleaning business, and waitressing in a tourist café down in Ironbridge.

I came from a very working-class family. My dad ran his own business. My mum was a childminder. One nan worked in an office, the other ran a bed and breakfast. There wasn't much emphasis on my parents' day jobs, though, in fairness, I probably would not have paid much attention even if there had been. But one thing I did notice, early on, was how adults introduced themselves. First, their name. Then their job. As if identity could be summarized by a payslip or a role description. I remember thinking how strange it was, this habit of giving ourselves a label based on what we do rather than who we are.

That observation stuck with me.

Across my working life, I have had more identities than I can count. If I owned a hat for every assignment I have taken on, I would be running a wildly successful millinery shop by now. I have worked in hair salons, restaurants, pubs, factories, gyms, ad agencies, government buildings, and start-ups. I have launched businesses, closed businesses, freelanced, consulted, and coached. I have worn the name tags of waitress, shop assistant, yoga teacher, PR manager, health coach, change consultant, paramedic trainee, vegan chef, energy healer, model, marketing lead, presenter, and now, author.

I am not listing this to show off. I am telling you this because if I had built my identity on what I did for money, you would probably assume I had multiple personalities. But there is one thing I became undeniably good at. Change. Not the kind you force, but the kind you become. I lived by a mantra. Anything is possible. And I meant it. If you want something badly enough and take aligned action, you will either get it or grow into someone who no longer needs it.

Change thrilled me. The idea that we could reinvent ourselves again and again, through desire, knowledge, and skill, was the ultimate high. It made me feel powerful, expansive, and alive. Until it did not. Until I realised that change was so easy for me, it became a habit: build it, burn it down, or move on and start over.

But I became fatigued with the energy it took to continually start over, and eventually I had to stop and ask myself the harder questions. Why am I chasing change like it is oxygen? What am I running from? What am I hoping to find?

When I became a change consultant, the title felt like a socially acceptable answer to the chaos of my CV. People stopped questioning my job-hopping. Recruiters did not blink at the patchwork of my LinkedIn history. The title of Change Consultant sounded impressive. Vague enough to intrigue. Respectable enough to silence.

But the truth behind the changes was not mysterious at all. I left companies because I could not move fast enough. Because I craved autonomy. Because I did not like the people. Because the culture sucked the life out of me. Because I was bored. Or burned out. Or because life whispered, This isn't it.

Underneath all of it, achievement had become my drug. My personal flavor of the Happiness Whore Habit.

And while achieving can be admirable, there comes a point when you realize you have been building castles on sand.

It looks good. It even feels good for a moment. But eventually, it sinks.

At some point, you have to stop leaping from one identity to the next and start building something true. Something rooted. You have to stop laying false foundations and finally ask yourself. What is all this success for, if none of it feels like me?

Here is the thing. Even when I was at the top of my game, consulting with the UK Cabinet Office or holding a leadership title at Charlotte Tilbury, something always felt slightly off. People respected those roles. I noticed their eyes lit up when I mentioned them. But what I noticed even more was this. How fickle the world becomes when your worth depends on your label. One minute, you are the cover girl. Next, you are a half-read mag in a nail salon toilet.

So I started asking bigger questions. Who am I, really? Who

am I not?

And underneath those. If I strip away all the roles, all the performance, all the borrowed definitions, what remains?

These were not just philosophical questions. They were invitations. Soul-deep summons to walk away from false identities and find something more permanent. Not fixed, but eternal. Not performative, but true.

I realized that even those not in the workforce are given roles. If you are a parent, a partner, a daughter, a "kept woman" (oh yes, that is a role too), or a friend, you are still navigating identity. Roles are not just professional. They are social. Relational. Cultural. And most of them are inherited, not chosen.

With every shift in identity, I saw how people related to me differently. They treated me with more curiosity or more caution, more warmth or more indifference, depending on what box I ticked. But what unsettled me most was this. I had started to relate to myself that way, too.

With each title came a new set of beliefs, images, and behaviors. I began living in the role. And in doing so, I moved further and further from my truth. My real purpose. My core.

But here is the liberating part. Once I started shedding those layers, peeling off the roles like old clothing, I found her. That version of me I had always sensed but never fully known. And when I did, I realized she had been there all along.

This part of me was the only part of me that was unchanged, untouched, and importantly unbothered by the hats or the haircuts or the highlight reels. This was the me behind the me.

It reminded me of a moment with my nan. I used to sit on her bed and ask, "How old do you feel inside?" She would laugh and say, "Twenty-one." And I would say, "But really, Nan?" And she would laugh again and say, "Young."

Her face was wrinkled, yes. Her body was slowing. But her essence was timeless. Her essence sparkled. There is something so precious in that, when life itself shines through age, through memory, through everything you have lived. It is not something you explain. It is something you feel. A knowing beyond words.

And that, right there, is what this chapter is about. Because when you strip away the roles and return to that inner steadiness, that unchanging, sovereign center, what you find is not emptiness. It feels like you, like coming home to yourself.

Discovering Your Mistaken Identity

To uncover who you truly are at your core, you must first understand who you are not.

I love this quote by the late Steve Jobs, "Your time is limited, so don't waste it living someone else's life."

Most of us build our identity without even realizing it, like layering outfits to match the weather of our lives. As children, we are "sporty," or "clever," or "creative." As teenagers, we experiment with rebellion or perfection. As adults, we collect job titles, partners, handbags, diplomas, and dinner party labels. We start to believe that the more impressive our outer life looks, the more valuable we must be. The layering becomes habitual until it becomes hard to tell what the mask is and who the real person is underneath. But then something happens. Life strips you.

A financial loss. A betrayal. A health crisis. Something collapses. Something you thought defined you disappears.

The career ends. The partner leaves. The role changes. Suddenly, the scaffolding that held your self-image in place is gone, and with it, your certainty. It is like your identity just went up in flames, and you are left sifting through the ash, whispering, Who the hell am I now?

That moment, the crumbling, is sacred. It's not comfortable, but it's the first brick to fall from the wall you have paved around yourself to survive this world. Because in the rubble of what you thought made you worthy, you have a chance to meet who you really are.

Here is the truth. Much of who you believe yourself to be is borrowed. It's based on conditioning and has been constructed by the society you were raised in. You have been shaped by culture, by other people's opinions, by systems built to keep you in roles that benefit them. Over time, you internalize the environment. You start to believe the lie that you are what happens to you. That if someone cheats, you are not enough. That if you lose your job, you are unworthy. That if you are overlooked, you are invisible. This is the false self in action, and it's easy to manipulate as it wants to stay safe and will conform in any way it can to ensure this is the outcome. The false self is driven by safety; it adapts, it performs, and wears "high achiever" like a crown, but it is secretly terrified of being average, overlooked, and misunderstood. These things feel like death to it. So it volunteers to always be the helpful one, it overdelivers, perfects, and takes charge of the situation. It does whatever it takes to stay on top and to be relevant. It thrives on competition and on being chosen. But beneath the hustle is a quiet, choking truth. The false self is always one wrong move away from collapse.

I lived as her for years.

I became the "super-helper," the rescuer, the woman who could fix everything and everyone. I overworked, overgave, and overachieved. The truth is, I enjoyed it, but what it did mean was that I became a pro at self-abandonment; I didn't have needs, I functioned to ensure everyone else's emotional needs were taken care of.

People pleasing became my mask. And like so many of us, I didn't even realise I was wearing one. I thought, *This is who I am. This is what I need to do to love my family and to be loved in return.*

But over time, that role began to suffocate me. I became the one holding everyone together, the father figure, the rescuer, the reliable one. My needs disappeared into the background noise of responsibility. And when I finally needed help to move forward in my own life, there was no one there. I collapsed under the weight of that truth, the realization that I had built my identity on being needed, not on being known.

It felt as though there was nothing solid beneath me. Until, slowly, I began to sense something greater, a power that holds each of us even when everything we've been holding falls apart. You'll come to meet that power in Part Two.

Back then, the pain of pretending became heavier than the pain of being misunderstood.

The false self goes by many names: the survival self, the ego self, the shadow self, the social self, the fictitious self. Freud studied it by examining the hidden architecture of the mind and uncovering how much of what we call "self" is built on defence, repression, and desire. Jung mapped it by exploring the vast landscape of the psyche and revealing that our masks and shadows are not flaws to fix but parts of ourselves longing to be seen. Ramana Maharshi dissolved it through self-inquiry, stripping away illusion with the question "Who am I?" until only pure awareness remained. Eckhart Tolle illuminated it through the power of presence, reminding us that the ego cannot survive in the light of consciousness.

Whatever name you give it, the essence is the same. It is not the real you.

It is you who is addicted to being liked. The you that clings to the illusion of success. The you who cannot relax unless she is being applauded. The you who would rather be impressive than intimate. The you who is constantly scanning the room to see how she is being perceived.

And it is exhausting. Because no matter how much you feed it with attention, possessions, status, or likes, it is never satisfied. It needs more. It must have more. And that is where the system wins because a false self is a dream client for consumerism. Insecure enough to buy, just confident enough to keep scrolling. It is how the machine keeps you small while convincing you that you are empowered.

But here is the invitation. What if you stopped feeding the false self? What if you paused the performance long enough to hear the quiet hum of who you really are?

Begin by being honest. Ask yourself. What roles do I cling to, and why? What do I believe makes me valuable? Whose love did I need to earn, and how did I learn to earn it?

Look around your life. The clothes, the car, the job, the titles. The curated identity. None of it is bad, per se. But if it all vanished tomorrow, would you still feel real? Would you still feel worthy?

That is the test.

The real you (the original you) is steady. She does not flinch when someone else wins. She does not chase applause. She does not need to prove. She knows. She remembers her wholeness. And she is waiting for you beneath the false self. Not with judgment. With love. Because this next part of your journey is not about becoming more, it is about undoing what you never were.

How You Formed a False Self

Your false self was not born. It was built. Thought by thought, layer by layer. Every time you adjusted who you were to earn approval, keep the peace, or fit in, another stitch was added to the costume. Eventually, it began to feel like you. But familiarity is not the same as truth.

This version of you (let us call it the false self) is a psychological construct, composed of your interpretations of the world. It formed through your earliest experiences, interactions with others, and exposure to social expectations. Some parts you chose consciously. Others were handed to you, like clothing you did not question. Over time, you were dressed in roles, beliefs, and identities, many of which no longer fit.

From the moment you were born, your nervous system began forming impressions. Your brain translated raw sensation (touch, sound, tone) into meaning. That meaning became belief. Those beliefs began forming your personality. For example, if you experienced inconsistency or rejection and concluded, "I must not be enough," that belief likely wove its way into your identity and silently shaped your boundaries, behaviors, and relationships.

This is how it works. A belief like "I am not good enough" becomes a lens. It dictates how you show up in the world. Maybe you over-give, over-perform, or tolerate poor treatment, because a part of you believes that is all you deserve. And when someone oversteps or fails to see you, it confirms the belief. The false self feeds on this cycle. It keeps you chasing, proving, and compensating.

One of the clearest ways to spot the false self is to listen to the voice in your head. The one that tells you that you are falling behind, not doing enough, not being enough. Sometimes it criticizes. Other times, it flatters you into chasing validation. But whether it is punishing or persuasive, that voice exists to protect the persona. It is trying to keep you safe by keeping you small.

This is where mistaken identity begins. You start to believe you are your roles. Your titles. Your relationship status. The clothes you wear or the number in your bank account. You attach your worth to how others see you. And when those things fall away, when you lose the job, or the relationship ends, or the mirror no longer reflects your youthful glow, you are left asking, Who am I without it all?

That unraveling can feel brutal. But it is also the beginning of liberation.

Your earliest sense of self was shaped through touch, safety, and closeness. The warmth of your mother's voice. The steady rhythm of her breath. Then came the awareness of objects and ownership, the first time you said the words "mine." Soon after came identity. *I am the good girl, the smart one, the helper.* Over time, these layers thickened and hardened. What began as innocent strategies for connection slowly became barriers between you and your true self.

Maybe your false self took shape after a moment of betrayal or loss. Maybe it formed the first time you realized being yourself was not safe. So you adapted to survive. You became the overachiever, the peacemaker, the invisible one. You earned love, not by being yourself, but by becoming who the room needed you to be. And that worked, until one day, perhaps today is that day, that you realise, this way of living is not working for you.

As an adult, those same strategies can feel suffocating. You stay in jobs that drain you. Relationships that shrink you. Roles that no longer feel true. Why? Because the false self is afraid. Afraid of being seen. Afraid of being rejected. Afraid that if you take off the costume, you will be abandoned and rejected, and no one will stay.

But here is the truth. You are not your coping mechanisms. You are not your polished image. You are not the identity you assembled to survive.

The world will keep telling you to fake it until you make it. But faking it is just another layer. Another mask. Another delay. It deepens the gap between who you are and who you are pretending to be.

The path back is not about striving. It is about undressing. Layer by layer. Story by story. Role by role.

You do not have to become yourself. You only have to return to the self that was buried beneath all the trying. And she is still there, waiting.

Why The Fake It Until You Make It Approach Doesn't Work

You may have been taught to fake it until you make it, a phrase that has been passed around as empowerment but more often functions as a spiritual sedative. The idea sounds seductive. Act the part, embody the vibe, dress the role, and the rest will follow. At first, it feels like a shortcut to confidence. A life hack for self-worth. But let's be honest, how long has this actually worked for you?

Have you ever told yourself you feel abundant while secretly wondering how to make rent? Have you practiced gratitude through gritted teeth while longing for something that does not feel so fabricated? Have you lain in bed pretending the space next to you was occupied by a soulmate while your heart ached with the weight of absence? Most of us have. We have lit candles, repeated mantras, visualized the life, and still gone to bed feeling like a fraud in our own skin.

"Faking it" is like wearing an outfit that almost fits. It looks convincing from a distance, but up close, the discomfort is palpable. The seams tug. The truth leaks. And eventually, the illusion starts to fray. You find yourself crying into a pillow, bingeing on old romcoms and popcorn, wondering why life still feels hollow even though you are doing all the things. You have been trying to believe your way into a new self, when what you really need is to undress the one you have been pretending to be.

Take the classic workplace example. Let's say you have been promoted into a leadership role you are not sure you are ready for. Your coach tells you to fake your confidence, to show up as the person who already believes she belongs. They guide you to dress the part, change your habits, and embody the energy of a woman who knows. And so, you do. You put on the heels, straighten your back, and practice your power pose. On the surface, it works. You pass. But deep down, you are trembling. Because you are not leading from truth. You are performing for safety.

This is the danger zone. When external polish hides internal panic. When confidence becomes a costume, not a calibration, you begin fearing the moment someone sees through you. Then impostor syndrome creeps in and you second-guess yourself, start self-monitoring your message and criticise how your voice sounds and whether you are pronouncing your vowels and sounding your t's. Then self-doubt creeps in. You exhaust yourself trying to uphold an image you never truly believed in. The more you fake it, the more disconnected you feel. Not because you lack anything, but because the moment you began proving your worth, you lost touch with the part of you that already knew it.

The reason the "fake it until you make it" strategy fails is that it doesn't address the root cause of why you don't feel confident in the first place. At best, it reinforces the false self instead of healing the attachments to the stories that keep your lack of confidence in place. The doubt is still there.

"Faking it" asks you to perform confidence rather than embody truth. You are still operating from a place of disconnection, trying to act like someone who feels whole rather than becoming someone who is. The nervous system doesn't lie. Even if you appear confident, your body still carries doubt, fear, and unprocessed emotion.

Instead of building authentic confidence, you strengthen the mask, layering performance over pain. Without addressing the root, your identity, your shame, and your nervous system, what you build is only cosmetic confidence.

It's not that "fake it till you make it" never works. It can help you practise courage in small, behavioural ways. But lasting confidence isn't something you perform. It's something you remember.

True transformation is not a costume change. It is a deep inner reconfiguration, which comes from remembering who you are beneath the mask. From the inside out. From shedding what is false, rather than adding more performance to the pile.

This is why my entire methodology begins with undressing, not embellishing. Not manifesting your next level by pretending to be someone you are not. But stripping away what was never yours to carry. The beliefs, the roles, the inherited identities. Only when the false self is dismantled can the real one rise.

You do not need to fake confidence. You need to dismantle the stories that told you that you were never enough.

This is not about becoming someone else. It is about returning to yourself. And when you lead from that place, from the clarity of your core, you become unshakeable. Not because you are flawless, but because you are congruent. Your power stops being conditional. Your presence stops being performative. You become magnetic, not because you are acting like a queen, but because you have all the qualities of one, when you are more aligned with the nature of divine intelligence.

Yes, undressing is vulnerable. It is raw. It is uncomfortable. But in that discomfort is your access point. Your turning point. Your real freedom and liberation.

So next time you feel tempted to fake it, to bypass the truth with a mask, pause. Ask yourself. What part of me is still trying to earn love? What am I afraid they will see if I stop pretending? And what would it feel like to be real, instead of right?

Because when you stop faking and start undressing, you stop chasing approval and start radiating truth. Here you will find the confidence and clarity you have been searching for all along.

Undressing the False Self (and why your "beliefs" aren't really yours)

When you stop faking and start undressing, you stop chasing approval and start radiating truth. That's where confidence and clarity live, and that changes everything.

Most of what you believe about yourself didn't begin with you. It was stitched together from family rules, school corridors, advertising jingles, heartbreaks, and the moments you felt too much or not enough. Over time, those impressions hardened into beliefs, which calcified into an identity. You began to wear them like outfits.

"I'm only lovable when I achieve."

"If I relax, things fall apart."

"It's safer to be small."

This is the false self. It's not "bad," just layered. It was formed to keep you safe. It helped you belong. But it also buries your brilliance. When you live from these inherited scripts, you dress in other people's expectations and call it "me."

Here's the truth. Beliefs are not facts. They're fittings. You can undress them.

A quick mirror check (read, don't overthink).

Which belief tightens your body the moment you think it?

Whose voice is it really, yours, or someone else's?

Where is this belief still running your day (work, love, money, body)?

If you'd never learned it, who would you be?

This is the beginning of remembering. The real you was never lost, only layered. The work now is simple, sacred subtraction.

Go Deeper in the Undressed Playbook

To do the full process (timeline mapping, core-belief inventory, gentle questioning, and a twenty-four-hour "belief spotter" practice), go to: https://www.gemdentith.com/playbook open the Undressed Playbook, and go to Inner Work Exercise: Exploring Your Limiting Beliefs and False Self.

Inside you'll get.

A printable Life Timeline template (age bands laid out for you).

A guided Influence Map (above/below the line prompts).

An Empowering vs. Limiting Beliefs worksheet.

The 5-Question Disbelief Drill to loosen inherited scripts.

A 24-Hour Observer Tracker to catch beliefs in real time.

You don't need to force a new you. You just need to undress the old story.

When my clients move through this practice, they often hit a tender edge. The realization that so much of their life has been quietly shaped by old, untrue beliefs buried deep in the body. Beliefs are inherited from the voices of childhood, moments of pain, or patterns of survival. These inner scripts often resurface in relationships with others, with work, and with self. And when the veil lifts, I often witness a wave of frustration wash over them. Not because they have done anything wrong, but because they suddenly see how much of their life has been lived on autopilot. How their deepest blocks were dressed in stories they never even knew they were wearing.

Suppose you are feeling that ache, pause, and just breathe. And know this. It is not your fault. You have done the best you could with the resources you had. The mind is built to protect, not punish. Your brain is designed for efficiency. It stores emotionally charged experiences like sacred blueprints, coding them into the subconscious to keep you safe. These memories become automatic programs. They whisper, do not trust, do not speak, stay small, try harder. Not because you are broken, but because at some point, that strategy worked. And now, it is simply outdated.

The truth is, every one of these beliefs, whether limiting or empowering, has shaped who you think you are. Your identity, or more precisely, your identities. Because we do not just have one, we wear them like outfits, layered and styled by our past. Some stitched by love. Some sewn in fear. And just like a beloved dress that no longer fits, many of these identities were never meant to last forever.

We are born naked. Not just physically, but energetically. Pure potential, untouched by labels or roles. But life, with all its lessons and losses, begins to dress us. Parents, teachers, culture, and media offer us outlets of meaning. And we wear them, often without question. Until one day, something tugs at the hem. A relationship ends. A role dissolves. A truth breaks through. And we realize, this does not fit anymore.

That is when the undressing begins. You peel off the borrowed clothes. The stitched-in expectations. The costume of perfection. Maybe you try on something new, another identity, another "better" self. But even that feels temporary. Eventually, you find yourself standing in front of the mirror again, asking. Who am I underneath all this?

This is the spiral path of the soul-seeker. It often starts externally, with changes in health, jobs, roles, and relationships. But eventually, it turns inward. Because the peace you crave cannot be found by switching outfits. It must be felt in the body, lived in the bones. The real you is not something to fabricate. It is something to remember.

So what about you? How many identities have you inherited or adapted just to survive? How many versions of yourself have you tried on in search of safety, success, or love? And how would it feel to gently undress them, not with shame, but with reverence?

As we move forward, this is your invitation. Not to strip yourself bare for the sake of performance, but to come home to the skin you were always meant to live in.

How Many Mistaken Identities Have You Had?

If you pause for just a moment, really pause and let the noise fall away, it becomes painfully and beautifully clear. The journey of self-discovery is rarely linear. It is layered, costumed, sometimes confusing, and almost always marked by a series of identities we have adopted, worn, and clung to like favorite coats in a storm. These "false selves," as I call them, are the roles and personas we have slipped into over the years, some consciously, some so unconsciously they feel like skin.

And much like me, you have likely tried on more than one outfit in your time.

Some people are fortunate enough to stay intimately tethered to their authentic essence from childhood, walking into adulthood wearing their truth like a second skin. But for me, that was not the case. I poured my energy into pleasing, into caretaking, into performing for the love I did not realize I was starving for. I was the good girl, the giver, the helper, the one who made sure everyone else was okay, even if I was not.

Looking back now, I can trace the stitching. I can see how, piece by piece, I abandoned the soft, sacred fabric of my true self and traded it in for something more palatable to the world. I offered my time, my body, my voice to others (my mother, my sisters, the stray animals I rescued from the roadside) long before I ever learned how to offer it to myself. Somewhere along the way, I absorbed the belief that my value was not innate. It had to be earned, proved, or delivered.

And when you lose touch with your real self, you do not just forget who you are. You become whoever the world tells you to be. You perform. You fit in and bend yourself to try to keep the love. You follow the rules handed down by family, religion, culture, and media. And when those rules conflict with your own values, you conform because you don't actually know who you are if you didn't."

You become an easy target for overwork, burnout, unbalanced relationships, and manipulative dynamics. You find yourself bouncing between jobs, lovers, and communities, searching for what fits. Knowing something is off, but not knowing what "on" would even feel like.

If any of this sounds familiar, let me tell you. You are not alone. Here is the truth no one teaches us in school. Unless you know your authentic, truest self, you will remain an actor in your own life. Playing identities handed to you by the system.

It is no wonder you are tired.

In my own journey, I realized just how many identities I had cycled through. By my early forties, I had counted nearly two hundred different identities, each one with its own posture, vocabulary, and energy. Daughter. Student. Mother. Boss. Yoga girl. Good wife. Fun friend. Spiritual seeker. Performer. Overachiever. Therapist. Rescuer.

These roles extended far beyond my job titles or relationships. They seeped into how I spoke, what I wore, how I made decisions, and how I received (or did not receive) love. They bled into every arena of my life.

Which is why so many of us struggle to answer the simple question. "Who are you?"

Without listing out our LinkedIn profile or the labels stitched into our current season of life.

But that is the invitation here. That is the deeper question beneath all of this. Who are you without the outfit? Without the costume? Without the socially acceptable role? Let's find out.

Imagine yourself standing before a magical dressing-up box, the kind children get lost in for hours. It is overflowing with colorful outfits, masks, wigs, and accessories. Each one carries a memory, a role, an era of your life. Some memories are sparkly and empowering. Others may feel heavy, outdated, or downright suffocating. Every single one tells a story. And together, they form the wardrobe of identities you have worn, consciously or unconsciously, to survive, to succeed, or simply to stay loved.

The Dressing-Up Box of Your False Identities

This next piece of inner work is not just reflective. It is revelatory. Like rummaging through that dressing-up box called *your lifeb*ox, this exercise is designed to help you name the parts of yourself you have outgrown, denied, or forgotten. With curiosity, compassion, and a little mischief, you will begin to tease apart who you have been from who you truly are underneath it all.

Throughout life, we pick up roles like we pick up outfits. Some fit, some don't. Some empower, others drain. Each carries beliefs stitched into its fabric. The achiever, the rescuer, the invisible one. Over time, these roles layer over your essence until you mistake the costume for the skin.

But here's the truth. You are not the outfit, the label, or the mask. Those costumes were survival. They gave you power, protection, and a sense of belonging. But they are not you.

They are not your essence.

Beneath them, there is a constant thread. A presence that has never changed. An essence that doesn't need a title to belong, doesn't need a costume to be seen.

That essence is what we are here to undress. For full "Inner Work Exercise: The Dressing-Up Box of Your False Identities" with prompts, journaling space, and a guided "costume release" visualization, visit Undressed Playbook at https://www.gemdentith.com/playbook

This practice is not about criticizing or rejecting the outfits you have worn. It is about recognizing that you are not the identity, the clothes, the roles, or the masks. Those costumes helped you navigate the world. Some offered you power. Others gave you protection. Some were placed on you before you were old enough to know you had a choice. But they are not you, not the real you. Although these costumes have shaped your experiences, they do not define your essence. They are part of your story, yes, but they are not the whole of you. By consciously unlayering them, you begin to reclaim the woman underneath. She is the one who does not need a costume to be seen. She is the one who does not need a title to belong. She is the one who has always been there, waiting to exhale, waiting to stand in her truth, waiting to finally be free.

Let this be your moment to loosen the grip of false identity. Let it be the moment you unzip the expectations, remove the labels, and make space. The real you has been there all along, simply waiting to be seen.

The Movie of Your Life

Think of your life as a grand cinematic masterpiece, with you not only as the leading star but also as the director, the writer, and at times the forgotten crew. Scene after scene, you have shapeshifted through timelines and chapters, slipped into roles, recited scripts handed down from family, culture, trauma, and desire. You have worn a thousand costumes, some dazzling and some threadbare, and played to a cast of characters who reflected back the versions of yourself you thought you had to be. It is no wonder that somewhere between costume changes and curtain calls, a quiet question begins to whisper from backstage. Who am I, really?

Is it the role I played so well that they applauded? The script I memorized until it felt like my own? Or is there something more honest behind the scenes, an essence not written by the world but remembered by the life force within you?

This metaphor is not simply poetic. It is revealing. It shows us that life is never static. It is fluid, flickering, always in motion. And like any film worth watching, your character evolves. You expand. You contract. You break. You rebuild. Unlike a screenplay with tidy edits and dramatic resolutions, real life does not give you clear scene breaks. There is no cinematic pause between the scene transitions. There is no backstage crew waiting to mop your sweaty brow. There is often just you and you. The lines often blur between which version is the real you, like you're arguing with yourself while standing on your head about which way is up. Most of the time, we can't clearly see which one is true. The makeup sinks into your skin, and before you know it, you are method-acting your way through a life that no longer fits, but you apply your hair and makeup in the same way anyway, hoping that somehow things will just work out.

But what happens when the script flips without warning? What happens when the plot takes a turn you did not see coming, when you lose a job, face a health scare, or enter into divorce, redundancy, retirement, or the quiet ache of an empty nest? These unscripted twists are often the moments that crack the illusion of the identity we once had. Suddenly, the lights dim, the role fades, and you are left on a raw, echoing stage, wondering who you are without the costume.

These are not just life events. They are identity ruptures. They leave you standing in the spotlight, uncertain whether the show is over or just beginning, and this, for many, creates so much suffering. Why? Because we try to hold on to what was, we resist change; we don't want to admit to ourselves that the moment has passed.

When Attachment to Identities Creates Suffering

This disorientation, confusion, ache, and collapse are not random. It often stems from the deep attachment we form to the roles we play. The labels stitched onto your name (founder, mother, wife, leader, healer) become more than jobs or dynamics. They become extensions of your self-worth. You do not just do the role, you become it. And then you guard it with everything you have.

Because if you lose the role, who is left?

In spiritual traditions, this is called attachment. But let us strip away the jargon. Attachment here is not simply sentimentality. It is survival. It is what happens when your inner sense of identity fuses with the external symbols of it. The title on your email signature, the wedding band, the praise, the purpose. These roles act like scaffolding, holding you up and holding you together. But they are also brittle. They require maintenance, approval, and performance.

And when they fall away, so does your sense of self.

Imagine working your whole adult life to reach a role of significance, only to lose it. Imagine your children growing up and no longer needing you in the same way. In those moments, you do not only grieve the loss of routine, you grieve the identity. It is a quiet death. A psychic disrobing. The kind no one sends flowers for.

Here is the sacred wound beneath the wound. When your sense of worth is tied to the role, losing the role can feel like losing yourself.

This need to protect the role and preserve the identity is not benign. It is the place where suffering lives. Wars have been waged, marriages have crumbled, and inner peace has been shattered, not because of truth but because of a desperate clinging to an identity. To an outfit that was always meant to be temporary. To a character that was never the whole of who you are.

The deeper truth is that roles, like seasons, are meant to change. They are meant to shift and evolve with the tide of your becoming. But we confuse the costume for the core, and that confusion costs us our freedom.

You are not the role. You are the shiny self-life force wearing it. And when you forget that, you suffer.

The invitation is not to strip yourself bare in shame but in reverence. See every role for what it was. A chapter, a lesson, a mirror. Lay down the costume without fear. Return not to who you were before the role, but to the one who was always underneath it. You.

Discovering Who You Are by Letting Go of Who You're Not

Before you can remember who you truly are at the raw, radiant, unshakeable level, you must first unlearn who you are not. This is not simply mindset work. This is identity work. This is the reclamation. It is the sacred peeling back of the false self, the identities, beliefs, roles, and stories that were never yours to begin with but that you have been wearing like skin.

I call this process undressing. Not because it is soft and aesthetic, but because it is exact. You are unclothing your psyche. You are removing the stitched-up layers of protection, performance, and pleasing that once kept you safe but now keep you small. You are taking off the roles that once gave you something to belong to, but that now suffocate the real you. These identities may have been formative, even necessary. But they are not the true you. They never were.

Think of it as stepping backstage after a long performance. The lights have dimmed. The applause has faded. And now it is just you, undoing the costume, unclipping the mic, wiping away the makeup. One layer at a time, you return to the essence beneath the act. The one who has been there all along. Always watching, always waiting, and ready.

Let us not romanticize this. It is not always a graceful shedding. Letting go of the false self can feel like losing a friend, or, worse, losing your identity entirely. Even when the layers are outdated or misaligned, they are familiar. They are comfortable in their own constricting way. They have kept you warm, protected, and praised. They have helped you belong, achieve, and survive. No wonder it is hard to loosen their grip.

But here is the truth. These layers were never designed to be permanent; they are just periods. They were seasonal. They were transitional. And when you keep wearing winter coats in summer, you not only overheat, but you also stop being able to move freely. You lose the fluidity of your expression. You lose the breath of your becoming and what the life force within you wants to express and experience next.

These roles and attachments cling not only to your behavior but also to your nervous system, to your body, and to your sense of self. While they may have served a purpose, their time is up, and you simply need to take them off. Gently, deliberately, and with reverence.

We have come to your next meditation, "Gently Dissolving Attachments to your False Self." Here, I will guide you to loosen your layer of attachment. Not by force, but through loving presence to support the uncovering, to dissolve the psychic glue that has held the false self in place, and to make space for your real self to shine. To listen to the guided meditation, visit https://www.gemdentith.com/playbook

How and Why You Abandon Your Real Self

When I was younger, I genuinely believed that love came with terms and conditions. I thought that to be loved meant to be pretty, polite, and pleasing. I believed the safest thing I could do with my aliveness was to tuck it away, fold it neatly behind a sweet smile and a pair of shiny shoes. I became a good girl in a well-behaved costume. The kind of girl who did not speak unless spoken to, who shone quietly, and who swallowed the rest.

But deep down, I wanted to burst. I wanted to sing, shout, and belly laugh. I wanted to storm a stage and take up unapologetic space. I wanted to be loud, expressive, and full of irreverent joy. Yet I feared rejection, especially from the people whose approval I hungered for the most. Somewhere along the way, I absorbed the belief that having a voice was dangerous. That being silly, sensual, or outspoken was unladylike. Vulgar, even. That joy was messy. And mess, I was told, was shameful.

So I kept myself small. I looked after everyone else's needs. I admired other people's talents as if I were only the supporting act in their one-woman show. I saw greatness everywhere except in the mirror.

That was my early wiring. That was the invisible script I was handed about love and worth. I learned to perform for affection. I learned that being easy to digest was safer than being fully expressed. Somewhere in my child's mind, I made the wildest connection. If I were not loved, I would be abandoned. If I were abandoned, I would be alone. And if I were alone, I would die. It sounds absurd when spoken out loud, but that is the primal logic of a nervous system trying to survive. It does not deal in nuance. It deals in belonging.

So I swapped aliveness for acceptance. I slipped into the costume of the Good Girl. I layered on the Achiever role. I zipped People-Pleaser onto my body like a second skin. These identities helped me move through the world. They got me praised, picked, and protected. But they also distanced me from myself.

And I see now, with hindsight and grace, that this is not just my story. It is ours.

If some part of you recognizes yourself here, you are not alone. In fact, you are human. The creation of a false self is one of the most universal responses to childhood conditioning. It begins subtly. A comment here, an expectation there, and we start to believe that certain parts of us are too much, not enough, or inappropriate. In response, we adapt. We play roles. We become versions of ourselves that are easier to love, easier to manage, and easier to digest.

Maybe you did not need to be pretty, but you learned to be useful. Maybe you were not the Good Girl, but instead the Carer, the Rebel, the Golden Child, or the Fixer. Maybe you discovered that the best way to get attention was to fall apart, to be ill, or to disappear altogether. These strategies made perfect sense at the time. They were survival tools. And they worked.

The problem is that we keep playing the role long after the curtain should have closed. The false self becomes fused with our identity. We forget that it was ever a costume. And as the years pass, we find ourselves in careers, relationships, and lifestyles that match the mask rather than the soul beneath it. We wonder why it all feels off, why we are restless, unfulfilled, or burnt out, even when life looks good from the outside.

As children, we traded authenticity for approval. As adults, we are still chasing that same validation, only now the stakes are higher, the masks more expensive, and the exhaustion more chronic.

This abandonment of the real self is not always obvious. It is not a dramatic act of betrayal. It is the quiet, cumulative cost of continually turning away from your own truth. Each time you swallow your voice. Each time you shrink to make someone else comfortable. Each time you say yes when your whole body is screaming no. Over time, you forget what you even want. You forget what you even like. You become a stranger to your own desire.

And none of this is your fault. It is conditioning.

Conditioning that began long before you were old enough to question it. So we learn to play along.

But when we strip it back, beneath all the inherited expectations and performance patterns, we find that at the root of it all is a need for safety, and when we do not get this need met, our body lives in a constant feeling of fear.

Fear is what keeps the false self stitched together. Fear of judgment. Fear of rejection. Fear of standing out. Fear of being abandoned. Fear is what makes us contort our essence into a form easier for others to accept.

We shrink. We edit ourselves. We abandon the parts that

feel too wild, too soft, too sensitive, too sensual, too honest, too real.

And to survive, we comply.

But to live, we must reclaim.

You may have been taught, quietly or overtly, that your real self was not safe. That speaking your truth was risky, that your bigness made people uncomfortable. That your softness made you weak. That your magic made you weird.

So you did what any adaptive child would do. You curated a self that fit the mold. You built a version of yourself that could win love, avoid rejection, and stay safe.

And yes, it worked.

But the price of that performance was connected to your own body, your own spirit, and your own life. And the only way back is through. Through reflection. Through remembering. Through the brave, honest act of undressing, layer by layer, belief by belief, costume by costume.

Because here is what I know in my bones, and what I want you to feel in yours. The self you abandoned is still in there. Waiting. Watching. Whispering. It never left.

And now she is ready to come home.

And that is exactly where we are headed next, once we get honest about the cost of abandoning our real selves.

The Cost of Abandoning Your Real Self

When you abandon your real self, the cost always shows up somewhere. In failed relationships. In overgiving and burnout. In the quiet ache of self-neglect and the endless search for fulfilment through new paths and identities. You keep trying to find the version of you that finally feels right, but each new chapter brings the same quiet whisper that follows you everywhere, reminding you that this isn't you.

These events are not random. They are symptoms of disconnection. They are the price we pay for performing a version of ourselves that is acceptable to others but suffocating to the truth of who we really are. When we abandon our real selves out of fear of being rejected, judged, or not loved for who we actually are, we unconsciously begin to live a life that is only half true.

But the biggest cost of all is living the wrong life. A life that may look fine on the outside but feels numb or empty on the inside. A life that never quite reaches the center of your soul. A life where your gifts stay dormant and your potential never fully blooms, not because you are not capable, but because the real you was never allowed to lead.

Let us break this down so you can see what is happening behind the scenes, in the places we rarely shine a light.

Mindset

When you are not living as your true self, a quiet discontent often lingers beneath everything. A sense that something is off. A feeling that you are missing the mark, even when you are doing all the "right" things. The false self, this curated version of you built to please, impress, and survive, has no real depth. It might get applause and even external success, but it will never give you peace, because peace is an inner quality of your true self, so you can't have something that you will not allow.

Suppressing your authentic desires, gifts, and voice creates a constant feeling that something is missing. And it is. What is missing is you. That disconnect can show up as restlessness, confusion, anxiety, or even depression. Most people try to solve it by changing their external life (new job, new partner, new goals), but the ache does not go away. Nothing and no one outside of you can fill the space where your truth is meant to live.

Only alignment can do that. Only presence. Only the return to your real self.

Health

This cost is not only emotional. It lives in the body as well.

When you continually abandon yourself to serve others, perform, or chase safety, you place your nervous system into a constant state of stress and survival. Even if your mouth is smiling, your body is bracing. Even if you appear to be holding it all together, your system is quietly falling apart.

There is never enough time. You are always on edge. And eventually, the body calls a time-out. You crash. You burn out. Or you break down.

This is the moment when your body takes the wheel, because it can no longer carry the weight of the misalignment. It forces you to stop, to reassess, and to rebuild. I call this the tower moment. Like a game of Jenga, you keep pulling blocks from the base, your truth, your needs, your boundaries, hoping the tower will still stand. But eventually, one more block gets pulled, and it all comes down.

The fall may look like exhaustion, illness, panic, or even a full breakdown. But beneath it all, it is your body trying to bring you back to truth. Not to punish you, but to free you.

Success

When you are not being your true self, it becomes almost

impossible to create success that is meaningful, lasting, or fulfilling.

Why?

Because you are building on shaky ground, you are suppressing the very parts of you that hold the key to your unique path. Your gifts, your truest desires, and your innate qualities. Instead of creating something powerful and rooted, you end up stuck in a loop. You change jobs. You change your mind. You start something new. You burn it all down again. Not because you are lazy, but because you are not aligned.

It is a painful cycle. Always starting over, never landing. The merry-go-round of reinvention. And slowly, it creates stagnation. Not the quiet stillness of peace, but the choking kind. The kind where you can feel yourself shrinking, where the life force energy in you is screaming for more, but you do not know where to focus it next.

You cannot build a purpose-led life on a performance-led identity. It does not work.

Relationships

This cost shows up in love, in friendships, and in family.

When you abandon your true self, you will always attract relationships that reflect your false self. You will meet people who love the version of you that you perform, but not the real you. And over time, that feels lonely, even if you are not alone.

You may notice this when you meet someone new and, without realizing it, start adjusting everything. Your routine, your voice, your style, your preferences. You bend. You blend. You become their perfect mirror. Yes, new relationships will always stretch you a little, but when you find yourself abandoning your own lifestyle, identity, and boundaries just to be liked, that is not love. That is survival.

And the cost is steep.

Because if you are not showing up as the real you, the people who are truly meant for you, aligned, truth-resonant, magnetic matches, cannot find you. They are looking for you, not your mask.

And here is the miracle hidden in the mess. If this strikes a chord, that is good. It means that a part of you, a strong and wise part of you, still intact, knows it is time to come home to yourself.

Reclaiming your authentic self does not mean burning down your whole life. It means slowly, gently, and honestly examining the parts of you that feel performative and daring, and letting them go. You begin to recognize which patterns are inherited and which are real. Which habits are coping mechanisms and which are truth? You get clearer, bolder, and more embodied.

And from that place, you build again. This time from truth. And what you build will last. It will nourish you. It will expand you. It will mirror you, because you are no longer hiding behind someone else's blueprint.

This is what real success feels like. Real health. Real love. Real wholeness. Not because you finally became someone new, but because you finally dared to be who you already are.

Congratulations, you've made it through this chapter.

What you have just done is no small feat. Taking the time to explore your false self, your attachments, and the layers of conditioning you have carried for so long is brave, potent, and profoundly uncommon. Seriously, take a moment to acknowledge yourself. Not everyone gets this far. Not everyone slows down long enough to feel what is really going on beneath the surface. But you did. You have begun the process of undressing, and that is no small thing.

Right now, you might be feeling a mix of emotions. Relief, clarity, maybe even a ripple of unease. That is not a sign that something is wrong. That is a sign that something is real. You have opened a door most people tiptoe past, and you have stepped into a level of self-inquiry that can feel exposing, confronting, or even raw at first. But this is the good kind of discomfort, the kind that tells you that you are on the edge of something powerful. Think of this moment like reaching the top of a rollercoaster. You have been clicking upward, peeling back layers, loosening the grip of old identities. Now comes the momentum, the plunge, the unravel, the sacred chaos before the clarity.

The truth is, the next part of this journey might feel darker before it feels lighter. As we go deeper, we will begin to look at the shadows, the hidden reasons you have stayed disconnected from your true self, the parts of your identity that were buried for survival, and the patterns that have kept you looping instead of living. Some of it might sting. Some of it might surprise you. But every single piece will be worth it.

This phase is the tunnel before the light. It is not a punishment, it is a passage. You are not collapsing, you are clearing. You are not losing yourself, you are remembering who you were before the roles, before the rules, before the performance.

Even if this next part of the path feels uncertain or intense, trust this. You are more equipped than you think. This is where real transformation happens. And you are exactly where you need to be.

So if you feel a little wobbly, I've got you. That is self-remembering. That is the nervous system making room for truth. Be gentle with yourself. Stay close to your body. Stay close to your breath. And know that I am walking this part with you, every step of the way.

Take a moment now to rest your hands on your heart, your belly, or wherever you feel the pulse of truth most alive in your body. Let this moment land. Let yourself know. You are not going back. You have already begun. The reclamation is in motion. The momentum is building.

And the best part? The most alive, aligned, undressed version of you is not in the past. She is up ahead, waiting for you to keep going.

Undressed Realizations

We have all been wearing roles, masks, and labels for so long that they have become skin. But none of them is the truth. Not really.

What you have uncovered in this chapter is the sobering, life-freeing reality that the identities you have worn were never you. They were adaptations, strategies, safety mechanisms that helped you survive, but cannot help you live. You have begun to separate your essence from your performance. And that is no small feat.

You have seen how abandoning your real self creates cracks in your foundation, draining your mind, body, and relationships. But you have also caught a glimpse of the deeper truth. Everything you have been seeking outside of yourself has always been waiting within, underneath the roles. This is the beginning of coming home.

Mirror Moments

In what areas of my life am I still playing a role that is not truly me?

Where am I still faking it to feel accepted, loved, or safe?

What am I afraid might happen if I stop performing and show up as the real me?

What would it look and feel like to be fully myself, with nothing to prove and no one to please?

Embodied Practice

Name the Costumes. Make a list of the roles, masks, or personas you have worn in different areas of your life, such as relationships, work, family, and online. Beside each one, note what it gave you (for example, love, praise, safety) and what it cost you.

Track the Performance. For the next three days, track the moments where you notice yourself shape-shifting, sugar-coating, or disconnecting from what is true. Where do you shrink, please, or posture? Bring compassionate awareness, not shame.

Practice One Undressing Moment. Choose one small area of life where you will drop the performance this week. Say the thing you usually suppress. Dress how you actually want to. Cancel something you agreed to out of guilt. Notice what freedom feels like in your nervous system.

Mirror Ritual. Each morning, stand in front of a mirror, look into your eyes, and say out loud. "I see you. I remember you. I choose to be you today." Let this simple act become a devotion to your real self.

Final Undressing Thought

The roles were never the problem. They were the training ground. But now it is time to outgrow them. Your real self, the one who was silenced, softened, or split, is not lost. She is intact. She is alive. She has been whispering beneath the noise, waiting for your return.

You do not need to build her. You do not need to fix her. You only need to undress until you meet her again.

Chapter 6:
The Body Doesn't Lie

Every time you chase what isn't real, you abandon what is.

Man sacrifices his health in order to make money. Then he sacrifices money to recuperate his health. And then he is so anxious about the future that he does not enjoy the present. He lives as if he is never going to die, and then dies having never really lived.

— The Dalai Lama

"Mummy, can you play with me?" Yasmin called from the living room, still surrounded by the magic and mess of freshly opened Christmas presents. I didn't even look up. "One second, darling. Mummy's just reading something," I replied, eyes fixed on the article I was researching for my next blog post, probably some piece on work-life balance or mindfulness or productivity hacks, if I'm honest. The irony wasn't lost on me.

There was always something more I had to do. Another deadline. Another launch. Another list. Always something that had to be finished before I could allow myself to live. But that moment? That request? That child is asking me to play. It's a moment I'll never get back.

This chapter is about one truth we keep trying to outrun. Your body always tells the story you refuse to hear. No matter how much you achieve, how many boxes you tick, or how convincingly you perform, your body will reveal the cost of the chase. Burnout, tension, fatigue, disconnection. These are sacred signals, alarm bells from your system; calling you back to what's real. This chapter invites you to strip away the illusion that fulfillment lives "out there" and remember that your deepest guidance is not in the next milestone, but in the whispers of your own body.

So, before we go any further in this chapter, I want to ask you to keep something in mind. The cost of chasing success, validation, or "enoughness" is never theoretical. It's not just some airy concept. It's paid in real time, real health, and real connection. It's paid in sleepless nights, aching bones, missed playdates, tension headaches, suppressed instincts, and a thousand stolen moments that will never return. Chasing shadows will cost you everything real.

The Sacrifices of Chasing Shadows

Chasing external validation is like trying to catch smoke. Or like playing that old childhood game of chasing shadows. Remember that one? You'd run wild, laughing hysterically, trying to step on someone's shadow even though you knew you never actually could. There was no real point to it, other than the thrill of the run. But eventually, the game ended. You got tired. You went home.

That's the difference.

As children, we knew when to stop. As adults, we often don't. We keep chasing titles, income brackets, followers, spiritual milestones, until we're bone-tired, soul-starved, and so far from ourselves that we don't remember how to come back.

This pursuit, relentless, addictive, and praised, leads to

disconnection from the only thing that matters. You and your internal alignment. That quiet knowing that whispers, This is who I am. This is what matters. This is what's real. But when we're caught up in performing for the world, being successful, being liked, being everything, we override that whisper. We abandon our body's signals. We trade truth for applause. And it's not a fair exchange.

Unlike children, we don't laugh our way to exhaustion and then collapse into safety. We delay joy entirely, believing we'll earn it at the next checkpoint. This is the Happiness Paradox, the dangerous lie that says, "I'll be happy when".

When I earn six figures.

When I lose ten pounds.

When I meet someone new.

When I finally slow down.

But let me be honest with you. This game has no finish line. And it has no winner. The more you chase, the further you run. The more you climb, the more the goalpost moves. And the more you perform, the less you feel.

The Trap of the "I'll Be Happier When" Belief

What makes this trap even more deceptive is how it can sneak into our so-called healing. The spiritual hustle is still a hustle. Just because you're chasing peace instead of promotions does not mean you've dropped the chase. The same addiction to striving shows up, only this time with palo santo and prettier packaging.

I see it constantly. In workshops. On retreat. In breathwork circles and "trauma-informed" spaces. People striving to go deeper, reach higher, and awaken faster. Swapping out their Type A goals for spiritual goals, but the nervous system hasn't shifted. The pace hasn't softened. The pressure just changed outfits.

I've watched clients trade corporate status for spiritual status. They stop collecting degrees from Stanford and start collecting teacher trainings, quantum certifications, and kundalini initiations. They ditch the suits and wear linen. They drop their morning coffee for ceremonial cacao. But the same belief hums underneath it all. "I am not enough yet."

If you scratch beneath the surface of even the most conscious-seeming lifestyle, you will often find the same anxiety running the show. The same need to prove. The same fear of not being good enough. It just hides behind better lighting and a healing hashtag.

So if you've ever looked around and thought, Why do I still feel this emptiness even after all the work I've done? This is why.

The Purpose Paradox

Here's where purpose comes into play. The act of chasing external markers of success, like money, recognition, or status, often creates a painful disconnect between who you are and what you truly desire. When this happens, it's like trying to climb an endless ladder. Every rung you climb just reveals another one ahead, leaving you dissatisfied and exhausted. Why? Because this kind of pursuit pulls you further away from your authentic purpose in life.

Purpose isn't about doing more, achieving more, or even being more. It's not something you measure by how much you've accomplished. It's about aligning with your deeper self, listening to the whispers of innate intelligence, and allowing your life to unfold in harmony with who you truly are. Purpose isn't out there waiting to be found. It's within you, waiting to be realized. And when you live in alignment with it, life stops feeling like a chase. It becomes a steady flow of clarity, ease, and meaningful action that comes naturally.

The modern world, however, has conditioned us to seek purpose outside ourselves. When we chase what society deems important (degrees, promotions, or even personal development "achievements" like meditating for eight hours a day or mastering a yoga pose), we might look successful on the surface. But inside, there's often a quiet emptiness. Why? Because we've mistaken these external markers for true purpose, and without that deeper alignment, the pursuit feels hollow.

This is where the happiness paradox sneaks in. The belief that "I'll be happy when" becomes a trap. When I get the promotion. When I lose the weight. When I buy the bigger house. When you reach the next milestone, it convinces you that happiness is somewhere in the future, always just out of reach. The harsh reality is that the finish line keeps moving. You might achieve your goal only to discover the fulfillment you were chasing isn't there. Or worse, it flickers briefly and disappears, replaced with yet another "when" to pursue.

This mindset doesn't only infect traditional goal-setting. It seeps into the spiritual world, too. I've seen people in coaching programs, retreats, and yoga circles fall into the same loop. They trade corporate pursuits for "spiritual" goals, counting meditation hours, striving to master advanced asanas, or chasing higher levels of enlightenment. The language changes, but the pattern remains the same. The underlying belief, "I'm not enough as I am," still drives them. They just wear yoga pants instead of suits and sip kombucha instead of lattes, but the chase continues.

If you pause to observe, it becomes clear that the problem

isn't the goal itself. It's the false belief that happiness and fulfillment live outside of you. That belief fuels the cycle of chasing, achieving, and then chasing some more. The key to breaking free is recognizing that true purpose and real happiness come only from aligning with your authentic self, not from endlessly striving to become someone else.

The Cost of Over-Achieving in the Wrong Areas

Here's the hard-to-swallow truth. You can be overachieving and underliving at the same time.

From the outside, your life might look like a glowing CV. Goal-oriented. Polished. Perfectly curated. The checklists are ticked, the titles are earned, and the image is flawless. But inside? You're starving. Not for food, but for feeling. For fulfillment. For realness. For rest. Despite all your effort, something essential is missing. You can't quite put your finger on it, but it haunts you in the spaces between accomplishments.

This is what happens when you're overachieving in the wrong areas. You pour energy into goals that don't feed your true self, performing a version of success that leaves you emotionally bankrupt. And because you're so capable, so good at pushing through, you don't question the system. You question yourself. You assume the emptiness must mean you haven't done enough, haven't earned your peace yet. So you hustle harder. You grind with more precision. You chase more credentials, more impact, and more validation.

But here's the deeper truth. It's not that you're falling short. It's that you're chasing something that never needed you to chase it in the first place.

When you misalign your energy, when your goals are built on

expectation rather than embodiment, you enter a toxic cycle of over-functioning. You become a master of the to-do list but a stranger to your joy. Your nervous system stays on high alert. Your calendar fills with things that look good but feel hollow. Slowly, your life becomes a theater of achievement with no soul in the audience.

And the cost? It's not just mental or emotional. It's cellular.

This overdrive erodes your vitality. It seeps into your relationships. It distances you from your intuition. It keeps you deferring joy for later, but later never really comes. The goalposts always shift. The "when" you were waiting for turns into another "if only."

This is the trap of deferring happiness.

It convinces you that peace is a prize for the future, something you unlock once you've perfected yourself or proved your worth. But that lie steals your now. It robs you of the moment your child asks you to play. It numbs the magic of ordinary mornings. It makes presence feel like a luxury instead of a birthright. And slowly, without even noticing, you become a stranger in your own home and with your own family.

Because chasing goals isn't the problem, the problem is that there is no endgame. It whispers, "Just do a little more", and that belief is the virus. It fuels the burnout, it kills relationships, but more importantly, it's a lie. Because doing more of the wrong thing won't give you the thing that you're doing more for. And when you keep pushing on in the wrong direction, it's always going to lead you to the wrong destination.

So ask yourself. Are you achieving your way out of alignment? Are you performing a life that the deeper intelligence in you knows it's time to break from? Because if you are, it's not too late to address it.

Ignoring Your Internal Alarm System

When you are chasing something you believe will make you happy, whether it is a promotion, a number on the scale, or the life you saw someone else post on Instagram, you tend to give it everything you have. All your time. All your energy. All your worth. Regardless of what it costs you.

And it does cost you.

You push. You stretch. You strive. Until your nervous system is on high alert, your boundaries collapse, and your connection to your own body gets buried under the rubble of your ambition. You override the signals. You postpone rest. You silence the whisper telling you something is off and instead listen to the pressure that says, "Keep going. You are not there yet."

But when you chronically neglect your physical, emotional, mental, and spiritual needs in the name of achievement, there is always a price to pay. And it is often your body that sends the invoice.

Your body is wise. It keeps the score. It speaks when you will not listen, and it never lies. While your mind might justify, dismiss, or delay, your body does not play that game. It is honest to the bone. It does not care about your deadlines or your title. It is not here to perform or to please. It is here to protect you. And if it needs to shut you down to get your attention, it will.

The mind-body system is a feedback loop, designed to keep you aligned. The problem is that most people are too busy surviving their day to actually listen. Between back-to-back meetings, overflowing inboxes, and the persistent hum of performance culture, we become masters of dissociation. We disconnect from the very signals trying to bring us back into balance.

You may recognize this in your own life. The tension in your shoulders that never goes away. The way that your sleep feels shallow. The headaches you push through. The breath you hold without even noticing. The emptiness that follows a "win." You tell yourself it is fine. Normal, even. Just part of being a high-functioning woman. But it is not fine. It is a sign.

And signs have a purpose. They exist to redirect you before you crash.

If you have ever said, "I don't know what's wrong with me," this might be it. You have normalized the warning signs so deeply that they have become part of your baseline. But that does not make them any less urgent.

Mentally, you may live with a crowded, noisy mind. Racing thoughts. A loop of self-criticism and worry. The inability to switch off, even when you are meant to be relaxing. Emotionally, it might feel like a quiet ache, a sense that something is missing even when everything on the surface looks good. You might find yourself more reactive, more sensitive, more anxious, and not even sure why.

And then there is the body. She speaks in her own language. Maybe it is fatigue that sleep does not fix. Tightness in your jaw or gut. A fogginess you cannot shake. Skin flare-ups. Bloating. Tension. A sense that you are not in your body anymore. You are just dragging it behind you.

Your relationships are not immune either. You might feel disconnected from your partner or children. You are physically present but emotionally absent, ticking boxes while your spirit checks out. Intimacy fades. Communication gets clipped. The people closest to you feel your absence even when you are in the room.

All of this is feedback. It is your system waving the red flag and saying, "Something is out of alignment." The question is not if your mind and body are speaking to you. The question is, are you listening?

Burnout does not always arrive with a dramatic breakdown. Sometimes it sneaks in through small betrayals of the self. A hundred little moments where you override your need for rest. Where you are numb instead of nurturing, but it does not have to get that far. If you learn to recognize the early signs, you can course-correct without ever needing to experience a big burnout yourself. Below are some of the most common signals your system sends to alert you to an imbalance.

Physical signs

Feeling chronically drained or fatigued, no matter how much you sleep

Frequent headaches or migraines

Tension, tightness, or unexplained aches and pains

Digestive issues, bloating, or appetite changes

Poor quality sleep, insomnia, or oversleeping

Frequent colds or illness, indicating low immunity

Emotional signs

Irritability, impatience, or short temper

Feeling anxious, restless, or overwhelmed

Inability to relax or feel off-duty

Emotional numbness, sadness, or emptiness

Hyper-sensitivity to criticism or minor setbacks

Loss of joy in things you used to love

Mental signs

Racing thoughts or mental fog

Difficulty concentrating or making decisions

Forgetfulness or frequent memory lapses

Constant worry or catastrophizing

Harsh inner dialog and perfectionism

A chronic sense of not enoughness

Behavioral signs

Turning to food, alcohol, or screens to cope

Overworking or, conversely, procrastinating

Withdrawing from loved ones or social interactions

Neglecting basic self-care or responsibilities

Avoiding rest, intimacy, or downtime

Losing interest in hobbies or creative expression

You might think you are being strong by pushing through. But strength is not the ability to ignore your pain. Strength is the courage to honor it. To listen when your body whispers instead of waiting for it to scream.

Ignoring your internal alarm system is like a circus clown seeing that his tightrope is fraying and stepping out to perform anyway. You might smile and juggle and convince the world you have it all under control, but deep down, you know, if you take one more step, you are going down.

The good news is you do not have to fall.

These signs do not need to be your downfall. They can be your awakening. They are not punishments. They are invitations. Invitations to pause. To reassess. To come home to yourself before your system forces you to.

Because burnout is not the end but a turning point, a releasing of an old version of you.

The Cost of Deferring Happiness

Have you ever felt like you were running on empty, chasing something you thought would bring happiness, only to find it never delivered? Maybe it was a promotion. A relationship. A body. A dream that turned out to be someone else's. Maybe you traded time, health, or your own presence in the name of success, only to realize the happiness you were banking on never truly arrived.

This next "Inner Work Exercise: Evaluate The Cost of Deferring Happiness" is your invitation to pause. To reflect. To finally account for the hidden costs of the chase and begin the tender work of realigning with what actually matters to you. Head to https://www.gemdentith.com/playbook to begin the exercise.

I wish I had this level of awareness when I began my own journey. Like many women who end up writing books about their healing, I learned the hard way. I had to break before I could listen. And I share all of this not because I got it right, but because I didn't.

If no one ever told you about burnout, let me be the one.

The term was first coined in the 1970s by American psychologist Herbert Freudenberger. He used it to describe the emotional collapse caregivers experience. Nurses, doctors, paramedics, those who gave so much of themselves that there was nothing left. He called it compassion fatigue.

But now, burnout is not limited to helping professions. It has become the silent epidemic of our time, affecting everyone from celebrities to stay-at-home mums, from consultants to creatives, to servicemen and women to students. It does not discriminate. If you keep giving and giving without ever replenishing your inner well, you are at risk.

In my own journey, I've discovered that knowledge is power, reflection is prevention, and alignment to your truth is the medicine.

My Burnout Story

In my late twenties, I was scouted by an interim recruitment agency to join a technology program turnaround team as the Change and Communications Lead within the law enforcement arm of the UK's Home Office. The day rate was too good to refuse. I instantly doubled my previous earnings. And having always wanted to call myself a "consultant," I jumped at the title with both hands. It was a dream on paper.

But the dream didn't last long.

Working in the public sector was an eye-opener. Even though I loved it. The environment was complex, charged, and deeply political, especially within a department entrenched in a chaotic IT transformation. This is where I thrive, in chaos. People weren't just stressed. They were flatlined. Staff members were burning out in real time, taking sick leave left, right, and center. Others were simply disappearing, resigning with no fanfare, no closure. The turnover was high, morale was low, and the systems were failing fast. Meanwhile, the rhetoric from leadership continued, tone-deaf and disconnected from the actual pain on the ground.

As someone wired to fix things (a "Miss Fix It" to my core), I couldn't help but feel pulled in. I started wondering what these people were carrying, what their lives must be like when they went home, what kind of fatigue you'd have to feel to stop caring about the job that once mattered to you. I was technically just a contractor, parachuted in to help and then move on. But for them, this wasn't a temporary stop. It was their career. Their life. I couldn't switch off the part of me that empathized deeply. And over time, that empathy began to cost me. Unprepared and, at the time, not knowing what I know now about resilience and leadership, this cost was huge.

I found myself emotionally invested in people I had never even met before joining the project. They'd pull me aside and vent their frustrations about the lack of direction, about leadership, about systems that didn't work. It wasn't just complaints. It was despair. They needed someone to hear them. And somehow, that someone became me.

Somewhere in the fog of all this, my sense of responsibility began to mutate. I wasn't just there to do a job. I had taken it upon myself to carry the torch. To be the light. I started pushing harder, trying to hold it all together. But the harder I pushed, the more inadequate I felt. The more I tried to fix, the more broken it all seemed. My self-esteem began to erode. I'd go home questioning my competency, wondering why I couldn't make any real progress. Every direction I turned, there was a blockade, a budget cut, or a bureaucratic delay.

It felt impossible.

To compensate, I worked longer hours. Skipped lunch breaks. Carried my laptop everywhere. I thought I was being committed. But in truth, I was becoming consumed.

And all of this was unfolding while I was pregnant with my second daughter and also trying to be a present mother for my then seven-year-old daughter, who also needed mummy time.

Despite the joy of new love with my partner, the relentless pressure from work eclipsed the lightness of that chapter. I was firefighting all day, every day. My nervous system didn't know what rest was anymore. And eventually, the signs started showing up in my body (hair loss, chronic fatigue, emotional withdrawal). Looking back, it's clear that I was running on survival mode. But at the time, I convinced myself I had to take it. I couldn't let the system beat me.

Until one day, my system beat me.

It was a crisp October morning, and I was on the 8:01 commuter train from St Albans City to London Blackfriars. The train was packed, as it always was at that hour (suits, coffees, unread newspapers, and weary eyes all around). I was wearing a black three-quarter-length military-cut wool coat, buttoned up tight to brace against the cold. Pinned neatly at chest height was my "Baby on Board" badge, a hopeful cue to those around me that maybe, just maybe, someone would offer me a seat.

That day, I hadn't eaten breakfast. I'd rushed out the door, jumped into my little Fiat 500, raced to the station, and made it just in time. My inbox was already pinging, so I did what I always did. I opened my phone to check the early chaos. A few angry staff emails. Some impossible requests. The usual dread set in. I instantly regretted looking. But by then, it was already in my body.

Out of nowhere, a wave of sickness came over me. My skin flushed hot, and my heart started pounding so loud it drowned out the announcements overhead. I tried to unbutton my coat and loosen my blouse. Still too hot. Still not right. With only a couple of stops left, I decided to get up and prepare to exit. I stood slowly and moved toward the doors. People jostled past me, but I barely registered them. I was clutching my coat in one hand and my laptop bag in the other, propping myself up against the train wall, trying to ground.

Then, my vision started to blur. The floor felt like it was rising, the ceiling like it was dropping. The space around me collapsed. And in that moment, all I could think about was my baby. I remember whispering inside, 'Please don't fall. Don't let me fall forward.'

With what little strength I had, I shuffled over to an empty seat and collapsed into it. And then (black).

When I came to, the train doors were open. It was my stop. I stood up, ghost-like (clammy, pale, and completely disoriented). I stepped off the train at Blackfriars, stood on the platform in a daze, and just stared into space. I felt like an empty shell. Something was very wrong. But I didn't yet have the language for what.

I called my partner. At first, I couldn't speak. Eventually, I said one word, "Blackfriars." That was all it took. He came immediately. Picked me up. Drove me back to Hertfordshire, straight to the GP.

The doctor saw me within the hour. He asked a few questions, nodded softly, and said the words I hadn't yet admitted to myself. "You've burned out." Emotionally. Mentally. Physically. System failure.

He gave me medication and signed me off. And just like that, it was over. The program ended. I went on maternity leave. The fire I'd tried to hold alone had finally burned through me.

But here's the thing about collapse. It creates a stillness. And in that stillness, if you're willing to listen, there is something to be found.

Burnout gave me space. It stripped away the noise. It left me with time, not just to recover, but to inquire. I asked myself deeper questions. Who was I trying to prove myself to? Why was my worth so tangled in work? How did I let it get this far?

And the biggest one of all. Was I willing to keep living like this?

I knew something had to change. No more chasing. No more saving everyone but myself. No more outsourcing my peace to titles, roles, or paychecks. It was time to come back to something. To me. To the version of myself I had buried beneath all the achievements. And that was the moment my true journey began.

A Breakdown of the False Self

In my experience, burnout had one sacred job. To dismantle the version of me that was never real to begin with. The self that kept pushing, performing, producing, until something had to give. And that something was me. Today, I achieve more than I did then, but now, armed with awareness, knowledge, and skill, I can produce more without ever feeling the effects of burnout because I'm creating from alignment, from the expression of my true nature.

Do not misunderstand me. Burnout does not happen because you are weak. It happens because you have been strong for too long in a way that is not true to you, and because you have not yet learned how to harness your inner power, mental focus, and physical energy. When the pressures of life pile up, when the pace becomes unsustainable, when your nervous system is stretched like a wire and no one sees the fray, it is only a matter of time before the whole structure collapses. And when it does, it does not just take down your energy. It takes down the version of you that has been pretending everything is fine.

What I have come to know, through my own healing and in guiding others, is that burnout is the moment when the false self finally breaks. It is the collapse of the identity we built to please, to prove, to survive. It is not a flaw. It is a threshold. And when the mask falls, something raw and real begins to rise in its place.

Burnout is often labeled a crisis, but in truth, it is a spiritual interruption. A forced pause. A sacred dismantling. It strips away everything that is performative and leaves us naked with the question. What now?

For me, that moment was both a rupture and a revelation. It made me question everything I had been taught to value. Status over stillness, performance over peace, material success over inner truth. I realized I had been living outward-in, hoping external achievements could fix something internal. But the body always knows. And my body was the first to speak the truth I had been avoiding.

That truth became the beginning of a different kind of journey. One rooted in curiosity, consciousness, and recalibration. I began to explore not just what I could achieve, but who I actually was without the roles, titles, and trophies. I started listening to my body as if it were the sacred instrument it is. I started walking more slowly, breathing more deeply, feeling more intentionally. I remembered that nature does not rush, and yet nothing is left undone.

Einstein once said, "Insanity is doing the same thing over

and over again and expecting different results." I saw myself in that quote. Chasing goals. Smashing deadlines. Earning praise. Then waking up empty. Again and again. Burnout showed me the loop I was trapped in and gave me the gift of stepping off the carousel.

For many, burnout becomes a portal. It initiates a deeper self-inquiry, one that breaks the trance of modern life and invites a new question. What if I built a life from the inside out?

It asks you to pause long enough to see that the old architecture (the beliefs, the conditioning, the borrowed expectations) is no longer fit to house your truth. It points you inward, toward the self that has been whispering beneath all the noise.

And this is the part I want to underline twice. <u>Burnout often comes when we have stopped noticing.</u>

We have stopped noticing ourselves. Stopped noticing our breath. Stopped noticing the ache in our belly or the lump in our throat. Stopped noticing the nudges and inner whispers that have been quietly guiding us home.

We get so busy tending to everything outside of us: tasks, emails, people, and pressure, that we forget to turn inward and simply ask. Am I okay?

So let me say this now, and let it land. You are always being guided. But you have to slow down long enough to notice. And maybe, just maybe, your breakdown is not the end. It is the sacred invitation back to who you really are.

You're Always Being Guided

But what exactly is doing the guiding? Call it what you like. Intuition, inner knowing, the organizing principle, universal intelligence, life intelligence, soul, God, grace. The name does not matter as much as the feeling of it. It is the compass that lives just beyond your intellect, yet always within reach.

Plato called it the daemon, a kind of inner genius whispering you toward your highest potential. Jung called it the Self, the deeper architecture of your psyche that is always reaching toward wholeness. I call it the intelligence of life. An unseen electrical rhythm that courses through your cells, breathes through your lungs, and nudges you softly but persistently toward alignment.

This force is not a prize reserved for the spiritual elite. It is always available. It's life's organizing principle, always guiding. But here is the catch. You have to slow down enough to listen or see the nudges.

Experiencing a breakdown, whether it looks like burnout, illness, or emotional collapse, is not a sign that you have failed at life. It is a sign that you have been missing the whispers. You have been tuned to the wrong station. The volume of your outer world has drowned out the quiet brilliance of your inner one.

Because you were being guided, you just weren't noticing.

The Happiness Whore inside you, the part addicted to applause, attention, and achievement, has been making choices from fear. Choosing from fantasy. Choosing what looks like joy but tastes like nothing. She keeps saying "yes" to destruction disguised as devotion. And she knows she is not listening to the truth. But she is too addicted to the toxic chase to stop.

Here is the gift. Even when you ignore the whisper, life will re-route you. Even when you take the wrong turn, it will build a bridge to bring you back. Even if your whole identity collapses, it can still serve as the compass.

Let me tell you about the moment I knew this to be true.

I had just left a coaching retreat, high on insights and low on fuel, literally. The conversation I had earlier that day was still echoing in my mind. What if life is always orchestrating exactly what we need?

The universe did not take long to test the theory.

A fire had broken out at a local petrol station. Every other station within a four-mile radius had been shut down. And I was running on zero. My dashboard was flashing. My heart was racing. The childminder was waiting. Cars were abandoned on the roadside like it was the end of days, and I could feel the panic rising in my chest.

I rang my husband. "You always red-line it," he snapped, tired of my tendency to push the tank to its limit. I could feel myself shrinking, shame bubbling beneath the surface. My mind flooded with images of being stranded, late, tearful, and helpless. And then something cut through.

A calm voice inside whispered. Stop panicking. Just notice.

Just notice.

It was not loud. It was not dramatic. It was simply clear, like a sliver of sunlight piercing through storm clouds. At the next roundabout, the nudge came. Go right. The sat nav insisted I go left. Logic told me to trust the tech. But my body leaned into the whisper. I turned right.

A steep hill lay ahead. No signs. No promises. No petrol stations in sight. My heart sank. I doubted. I cursed. I almost turned around. But the pull was stronger than the panic. I kept going.

About a mile later, there it was. A tiny independent station, tucked away out of view. No queue, fully stocked, it was as though it had been placed there just for me.

I exhaled. I filled the tank. And then I cried. Not because I was sad, but because I knew this was more than luck. More than coincidence. This was guidance. This was life speaking through me. And this time, I was quiet enough to listen.

When your mind is too clouded to see clearly, life will still show you the way if you are willing to tune in. And that is the shift I want you to claim. Guidance does not come from force. It comes from surrender. You do not have to earn it. You do not have to hustle for it. You only have to be still long enough to receive it.

So the next time you find yourself spiraling, gripped by fear, control, or that frantic need to push, pause. Just pause. And ask yourself. What if I just stopped and noticed? What if, instead of reacting, fixing, or forcing, I allowed myself to get still enough to hear what life is actually whispering beneath the noise?

What might life be trying to show me? What if I trusted the nudge instead of the narrative? Because here is the truth that is so easy to forget when you are spinning.

You are always being guided, even when the path is foggy, even when the sat nav tells you to turn back. Even when your tank feels empty and you are not sure you can keep going.

Especially then. That is when the deeper wisdom arrives. Not in the doing, but in the stopping. In the noticing. In the surrender.

The Intelligence of Life

This experience was more than luck. It was proof to me that life is always guiding us, if we are willing to notice.

It is vital to realize that even in your seemingly darkest moments, life is trying to re-route you. Often, the whispers of guidance are too faint to be heard over the loudness of an overthinking, overly attached mind.

But if you allow the dust to settle and your mind to quiet, you begin to hear a new frequency playing in the echo chambers of your thoughts. This subtle glimmer of truth holds the clarity you need, gently guiding you toward the course of action you are meant to take.

Later in this book, you will learn more about how this guiding force, the intelligence of life, shows up as intuition. It is not mystical or abstract but a natural part of your being, always working in the background, waiting for you to notice.

As Eckhart Tolle wisely said, "Life will give you whatever experience is most helpful for the evolution of your consciousness. How do you know this is the experience you need? Because this is the experience you are having at this moment."

Before we move on, I invite you to take part in another Inner Work Exercise. Life's Growth Gifts. This one is for you to reflect on the growth gifts that came from your challenges. Through reflection, you will uncover the wisdom and opportunities for growth that emerged from your seemingly darkest moments, not by reliving the pain but by focusing on the new strength, qualities, and wisdom those experiences gifted you. Head over to https://www.gemdentith.com/playbook to complete the exercise.

By recognizing the growth that has emerged from your challenges, you can appreciate the transformative power of difficult experiences. This exercise is here to honor the growth that has already occurred and to help you step into the next chapter of your life with clarity and strength. Often, these moments either strip away a layer of your old identity or help you embody a new quality, bringing your true self forward.

Rising from the Ashes

"I rise from the ashes, stronger than ever before."

— Albus Dumbledore, Harry Potter and the Goblet of Fire

This line, whispered by one of fiction's wisest wizards, carries more than literary charm. It carries the sacred pulse of rebirth. It speaks to resilience. To the kind of transformation that does not come from a tidy personal development plan, but from being brought to your knees. Dumbledore, having faced losses, truths, and inner reckonings of his own, reminds us that our power is not in avoiding the fire; it is in rising through it.

The image of rising from ashes, like the mythical phoenix, embodies a deeper truth. To truly become, we must be willing to let something die. The old identity. The performance. The illusion. What once defined us must break down, not as punishment, but as a necessary rite of passage. And through that fire, something far more real is born.

Even the most significant setbacks, such as burnout, heartbreak, a crumbling friendship, or a career collapse, can hold a coded invitation. Not to return to who you were, but to become who you truly are. To rise, yes, but as something wiser. More rooted. More whole.

This is the essence of transformation. The reminder that endings are not failures. They are thresholds. Entry points. Sacred beginnings that are mini-resets of reorganization disguised as loss.

Just as the phoenix does not fear the flame, you too are wired for rebirth. Each time life brings you to your knees, you are being invited to recalibrate your perception, soften your grip on outdated beliefs, and realign with the truth of who you really are. Not the version shaped by survival, but start to see how life is trying to reorganize and reorient you back to its original nature, because you'd steered too far off course. I liken this to my car's lane-keep assist, where my Tesla auto-corrects and nudges me back if I drift too far left. It also gives out a beep, which sure does wake me up. Wouldn't it be great if, in life, when we drift too far off track, a little horn beeps to get our attention, for us to live correctly in that moment? Therefore, your breakdowns are not random. They are your in-built life corrections when you sway too far off center.

They also often arrive when the organizing intelligence within you is ready to evolve, so it's inevitable that you have to transform. Like a butterfly transforming from a caterpillar, it's inevitable. You don't see a caterpillar negotiating with its old life that it must stay a caterpillar. No, it has no choice but to evolve, as this was written in its divine DNA.

Burnout, betrayal, breakdowns. They do not signal the end. They signal a shift back to life's organizing intelligence. They offer the opportunity to examine the stories you have been living in and holding on to, to justify your existence, the lenses through which you have been seeing yourself and the world. And if you are willing to get honest, allowing the breakdown and the losses that come with it to happen, will guide you back to something far more aligned. Your true divine expression.

So as you continue reading, and as you move through the chapters of your own life, remember this. Things you see as going wrong are not actually things going wrong in your life. They are life's nudges and recalibrations. They are how the intelligence of life steps in to reorganize and realign you when you've drifted too far from your path.

The outer world is a mirror of your inner state. In the next chapter, we will explore how this mirror works and how your reality reflects your alignment, your frequency, your truth. When you shift your internal world, when you rise from your own ashes with clarity, softness, and presence, the world around you responds in kind. That is when life begins to feel like home. Not a performance. But a reflection.

Undressed Realizations

The chase always promises more. More success. More status. More happiness. But beneath the shine, it starves you of the one thing you actually crave. Wholeness. It disconnects you from your body, your breath, your presence. And over time, it costs you more than it gives.

What we have unpacked in this chapter is not just a personal truth. It is a collective pattern. So many of us have been conditioned to believe that fulfillment is something to achieve when, in fact, it is something to remember. To reclaim.

Because true contentment does not come from ticking boxes or climbing ladders, it comes from coming home to your now, to your truth, to the innate wisdom that you already know.

Burnout is not a sign of failure. It is a flare sent up by the deeper intelligence of life. A signal that something you have built no longer fits, and that there is something far deeper, more honest, more alive, waiting to be claimed.

You do not need to do more to access that version of you. You need to undress what is in the way.

Mirror Moments

Where in my life am I still chasing external success, believing it will bring me happiness?

What personal sacrifices, such as time, health, or

relationships, have I made in pursuit of those goals?

What warning signs, whether physical, emotional, or energetic, has my body been giving me that I have ignored?

What truth has been whispering beneath the noise, waiting for me to hear it?

What part of me is ready to rise, if only I would let her?

Embodied Practice

Recognize your early warning signs. Reflect on the last time you felt burned out or misaligned. What did your body, your energy, or your relationships try to tell you before things broke down? Journal the signs so you can catch them sooner next time.

Identify one misaligned goal. Choose a goal you have been chasing that now feels hollow or heavy. Ask yourself honestly. Was this goal ever mine, or was it borrowed from someone else's dream, expectation, or timeline?

Return to the now. For one full day, practice micro-presence. Every hour, pause for two minutes and drop into the moment. Feel your breath, your body, your environment. Ask yourself. Am I here, or am I chasing? You will start to notice where you are alive and where you have gone missing.

Final Undressing Thought

You do not need to be more. Not more successful, not more healed, not more perfect. You just need to be here. In your body. In your breath. In this unrepeatable now.

Because here, beneath the noise, beneath the proving, is where your truth lives. It is where the phoenix rises, not through effort but through surrender. Through the ashes of what no longer fits.

Here is where life begins again. Not as a performance, but as a presence. Not through strategy, but through embodiment.

Let what burned you teach you. Let what is whispering guide you. And let this be the sacred threshold, the moment you stop chasing and start deeply, unapologetically living.

And remember this. Your body is not the enemy. It is the oracle. It never lies. It will always show you when you are out of alignment and always call you home. The question is, are you willing to listen?

Chapter 7:

Undressing Survival

From survival to awakening, your mind isn't the enemy, but it's not your home either.

"The energy of the mind is the essence of life."

— Aristotle

As the room begins to fill, bodies ease into seats, some clutching coffees, others scanning for familiar faces. I press play on M People's Moving On Up. Before I have said a word, I am already lip-syncing in my head: "I'm movin' on up, you're movin' on out. Time to break free, nothing can stop me."

It is more than a feel-good throwback. It is an anthem for what is about to unfold. Because once you see how you have been trapped in lower-level patterns of thought, energy, and perception, the only thing left to do is move up. The realization alone is enough to shift your chemistry. You suddenly feel lighter, clearer, more alive. You realize: oh shit, I am not stuck. I have just been living on a lower level, and with that, a lower vibe of reality. And that insight doesn't come in gently. It hits with holy-fuck energy. A cellular-level wake-up call.

This chapter might feel like that. A rollercoaster of truth, sobering and electrifying all at once. We are going to unpack why life feels the way it does, why certain patterns repeat.

Why the same arguments, the same money stories, the same emotional hangovers keep circling back, no matter how many books you read or podcasts you devour. And spoiler alert: it is not the outer world doing it to you. It is the level of awareness you have been operating from within.

At a retreat I was hosting for a roomful of midlife women (successful, exhausted, quietly seeking something real), I opened with a question: "What do you think determines the quality of your life experience? I don't mean your achievements. I mean, how you feel, day to day, moment to moment. What shapes the actual lived experience of your life?"

Hands shot up.

"Other people and how they treat me," said one.

"The weather. Especially sunshine," laughed another.

"My bank account," said a third, bluntly.

I nodded. "Okay, so let's name that. Relationships. Circumstances. Money. Can we agree that those are all external to you?" They nodded again. "Let's call them external objects, things that exist outside your mind and body."

One woman, a repeat attendee, chimed in thoughtfully: "But it's also how I feel about those things. I don't mind the rain, but my husband can't stand it. We have totally different views on money, too, on how much we need and how to spend it. So it's not just the thing itself, it's what I think about the thing."

"Yes," I smiled. "That's the key."

Because here's the twist: the outside world doesn't hit us raw. It is filtered, processed, and interpreted through the beliefs, stories, and emotional patterns already stored inside us. We don't experience the world as it is. We experience it as we are.

I pushed the group a little further. "If you had to estimate, what percentage of your experience is shaped by the outside world, and what percentage is shaped by your own thoughts and beliefs about it?"

One woman, still entangled in marital tension, didn't hesitate. "Ninety percent external. It's him, not me. The way he treats me makes me feel like shit."

Another offered a more balanced view. "For me, maybe fifty-fifty. I know I'm opinionated. But other people's behavior still affects me."

I nodded. "Totally valid. But here's something to consider. Many psychologists and researchers suggest the 80/20 rule, also known as the Pareto Principle. And when it comes to your lived emotional reality, it suggests that eighty percent of your experience comes from within (your thoughts, your beliefs, your emotional responses). Only twenty percent is based on what is actually happening outside of you." But I said, "I take this further and I would argue that all of your life is shaped by what's happening inside of you."

The room went silent.

Because if that is true, if most or all of your life is shaped by your inner world, then trying to control the outside is like rearranging deck chairs on a sinking ship. Futile. Exhausting. And it keeps you stuck at a lower level of living. A level where blame and lack of accountability seem more natural than taking responsibility. Where reaction feels safer than reflection.

Then came the moment that always comes. One brave woman raised her hand, face soft but serious.

"So… are you saying it's my fault I feel the way I do about my husband? That it's all in my head?"

I met her gaze. "No. Not fault, but it is a reflection of the level of awareness you are currently living from. So no, there is no blame, only feedback. And that is where the power to shift exists."

Because once you can name the level you are living from, you can choose to rise above it. That is the invitation here. To leave behind the lower Happiness Whore Habits (the ones built on fear, blame, guilt, and control) and reclaim your seat at the table of your own awareness. The table where peace, perspective, and sovereignty sit waiting.

As we open this chapter, I want you to sit with one uncomfortable but liberating truth: You are not experiencing life as it is. You are experiencing life as you are. The question is: what level of reality are you living from?

What Level Are You Living From

Before you can truly shift to a higher level of conscious awareness and change your life, you need to understand the lens through which you are living it. I am not talking about your personality type or how much yoga you do. I am talking about something far more subtle, yet far more powerful. Your level of consciousness. The internal frequency that determines not just what you experience, but how you experience it.

Let's get one thing clear: this is not about spiritual superiority. You are not better or worse for living at one level of conscious reality or another. You are not being graded by the universe. But it is about perspective, and perspective changes everything.

Think of the levels of conscious reality like a building. On the ground floor, all you can see is the street. The bins. The traffic. The chaos. It is loud. It is reactive. It feels like life is constantly happening to you. But as you rise, floor by floor, your view widens. You start to see things from above. You are no longer just reacting to what is in front of you; you are understanding it, moving with it, maybe even seeing patterns in the chaos. By the time you reach the top floors, you are not in the noise anymore. You are in the stillness. The clarity. The wisdom.

Each floor of this building represents a level of awareness. And you then live in this reality. Everything on this floor looks real to you. And here is the kicker: it is not your life that needs to change, it is the floor you are living on.

We can spend decades redecorating the ground floor of our experience. Different job. Different partner. New goals. More therapy. But if the level stays the same, the energy stays the same. And the patterns? They repeat, just with better furniture.

To help you locate where you might currently be living, let's explore the three key levels of consciousness that shape how we experience ourselves, our lives, and everything in them.

First, there is the Low Level, operating at the personal, survival self, and the physical level of reality with a survival-based consciousness. This is where most people start, and where many stay. It is rooted in fear, control, urgency, and lack. You are in constant reaction mode. Life feels like a fight. Everything is a personal attack. You are scanning for danger, hustling for safety, performing for approval. Your nervous system is shot. You are doing your best, but everything feels hard. Success feels temporary. Peace feels impossible. You measure your worth through output. You live for the next dopamine hit of validation. And if you are honest, it is exhausting. You know there is more to life than this, but you don't yet know how to access it.

Then, there is the Mid-Level, the more impersonal level, operating at the mental level of reality with an observing mind. This is where awakening begins. You start to realize, wait, maybe it is not just what is happening out there, it is what I believe about what is happening. You become aware of your own mind. You understand that your thoughts shape your experience. Life feels less personal and more impersonal. You learn to reframe, rewire, and reflect. It is empowering and yet still limiting. Because even though you are no longer reacting blindly, you are now trying to control everything through your mindset. You try to think your way into peace, productivity, and power. But thinking only takes you so far. You may feel more in control, but you are still striving. You are still exerting. You are still operating from identity.

And then comes the higher level, the awakened self, where you move beyond survival mode into a more expansive state of being. This is where the veil lifts. You stop operating from a survival personality and begin to live from the qualities of Life Intelligence. In this state, the deeper intelligence of life expresses itself through you. You do not need to prove, chase, fix, or control. You remember who you are, beyond your story, your strategy, or your survival script. You live from your brilliance, not scarcity. You begin to listen to your life rather than fight it. Your energy becomes clean, clear, and congruent. You speak from knowing and certainty, not from needing. You no longer hustle for alignment. You are the alignment. And you attract a reality that reflects it. We will cover this level later in detail in Chapter 9.

This part of the book, and especially this chapter, is your bridge from the first level of reality to the second. From unconscious reaction to conscious reflection. From identifying with your circumstances to realizing you are the one shaping them. From "Why is this happening to me?" to "What is this showing me?"

We are preparing the ground for the deeper embodiment

work that comes in Part Two. But first, we have to clear out the survival programs that keep you spinning on the lower floors. We have to name the patterns, question the thoughts, and challenge the stories that are still running your show. Because until you do, you will keep mistaking the noise for the truth.

Low-Level Awareness: Living in Survival

Imagine living your entire life on the ground floor of a building. Your view is narrow. All you can see are passing cars and chaotic movement. The traffic is loud, the neighbors' voices seep through the walls, and everything feels like it is closing in on you. You are so close to the noise that it becomes hard to think, let alone feel. It is not peaceful. It is not expansive. It is reactive, cramped, and exhausting.

This is what it feels like to live in survival mode. At this level of awareness, life happens to you. You are not steering the ship; you are just trying not to drown. Every situation feels personal. Every challenge feels like an attack. You are stuck playing emotional dodgeball with people, problems, and patterns that never seem to let up. Your nervous system stays on high alert, scanning for threats. And because you are so consumed with managing the chaos around you, you forget that you are allowed to look up and ask: Is this even the life I want?

From this level, you do not see clearly. You only see what is right in front of you, and most of it feels urgent, unfair, or out of control. Your energy is constantly being used to protect, perform, or please. So it is no wonder you are exhausted. You may feel ashamed that you cannot keep up. Or angry that others do not understand how hard you are trying. There is no space for softness here. No room to breathe. You are either clinging to control or collapsing under its weight.

And the hardest part? You do not even realize you are doing

it. This level of awareness becomes your normal. You over-function, over-analyze, over-please, or overwork, believing that this is just the way life is. You think the exhaustion is because of your schedule. But it is actually because you are living at war with your own system.

The Survival Self is deeply human, but it is not your real self. It is a temporary operating system designed to keep you safe, not to lead your life. And yet, most people build their entire identity from this place. Let's undress it so you can see it in action.

The Survival Self: The Trance of the Physical

Let's call it like it is: survival mode is not a high vibe. It is a trance. You have been told that life is physical. That your senses are the ultimate truth-tellers. That, what you see, hear, and touch, is the whole of reality, and everything else is fluffy or spiritual nonsense. This is the level of awareness most of the world operates from: the concrete, the visible, the explainable. What you see is what you get.

But let's go deeper. When you live from this level, what I call the personal Survival Self, you are functioning from the ground floor of consciousness. You are looking at life through a fogged-up window, trying to interpret the world based solely on what you can physically perceive. It feels real because your body feels it. But what you are experiencing is not the objective truth. It is a filtered, incomplete version of reality shaped by conditioning, survival instincts, and old programming.

Here, your body becomes your primary interface. The nervous system is constantly on edge, scanning for threats. Your senses are overloaded. Your emotions are misunderstood. You respond to stimuli like a machine (reactive, bracing, exhausted), believing that life is happening to you and your only role is to survive it. You do not realize you are reacting not just to the event, but to the meaning your mind has made about the event.

At this level, everything is personal. Your boyfriend didn't call. You must not be lovable. The hotel wasn't as nice as expected. The whole holiday is ruined. Your boss gave you feedback. You spiral into shame. You are wired to outsource your peace, constantly looking to the external world for proof that you are okay, that you are safe, that you matter.

This is the level where most people live, stay, and suffer most. Not because they are weak, but because this is how they have been trained. Parents, schools, media, society, all reinforcing the same belief: that your circumstances dictate your wellbeing. That your emotions are caused by what is happening outside of you. That, if you want to feel better, you need to change your body, your relationship, your job, or your bank account.

But here is the secret most people never learn: it is not the thing, it is the meaning. Always.

Imagine you and three friends go to see the same film. You walk out, and one person loved it, one was bored, one was triggered, and the fourth says she is just "happy to be included." It is the same film, but four different experiences. Why? Because you weren't reacting to the film. You were reacting to your perception of it. This is true in every moment of your life.

That moment changed everything for me. It made me less interested in what people said about the world and more interested in how they thought about it. What filters were shaping their view? What conditioning was narrating their reality? And then I turned that same curiosity back onto myself.

This is when things start to crack. When you realize that reality is not objective, it is constructed. Your senses, while powerful, are not the full picture. Your survival self has been doing its job, trying to keep you safe in a world that rewards performance, perfection, and control.

But staying here has a cost. Living from the Survival Self means you are always on alert, always burning energy, always clinging to people or pushing them away based on how they make you feel. You become addicted to validation. You need the likes, the praise, the wins. And when they do not come? You turn on yourself. Or worse, on others.

Eventually, this creates one of two reactions. You either double down on control, trying to manage the world around you to make sure it does not hurt you again. Or you collapse, feeling helpless, victimized, and resentful that life just keeps happening to you.

Neither of those options is power. They are trauma responses dressed up as personality.

Let me be clear: this is not your fault. You have been conditioned into this worldview. Conditioned to believe that life is external, that emotions are inconvenient, and that success will finally fix your emptiness. But here is the uncomfortable and liberating truth: the physical world is not the full story, and it never was.

Living from the Survival Self might feel normal, but it is not natural. It is not your truth. It is not where your power lives. This is where we start to level up.

Challenging the Belief in Objective Reality

One of the most destabilizing and liberating truths we can

confront is this: you are not experiencing life as it is. You are experiencing life as you are.

Most people move through the world assuming that their view is the view. That what they see, feel, and react to is not only valid but also universally true. This is the illusion of objectivity. The idea that what you are experiencing is a direct, unfiltered reflection of reality, rather than a mirror of your internal perception. But the deeper truth is that your experience of life is shaped by the meaning you give it. Your reality is not a neutral broadcast. It is a curated projection filtered through your beliefs, biases, body, nervous system, and past.

When you assume that everyone sees what you see, or that your interpretation of events is the truth rather than your truth, you become trapped in a narrow, ground-floor existence. You forget that perception is deeply personal. Two people can walk into the same room, hear the same comment, witness the same event, and walk away with entirely different stories, emotions, and memories. Not because one is wrong and the other is right, but because we each live in the world through our own lens.

This is not a philosophical idea. It is the foundation of freedom. Because if how you feel is not determined by what is happening, but by how you are seeing it, then suddenly your power comes rushing back to you. You are no longer at the mercy of other people's actions, unpredictable circumstances, or external validation.

But let's not just intellectualize this. Let's live it. Let's challenge this belief in real time, go to https://www.gemdentith.com/playbook to the "Inner Work Exercise: The Rain Experiment."

Now that you've stretched the frame of reality, we're ready to rise. It's time to move up to the next level of awareness and meet the version of you who lives from a higher floor.

Together, we will move to the mid-floor. The mid-level of awareness. The mental self.

Seeing the World Through Tinted Glasses

In this section, we will explore how your experience of life originates from within, not from what is going on out there. You will see that the level of awareness you operate from acts like a filter for how you interpret, respond to, and engage with everything around you.

Everything is available to you. You are just viewing it from the ground floor.

It is like wearing tinted glasses. Your thoughts, beliefs, and emotions shape the color of your world. If your lenses are dark and cloudy, life feels heavy, unclear, even hostile. If they are rose-tinted, everything sparkles with hope and potential. But here is the kicker: the world itself has not changed. Only your perception has.

That is the essence of mental-level awareness. You are not reacting to reality; you are reacting to your interpretation of reality. And those interpretations are not fixed. They are filtered.

A higher level of awareness is about cleaning the lenses, removing the smudges left by fear, conditioning, comparison, and old attachments. Because, whether you realize it or not, you are continually shaping your experience through the beliefs and perceptions that color your view.

So, what shade are your glasses right now?

If your state of awareness creates your world, and your reality is dictated by the lens you are looking through, then the question becomes: what within you has the power to shift that lens?

At the surface level, it is your conditioned beliefs, what you have been taught to accept as truth about yourself, others, and the world. But if you go deeper, you will see it is not just what you believe that matters, but how you believe. The mechanics of the mind, not just the content, are what shape your lived experience.

And if you have ever tried to change one thought at a time, you will know how exhausting that is. It is like playing a never-ending game of cat and mouse. What you need is not a better trap, but a new paradigm.

When you shift your framework, when you stop trying to control every individual belief and instead understand the architecture behind how they are created in the first place, the old patterns begin to dissolve on their own. You see the game, and the game changes, and so does your world.

This chapter is a turning point. A quiet revolution. Because the moment you realize that the weather, your partner, your job, your income, or the political climate are not actually what is causing you to suffer, an opening appears in your mind, you stop filling your mind up with the same conversation, and when you stop having this conversation with yourself, then naturally there's more space.

Have you ever wondered why two people can be at the same event or watch the same film and have completely different experiences? You are about to find out why.

The Mental Level: The Mind That Makes Meaning

Once you have dissolved the illusion of an objective world,

that universal, fixed, one-size-fits-all truth, you naturally begin to explore the next terrain: your own mind. This is the mental level of awareness. The interpersonal realm. The psychological plane. The moment you realize: I am not just in a world; I am interpreting it.

At this level, you begin to acknowledge that you live in a constant relationship with others, but those relationships are not experienced through pure truth. They are experienced through perception, through thought, through belief. You recognize that your experience of life is not simply the weather, the traffic, or the words spoken in the room, but what your mind does with them. You start to notice that no one around you is seeing the world in quite the same way you do. They cannot. Everyone is perceiving through their own mind stream.

This is where subjective reality begins. You start to see how much your experience is filtered through your thoughts, beliefs, emotions, and cultural frameworks. You move from "what I see is what I get" to "what I believe is what I experience." You begin to believe, consciously or unconsciously, that if you can just think the right thoughts or hold the right beliefs, you can change your life. Life becomes a mirror, and you become the mind behind it.

At first, this shift feels like liberation. You feel powerful. You begin editing your inner monologue like a director on a deadline. You swap negative thoughts for positive affirmations. You try to think your way out of fear. You believe that if you manage your mind well enough, you can rise. And for a time, this seems to work.

But here is what most people do not tell you: trying to control your thoughts can become its own form of imprisonment.

You spend so much time scanning your mind for misalignment that you begin to fear your own thoughts. You try to stay "high vibe." You try to think your way back to joy. You try to outwit anxiety by changing the story. But if you are constantly trying to reframe, you are still inside the belief that your power lies in performance. You are not really free. You have just upgraded your tools.

One way I explain this to clients is through the concept of the mental body, the energetic layer through which thoughts, beliefs, and emotions are processed. When you are thinking "I am confident," your mental body relaxes, and your emotional state follows. But when you are looping in "I am failing, I am behind," the entire field of your experience contracts. The mental body is the bridge between the physical self and the emotional self, and most people live stuck in the traffic jam between the two.

This is why the personal development industry became obsessed with positive thinking. But the truth is, slapping a new thought on top of a false identity does not resolve the issue; it just layers it. That is why this level of awareness, while profound, is still limited. You have not yet touched the root of the thought. You are still playing in the theater of the mind.

When you live at the mental level, you are still trying to figure it out. You are intellectualizing your way through emotion. You have shifted from "the world is happening to me" to "I am happening to the world," but you are still operating from a place of control. The reins have changed hands, but you are still gripping them tightly.

And yet, the breakthroughs here are potent. You begin to realize that perception is malleable. That thoughts are not facts. That belief systems can be rewritten. That you are not experiencing reality, you are experiencing your version of it, shaped by filters you rarely question: childhood imprints, cultural narratives, unspoken fears. You see that your life is less about what is happening and more about how your mind is processing it.

Imagine standing in a glass elevator. At the ground floor, your physical self, you could only see what was right in front of you. But now, as you rise into the mental floors, the view starts to expand. You begin to observe the lens through which you are looking. And if you are honest, sometimes the lens is distorted. Rose-tinted, fogged up, cracked from old stories. You start to notice how your beliefs tint your perception, how your thoughts shape your relationships, how your reactions are often responses to an inner story, rather than an outer truth.

This new vantage point allows you to relate differently. To yourself. To others. You realize that every person is living in their own version of the world, not just yours. The way your partner sees that conversation, the way your friend hears your silence, the way your boss interprets your tone, it is all filtered through their mental landscape, not just yours. This awareness, while initially destabilizing, opens the door to compassion. Suddenly, you stop trying to win arguments and start trying to understand realities.

And if you are wondering how to really feel this, not just grasp it intellectually, there is a practice that will help you see it firsthand. Let's take what we've just explored about the mental level, and now feel it. Because it's one thing to understand that reality is filtered through the mind, and it's another thing entirely to witness it unfold in real time through conversation, observation, and reflection.

Try this: With a small group of people, place an ordinary object in the middle of a small group, a coffee cup, a pen, a slice of toast. Look at it silently for one minute. When you share, describe not just what you saw but how you saw it: did you judge it, admire it, or ignore it? Notice how five minds create five realities. This isn't about being right; it's about seeing the filters that shape your reality. For the full Group

Awareness Practice: Seeing the Mind at Work, go to the Undressed companion playbook: https://www.gemdentith.com/playbook

This exercise is deceptively simple, but it's potent. It helps you recognize how uniquely we each perceive reality. It also highlights the invisible frameworks we carry: biases, memories, emotional overlays, and unspoken assumptions. Some may think: "Just a pen." Others may think: "I remember signing my divorce papers with one of those." You get the point.

This is the crux of mental-level perception. We're not experiencing reality; we're experiencing our interpretation of it. This exercise reveals that truth in a way no theory ever could.

Now, if you're feeling brave, you can level this up. Choose a subject that naturally carries more emotional weight: politics, parenting styles, spirituality, or even the topic of veganism. But be warned, this is not a debate. The goal is not to prove who is right. It is to witness how differently we all arrive at "truth." You'll notice how our beliefs shape our tone, how our tone shapes the room. How even our posture changes depending on the story we're telling.

If emotions rise, stay. Don't fix. Just observe. Let the heat of conviction expose the structure beneath it. Ask yourself silently: What belief is sitting underneath this reaction? What filter is shaping this view?

Once the conversation closes, take yourself away to a quiet space. Journal your experience. Reflect on the exercise, not just what was said, but how it landed in your body. Ask yourself:

What did I assume? What did I project? What was I unwilling to hear? What surprised me? What stayed with me?

Notice if you agreed with certain people. Ask yourself why. Did you grow up with similar values? Are you both conditioned by the same systems or cultures? Notice how agreement does not necessarily mean truth. It might just mean a shared lens.

This group awareness practice doesn't just help you understand others; it helps you become more conscious of yourself. You start to see that you're not reacting to people, you're reacting to your perception of them. To the meaning you've made. To the beliefs you've stored and replayed, sometimes for decades.

And this realization is everything.

Because the moment you see your filters is the moment they loosen. You no longer need to defend them. You no longer confuse opinion with identity. You stop trying to control the room and start learning how to hold it. You become more fluid. More curious. More sovereign.

This is the true gift of the mental level: not perfect thinking, but conscious relating. Not mastering the mind, but understanding its influence. Not creating the perfect thought, but noticing which ones are quietly running the show.

Now, take a breath. Let that settle. That was quite a swallow. But now, you've begun to see behind the veil. And once you've seen it, you can't unsee it.

Implications of the Mental Level

Once you understand that your mind is not just receiving reality but creating it through thoughts, interpretations, and past experiences, you begin to live life differently. You stop looking for one absolute truth and instead start listening to the symphony of truths playing out through different people. You realize that your senses are not the full story. They are only the starting point. It is what your mental and emotional filters do with that data that creates the story you live inside. And when you truly understand that, you stop trying to win arguments and start trying to understand perspectives. You stop outsourcing your peace to other people's behavior and start taking responsibility for the lens you are looking through. That is when life gets interesting. That is when your relationships deepen. And that is when your power returns, because you know: if I change my thoughts, I change my world.

There may be nearly eight billion of us on this planet, but no two of us live in the exact same reality. That is not a problem. That is a miracle. And the moment you can honor that, without needing to fix, convert, or defend, you have arrived at a level of freedom most people never taste.

Up and Down the Survival and Mental Levels

Let's debunk a sweet little illusion while we are here. We love to think that once we have seen a fraction of the truth, we will never forget it. Once we have "upgraded" from survival mode to mental awareness, we will stay elevated like an ascended guru floating above petty drama and flight delays. But here is the truth:

Awareness does not make you better than being human. It just makes you more aware, as a human.

You do not graduate to the next level and stay there. You oscillate. You dance. You fall flat on your face. Then you remember again.

Some days, you catch the flavor of your thoughts as they season your entire mood. You see the projection, the pattern, the loop. You breathe. You choose differently.

Other days, you are in the thick of it, reacting your damn ass off, emotionally hijacked, huffing like a volcano goddess in leggings. You blame your partner, your child, your ex, your inbox. (Ask any life coach where they still react from their survival self. They will say, "My mum, my lover, my child." Welcome to the club.)

This is not a failure. It is a rhythm. So, rather than judge yourself for slipping, get curious.

Where are you relating from today? The ground floor of reactivity, or the first floor of mental awareness? And can you love yourself in both places?

I have designed a simple thought experiment meditation to illustrate more clearly how we often oscillate between different states throughout the day, or, as you will discover, throughout this next "Guided Meditation: Going on Holiday." Head over to the meditation section of https://www.gemdentith.com/playbook

When my clients have done this exercise, they tend to realize the same things. I have summarized these insights below. As you read through, see if they are like your own.

They see that their experience is created moment by moment, shaped not by the event but by the story they tell themselves about it.

They notice that feelings are not caused by other people or delays. They are generated from their own thoughts in response to what is happening.

They realize that while their experience feels real, it is not the only truth. Every person around them is living in their own world, formed by their own meaning-making mind.

They understand that thoughts are always present, like a

stream running beneath everything, and that those thoughts are transient, fluid, and ever-changing.

They become aware that trying to control every thought is exhausting and unnecessary. Sometimes, just letting a thought pass through is enough to shift everything.

They realize that while awareness does not promise perfection, it does offer freedom. The freedom to respond instead of react. To witness, rather than wage war with reality.

I hope you found this exercise helpful. The intention of this meditation, and my clients' observations, is to highlight the significant role that thoughts play in shaping your experiences, and the dynamic nature of your inner world.

Understanding the Mechanics of Your Experience

If you want to change your life, you have to get intimate with the mechanics of how it is being created.

We obsess over the inner workings of things we love (watches, cars, tech). We take them apart, inspect the parts, and figure out how to make them work better. But when it comes to our own minds, most people never stop to ask: how does this actually work? You have a built-in operating system running the entire show, yet you are walking around as if you do not have the manual.

Your mind is not you. It is a system, a human computer, a thought stream system. And just like any system, it comes with default settings, you can add software to it, and it needs a power source. As you start to see how it operates, you not only gain leverage over your experience, but you also become its designer. But if you never look under the hood, you will keep mistaking the ride for reality. Let's break this down in the way that I see it.

Raw data, as sensory input. It all begins with the body. Your five senses constantly feed raw, unfiltered data into your system: light, sound, texture, temperature, taste. At this stage, there is no emotion, no meaning, no story. It is just neutral input.

Think of it like a camera lens capturing light. The camera does not flinch or analyze. It just receives.

The mental processing filter. Next, that raw data gets filtered through your unique internal lens: your past, your beliefs, your current mood. Your mind does not just receive information; it distorts, edits, and colors it.

If you are carrying old stories, unresolved trauma, or inherited belief systems, those become the tinted glasses through which you see the world.

Fear tint? You perceive a threat where none exists. Worthiness tint? You see rejection in neutral glances. It is not the world. It is the lens.

Meaning plus Emotional Reaction. You do not respond to life. You respond to the meaning you have assigned to life.

Let's say someone cuts you off in traffic. Raw data: "A car moved in front of me." That is the camera shot. Now the lens kicks in. Maybe you think, "What an asshole." Boom (anger). But what if your lens said, "Maybe they are rushing to the hospital"? Suddenly, it is compassion. Same event. Different filter. Totally different experience.

Your thoughts are the movie reel. Your life is what plays out on the screen.

The Loop. Every time you reinforce that mental filter (every time you repeat a story), you hardwire that interpretation deeper into your system. Now your mind scans for more proof. And guess what? It finds it. Welcome to the self-fulfilling loop.

But here is the truth bomb that breaks the spell: you are not experiencing life. You are experiencing your thoughts about life.

When you start to witness the process, rather than just being inside it, you reclaim your authority. You shift from actor to director. From character to consciousness.

But What Even Is Experience?

Unless you are a psychologist, philosopher, or someone with a casual crush on consciousness, it is rare that you stop and ask: What actually creates my experience? Not just in a general, "how was your day?" kind of way. But moment by micro moment. Right now. And now. And now.

We are so busy having experiences that we forget to ask what they are made of.

And yet, if the quality of your life is shaped by the quality of your moment-to-moment experience, is it not odd that we spend more time planning holidays than we do investigating the very mechanism that determines whether life feels like one?

Let's make this personal. Do this now. Don't just read it, feel it.

Count to one. Again. One more time.

That is a moment. That is how quickly it passes. That is what your life is made of. Not weeks, not seasons, not phases. Just the sacred flicker of right now, layered one upon the next like notes in a symphony.

We like to romanticize the idea of "being present," but presence is not some big mountaintop moment. It is that one-second click of awareness when you are actually here. And if experience is happening in these tiny windows of now, why are we not more obsessed with what is inside those windows?

Because the truth is this: you cannot change your life if you do not understand how your experience is created.

The Misconception About Experience

Here is where we have been duped. Most people assume experience is dictated by the outside world, by what is happening around them, who said what, how smoothly the day goes, and whether their plans unfold without interruption. We have been raised on the myth that experience equals circumstance. But that is only part of the picture.

Yes, your senses are constantly collecting data. But they are just the delivery service. They bring raw, neutral information, such as light and sound waves, into your awareness. They do not interpret. They do not assign value. They do not decide what it means. That part is all you.

Here's an example. You are in a conversation. The person in front of you is the "objective" reality, or so you think. But notice where your attention really is.

Are you listening deeply, or mentally formulating your next sentence? Are you noticing their tone and judging whether they sound confident, certain, or sexy? Do their words remind you of someone from your past? Are you hearing their voice, or your inner voice interpreting what they meant? You are not engaging with them. You are engaging with your mind's version of them and the meaning you associate with them through interaction.

So in fact, you have never actually experienced the person in front of you. Only your perception of them. That is the illusion. That is the mind's sleight of hand.

Through the Lens of the Mind

Imagine your mental framework as a pair of glasses you forgot you were wearing. The color of the lens changes everything. Dark, rose-tinted, scratched, smeared. It does not alter what is in front of you. But it completely alters how you see it.

Your beliefs, past experiences, emotional state, and cultural programming all shape those lenses. That internal framework filters what you notice, how you feel about it, and what you do next.

It works like this:

Past experiences condition you to expect certain outcomes. Core beliefs inform what you think is true about yourself, others, and life. Emotional state shifts your interpretation. Are you reading this with anxiety, calm, or curiosity? Social conditioning tells you what is acceptable to feel, say, or want.

And here is the thing. Your brain is exposed to around eleven million bits of information every second, but it can only consciously process about fifty. So how does it choose what to keep?

It filters based on what matches your existing worldview. Confirmation bias is not a glitch. It is how your mind stays "efficient." So you are not seeing reality. You are seeing the parts of reality that align with your beliefs. You are not experiencing the world. You are experiencing yourself projected outward.

So... What Is Experience, Then?

Experience is not something that simply happens to you. It is something you generate from the inside out. Contrary to what most of us have been taught, experience is not dictated by external circumstances, people's behaviors, or even how successful or safe your life looks on paper. It is shaped internally by a complex interplay of thought, attention, emotion, memory, and perception, all filtered through the unique lens of your awareness.

Here is how it actually works. Experience begins with awareness. The more aware you are of your thoughts and sensations, the more agency you have in how you respond. Without awareness, you are reactive (thinking, feeling, and behaving on autopilot).

From there, experience moves through your mental conditioning. Every interaction is filtered through your beliefs, emotional history, and subconscious interpretations of what something "means." This is why two people can have the exact same external experience but walk away feeling completely different.

Finally, your experience crystallizes into perception (the internal story you tell yourself about what just happened). That story becomes your reality, whether it is accurate or not.

This is the mechanism: your reality is not what is happening. It is what you think is happening. Life unfolds moment by moment, but what determines the quality of your life is not the moment itself. It is the quality of your mind at that moment. This is the invisible framework that governs your emotional world.

So the real question becomes: what is shaping your lens right now? And more radically, what might open up for you if you stopped believing every thought that passed through your mind?

Shift the Lens of Your Mind

If you recognize yourself in this (if you've been living reactively, swinging between emotional highs and deep dissatisfaction), it's not because you're broken or behind. It's because you've been navigating life from an awareness that's too small for the truth of who you really are. The good news is, awareness is not a fixed trait. It's a state or capacity that can expand or contract based on where you place your attention and how much you realise the inside-out nature of your experience.

You don't have to escape your current life to feel mentally free. You just have to remember the origin of what's creating your experience in that moment. The moment you begin to observe your mind rather than unconsciously identify with its content, a powerful shift begins. You become less entangled in the mental noise and more available to the deeper intelligence to rise within you.

To begin shifting from lower to higher awareness, ask yourself a few questions. What do I believe is causing me to have this experience right now? The only answer should be your thoughts. What thoughts am I gripping onto right now? What beliefs might be coloring my interpretation of this situation? What story am I telling myself about this person or outcome? What would happen if I let go of my need to be right or in control? And how might I see this differently if I zoomed out and softened my grip? These aren't just reflective prompts. They are actual tools to unhook you from the trance of thought and reorient you to a place of clarity and spaciousness.

Each time you pause and question the narrative your mind is running, you reclaim your sovereignty. You stop performing your false identity and orient to your true self. And when that shift happens, you begin to experience your emotions, your relationships, and your choices from a much more grounded, empowered place.

The Power of Understanding The Nature of The Mind

Instead of simply being in the experience, you can step back and observe how it is being formed. By dissecting the elements that shape your reality, you gain a new level of self-awareness, one that allows you to navigate challenges with clarity and intention.

This is especially powerful when life takes a nosedive. Rather than feeling powerless, you develop the ability to see what's really happening beneath the surface and recognize what needs to shift in order to realign yourself. Likewise, when things are flowing effortlessly, you begin to understand why, which allows you to sustain and expand those moments.

When you begin to watch your mind in motion, you develop the ability to take conscious action rather than operating on autopilot. From this elevated perspective, you move through life with greater ease and grace (responding rather than reacting, creating instead of consuming, and experiencing life as something you actively design rather than endure).

Until you grasp the true nature of your experience and can identify what level of awareness you are operating from, you will remain at the mercy of external circumstances, events, and distractions. You will feel like life is unpredictable, that you are constantly bumping into challenges, and that you are overwhelmed. Or, on the other end of the spectrum, you may find life predictable because you are controlling and manipulating everything around you just to feel safe.

However, when you shift into a higher level of awareness, everything changes. You rise out of victimhood or the need to control and instead begin working with the flow of life. You free yourself from unnecessary suffering, conflict, and the internal battles that have kept you spinning in cycles.

If you find yourself dissatisfied with your current reality, the first step toward transformation is realizing that your experience of life is created from within you (not by external conditions). Once you recognize this, you can begin the process of transcending lower levels of awareness and stepping into a more fulfilling, empowered way of being.

Why You Still Get Knocked Off Center (Even When You're "Doing the Work")

Let's be honest. You can journal every morning, say your affirmations, meditate with all the right apps, and still spiral when someone cuts you off in traffic or sends a passive-aggressive text. You can think all the "right" thoughts, do all the mindset work, and still find yourself triggered, resentful, or quietly collapsing into guilt or shame.

This is because you're still living inside the limitations of the mental level of awareness. You're working on yourself, but you're still doing so from a place that's dependent on outcomes. You're trying to control your internal state by controlling your environment, managing your reactions, and over-analyzing your thoughts. But it's all still happening inside the same loop.

Even "positive thinking" becomes performance at this level. You feel better when you meditate or when your morning goes to plan, but the moment the outside world disrupts your carefully curated internal state, you're back in survival mode. Which means: it's not real freedom. It's just mental management. And while it may look good on the outside, it's still exhausting on the inside.

Undressed Realization

Remaining at the mental level of awareness helps you transcend the victim mindset and begin playing with the creative power of thought. But both the physical and mental dimensions are still limited by circumstance (by your environment, other people's behavior, and the constant effort to manage your own mind). You may reach moments of joy or empowerment, but they are often temporary, conditional highs. As soon as the outside world interrupts your carefully curated state, you find yourself thrown back into old patterns of control, frustration, or collapse.

This is the limitation of stopping at survival or mental awareness. They are stepping stones, not destinations. True liberation begins when you move beyond perception alone and awaken to the deeper, multi-dimensional nature of who you are. That is where the real freedom, self-mastery, and alignment live. And that is what we will explore in Part Two.

For now, take this with you: you have already come a long way, and the best is still ahead. Surviving isn't enough. Life is meant to be lived with purpose, joy, and full engagement. Thriving begins when you realize that nothing is ever truly personal. The more you embrace this, the more life opens into alignment, growth, and deep satisfaction.

Shifting into higher awareness is not about positive thinking. It is about seeing life from a new vantage point. From survival to flow. From control to trust. From resistance to creation. And when you live from that expanded state, life begins to feel effortless (not because circumstances change, but because you are no longer confined by the lens of your old perceptions).

Mirror Moments

How much of my life is currently spent in survival mode, just getting through the day?

What beliefs or habits are keeping me from fully thriving?

What would it look like for me to truly level up my awareness? What small changes could I make right now?

Embodied Practice

Identify Survival Patterns. Spend a few minutes each day for the next week noticing moments where you feel like you are simply surviving. Write them down and note how you can start shifting toward thriving.

Shift Your Mindset. Choose one belief that keeps you in survival mode (e.g., "I don't have enough time or energy"). Reframe it to support growth (e.g., "I have the time and energy to do what matters most"). Practice this new belief daily.

Take One Action to Thrive. Choose one area of your life where you can take action to thrive rather than survive. It could be self-care, boundaries, or pursuing a passion. Notice how this small shift changes your overall energy.

Chapter 8:

Turning inward

The First Step To Real Change

What lies before us and what lies behind us are small matters compared to what lies within us. And when we bring what is within, out into the world, miracles happen.

— Henry David Thoreau

For as long as we have been alive, we have been sold a promise. That happiness waits for us out there, in the dream job, the soulmate, the dream house, or the next orgasm. That if we could just earn more, do more, become more, then we would finally feel whole.

But the truth?

Here is the deeper truth: no one hands you your degree, your medal, your engagement ring, or your morning coffee: happiness was never out there. It has never been something to achieve. It has always been something to uncover.

It lives in the stillness between breaths. In the pause before the performance. In the quiet voice that whispers beneath all the noise: *I'm already here.*

Happiness is not out there waiting for you. It is already here. Inside you. Not in your future. Not in your past. Only ever in the now.

And the moment you stop reaching outward and turn inward, a doorway opens. Like a hidden portal, this space is quiet but alive. Wise but wordless. Entirely sacred.

But here is the catch: you cannot access it from the outside in. You have to turn inward. You have to stop. What no one tells you is that you do not need to find happiness. You need to undress what has been blocking it.

For most of my life, I did not know any of this. I bought into the same myths the world sold to all of us. That happiness existed outside of me. That I had to go somewhere, be someone, do more, in order to feel it.

But somewhere deep in my knowing, I already knew this; there was already a glimpse of light guiding me, I had just forgotten. It wasn't until I recalled a time in my childhood when an unlikely woman stopped me in my tracks. She planted a seed that would later change everything.

The Woman Who Sparked It All

I was no older than twelve when she found me.

A typical grey-skied day in Telford, the kind where even the air felt damp with disappointment. I was standing near the bus stop, waiting for my mum, when a woman appeared out of nowhere. She walked straight toward me like she was on a mission. No hello. No smile. Just a voice that sliced through the silence.

"What are you doing with your life?"

Her eyes locked on mine. Not with judgment, but with urgency. Like someone who had witnessed too much and could not bear to watch it happen again. There was something in her stare, intense but wise. Unapologetically honest. Her words did not feel random. They felt like a warning from a future I had not yet lived.

"Telford is the place people come to die," she said flatly. "Get out while you can."

I blinked. Frozen. A little confused. Not sure if I should move or run. But something in me knew she was not mad. She was medicine. So I stayed. Her presence was not threatening. It was prophetic. Her words did not land like an insult. They landed like a sacred interruption in a town too used to sleeping through wake-up calls.

Her name was Maggy.

She wore layers of worn-out clothes and carried the kind of weathered face that told stories no one had asked to hear. Her silver-streaked hair was tied loosely, fraying at the ends. But when she spoke, her voice stopped time. It was clean. Clipped. RP English. The kind you would hear on an old BBC broadcast, not echoing from a woman on a wet pavement in Shropshire. It did not match her appearance, and that is what made her unforgettable.

She spoke like someone who once held something precious and lost it.

"I used to run businesses," she told me. Her voice had thinned with time, but her tone was still sharp. "Then I met my husband. Charming, but dangerous. I lost myself in him. And when I lost myself, I lost everything. My work. My home and dignity."

She looked around with disdain, waving at the town like it was an inside joke she no longer found funny.

"Have you seen the new TV ads? 'Come to Telford,' they say. It should be, 'Come to Telford and die.'"

And just like that, she winked, boarded the bus to Brookside, and vanished.

No goodbye. No turning back.

I stood there, silent. Watching the bus pull away. Watching her disappear into the fog of forgotten lives. Around me, the town pulsed with its usual fatigue. Slumped shoulders, grey faces, the slow, lifeless shuffle of people who had accepted too little.

And in that moment, I saw it clearly. If I stayed here, I would become her.

She had spoken it like a curse. But I received it like a prophecy.

That realization, that I could die in this town with my dreams still buried in my bones, terrified me more than death itself.

Leaving Telford, Looking for Light

After college, I worked as a fitness instructor, but it did not take long before the repetition of four white walls and protein shake routines left me craving something deeper. I wanted to expand my health knowledge, so I joined the Ambulance Service. By my late teens, I had become the youngest medical emergency services responder in the West Midlands.

Thrown into the deep end of blue-light emergencies, back-to-back trauma calls, and raw human fragility, I witnessed what it meant to live on the edges of society. The poverty. The pain. The hopelessness. And somewhere between the sirens, the sterile corridors, and the late-night breakdowns on backstreets of council estates, a brutal realization hit me like a defibrillator: if I do not leave now, I will lose the light in me.

I started to see what Maggy had seen. Telford was not just

a postcode. It was a place where dreams came to die in silence. And I was not ready to become another woman who had given up.

I knew I needed to get out of the health care system in order to ever truly help it. After every shift, I would stay up late scrolling through university websites and city maps, quietly plotting an escape. The decision arrived with clarity: London.

It is true what they say. Bright lights attract starry eyes. I started to imagine a new life, one far beyond these grey-lit streets. I pictured the buzz of the city, the people I would meet, and the endless possibilities. "It is only a three-hour train ride," I told my mum, who was beside herself at the idea of one of her daughters flying the nest. I was the first to leave, but not the last.

The day I left, I carried no backup plan. Just a suitcase, a spine of fire, and a stubborn sense that there was something more. I moved to London with nothing but my drive and my desire for a different kind of life. I studied. I worked. I sacrificed. I climbed the corporate ladder in heels and hustle, believing, like so many do, that if I just worked hard enough, happiness would eventually arrive. That someday, success would save me.

Cracking the Illusion

Ten years later, with a resumé full of wins and a body full of exhaustion, I was not happy. I was burnt out. Disconnected and numb.

I reflected on my ten years in London and asked myself: What am I missing? Was Maggy right? Why am I not happy with all that I have achieved?

"On the outside, I have everything a woman wants."

That thought stopped me. "On the outside," I repeated under my breath.

Then a flood of questions poured out of me. Why am I dissatisfied on the inside? Have I been doing life wrong? Have I missed what is happening within me?

The question cracked something open. What followed was collapse. All those years, I had been too busy and too distracted with building businesses and relationships to see that the answer had been within me the whole time.

Happiness or contentment could never come from my achievements, my possessions, or my relationships. It had to be uncovered on the inside. It had to be undressed.

It was an inside job. The penny dropped.

The First Time I Met My Real Self

I had heard that yoga students often meditated after their practice, something about settling the body so the innate wisdom in me could speak. I was not a yogi, not then. I was not even sure I believed in it at the time. But one evening, hollowed out by the noise of city life and my own constant striving, I decided to give it a try.

I found a quiet room. Opened Spotify. Typed in "meditation music," a search I had never made before. I sat cross-legged, spine upright, with no idea what I was doing. But I did it because I needed to stop. Stop performing. Stop chasing. Stop spinning all the plates I no longer wanted to carry.

For the first time in my adult life, I stopped.

No deadlines, deliverables, or curated smile. Just me, sitting in the stillness, breathing.

And then it happened.

Not all at once, but gently, like light rising before the sun breaks through. A soft wave of peace began to move through my body. Not the kind I had ever felt from a glass of wine or a holiday. This was cellular. Soul-deep. The kind of calm you do not earn, but remember.

The stillness wrapped around me like a cocoon I never knew I needed. Time did not just slow; it dissolved. The city, the noise, the endless proving, all dropped away. And with it, the identities I wore like tight clothes: Gem the consultant, the daughter, the doer. They all fell like ash.

For a moment that felt like forever, I was nothing. And somehow, I was everything. I was space. I was a living thing that could shine awareness on absolutely anything and was connected somehow to everything, like the fabric of life itself. And, in that moment, I felt as if I was home within myself. For the first time, just present, still, and feeling full from the inside, as if I was going to burst with all the good emotions that you can roll off your tongue. Pure bliss.

Tears spilled down my cheeks, not from sadness, but as if my soul finally exhaled for the first time. And then a deep-level sigh whispered through my being: You have returned.

In that moment, I realised the end of searching is not the end of desire. It is the beginning of wholeness. It is the radical recognition that within the infinite well of the now lies the possibility of everything. It was never out there. It was always in here, beneath the armour, beyond the ache, waiting for me to get quiet enough to hear it.

The Day I Stopped Trying to Earn My Place

From that moment, I stopped trying to prove I was alive. I just gave my awareness to it. I saw that wherever I directed my attention, that reality grew stronger. So I chose to focus on the deeper intelligence of life itself.

From here, I no longer outsourced my worth to validation or applause. I no longer curated my personality to be digestible. I no longer seduced belonging through performance. Something had cracked, and through that crack, my true self poured out.

What emerged was not the polished woman I had been trying to become. It was the whole woman I had been running from. She was quiet. She was powerful. She was undeniably enough.

That shift gave birth to a new kind of freedom. Not freedom rooted in rebellion, but in remembrance. It was not loud. It did not announce itself with glitter or fireworks. But it was seismic. For the first time, I stopped living for the next version of myself. I stopped shaping my life around who I thought I should be and started sinking into who I already was.

And in that presence, I felt something I had chased for decades. Real joy. The kind that does not need an excuse to exist. The kind that wraps itself around your breath and meets you in the mundane. Every step, every inhale, every ordinary moment began to feel sacred, simply because I was in it.

The town that once symbolised limitation, Telford, with its grey skies and slower pace, no longer held power over me. When you stop trying to escape yourself, everything around you becomes a mirror instead of a prison. What had once felt like exile transformed into an invitation.

The end of searching revealed the secret I had been missing all along: true fulfilment is not found in the chase. It is revealed in the return.

It is not a finish line you cross. It is a field you surrender to. The more I sat with myself in stillness, the more I found that happiness was not a prize I had to hustle for. It was already available to me, rising like breath, emerging without permission, unconditional and free.

I would sit in meditation and feel time dissolve. Identity would fall away. There, in the spaciousness of presence, I was naked. Not vulnerable, but available. Not empty, but whole. Nothing but an awareness suspended in nothingness, yet complete.

That space became my portal. A gateway. The place where death and birth coexisted. Where old selves could dissolve, and new truths could emerge. Each time I returned to it, a layer would fall away. Each time, I undressed a little more. Until finally, I sat bare, soft, surrendered, and entirely myself.

These experiences, and the insights they birthed, changed everything. And they will for you, too.

But, that's enough about me – what about you!

Well done. You've made it here. And you didn't just get through pages, you got through yourself.

You met truths you didn't expect. You saw through the stories you thought were yours. You began to hear a voice inside that has been whispering for years, beneath the noise, beneath the mask, beneath the over-functioning girl who learned to survive by performing.

And now, something has shifted. Quietly. Powerfully and irrevocably. Because once you see through the illusion, you cannot unsee it.

No one teaches us how to be with ourselves. We are taught to be good. To be pretty. To be productive. To be liked. But not to be with ourselves. Not to sit in silence and listen. Not to ask the deeper questions without rushing to fix or perform.

But here you are. You didn't just read this book; you let it read you. You let it mirror something back that you were finally ready to meet.

So let's take a breath together.

The Turning Point

The turning point is the moment you stop looking outside of yourself for the answer to your inner ache. It is when you stop chasing the next thing to finally feel "enough," and instead begin to turn your attention inward, toward what has been waiting beneath the noise all along.

To turn in is to remember where your real power lives, not in your productivity or perfection, but in your presence.

It is a subtle shift. But it changes everything.

Because, as you begin to turn in, you begin to turn on. It is like a light switch flipping in the body. A pleasure switch. A presence switch. And that aliveness, that current, is not coming from the outside. It is coming from you.

When I started activating this inner current, I didn't just feel peace; I felt pleasure. Undeniable, wordless, unconditional pleasure. The kind that doesn't depend on whether someone texts you back. The kind that lives in your cells.

It is hard to explain in words, because the best parts of this journey are not intellectual. They are felt. They have to be experienced and lived.

Summary of Part One

In Part One, you began the sacred work of undressing. You shed the layers of conditioning, performance, and pretense that once covered your connection to self. You walked through the first arc of your return, stripping away the false identities that separated you from presence, from possibility, and from the magic that only becomes available when you stop chasing and start remembering.

This part of the book was not about demonising success, beauty, or ambition. It was not about giving up the glow-up, the good man, or the next-level life. It was about waking up to the wild goose chase underneath it all. The performance patterns that had you sprinting toward things that were never meant to hold your wholeness.

You began to see the clues. The traits. The compulsions. The quiet ache beneath your over-functioning. The moments you caught yourself trying to prove you were enough through your to-do list, your image, your relationship status, your Instagram grid. You started to recognise the addictive nature of the "happiness whore habit," that performative pursuit of joy that leaves you more burnt out than blissed out. And you realised: this was never your fault. You were taught to live this way. You were raised in a world that profits off your disconnection.

We went deep into the lie of consumerism. The sneaky gospel that sells you your own worth, one branded object at a time. We exposed how society does not just market products, it markets identity. And how, somewhere along the way, you internalised the idea that by wearing, buying, dating, or doing the right things, you could finally feel like you were something. That is a lie. You were born valuable. You were simply programmed to forget, so you would keep opening your wallet and closing off your attention from listening to the deeper wisdom within you.

You traced the roots of your pursuit. You saw how culture conditioned you to measure worth through output, image, productivity, and prettiness. You began to catch the consumer matrix feeding on your self-doubt. Whispering, *buy this, fix that, be her.* You started to reclaim your attention.

We also explored the two levels of reality most people unconsciously live in: the objective and the subjective. You learned that you are not seeing the world as it is, but as you are. That every thought, emotion, and belief is shaping your experience like a filter on your lens. And that is when you shift the quality of your attention; you begin to shift the entire frequency of your life.

With every mirror moment, every guided meditation, every breath into the stillness, you began to experience a different truth. A quieter one. One that does not shout, or sell, or seduce. One that lives deep within your soul.

Because lasting happiness is not something you build like a business plan, it is not something you buy. It is something you uncover.

The Flip: From Chasing to Remembering

We have spent this first part of the book undressing the external: the conditioning, the distractions, the quiet lies that sounded like truth. We have exposed the illusion that your joy lives in the next achievement, the next man or woman, the next glow-up, or next season's wardrobe. We have seen how society grooms us to be good humans with great potential, just so we can spend our lives proving it. We have named the burnout. The performative pressure. The invisible grief of losing yourself while trying to become someone worthy.

And now we name something else: you are not missing anything.

That quiet ache in your stomach, the longing, the low hum that has been with you since you were old enough to perform love instead of receive it, is not a flaw. It is a flare signal. It is your truth, knocking. It is the deeper intelligence in you saying, *I am still here. You did not lose me. You just forgot how to listen.* And it is the only way it can communicate with you to tell you that you need to reconnect.

What we label as self-doubt or insecurity is often nothing more than disconnection, from presence, from the moment, from our real self. We misinterpret that gap as though there is something wrong with us or our life, when it's really just a loss of connection. We mistake it for lack. So we chase: clothes, praise, knowledge, women, men, mentors, experiences. All the while, the real you is sitting quietly at the centre, untouched and unamused, patiently waiting for you to return.

And here is the twist. The thing you thought you had to earn, you already have. The peace you thought you would find once you arrived is here, now. The happiness you keep trying to construct like a business plan was never meant to be built. It was meant to be remembered.

This is the sacred flip. The moment your attention shifts from the outer to the inner. From performance to presence. From the survival self that always needs more, to the deeper self that knows you are already enough.

When you reconnect, you do not have to transcend your life. You do not have to ditch your desires or burn your vision board. You do not need to renounce sex or stop loving beautiful things. You only need to stop outsourcing your worth to them.

You can have the house. You can build the brand. You can

fall in love with a man or woman who worships your truth. But not because you are trying to become someone worthy of it all. Because you have already remembered: you are.

So let us talk a little more about this phantom missing piece. That ache. That sense that something is off, that something is missing, that if you could just figure out what, everything would click into place. Maybe you have told yourself the missing piece was a soulmate. Or more money. Or clarity. Or a new body. But what if the missing piece is not missing?

What if it is only covered? Covered by thoughts. Covered by stories. Covered by years of trying to be what you thought was required.

The truth is that the real you is still there. Always has been. But like a satellite signal dropping, sometimes we lose connection. That does not mean you are broken and you need to go to the doctors to get something to fix yourself or numb the ache.. It means you need to pause long enough to reconnect. You need more meditation than medication.

When you live in a constant loop of negative, fearful thoughts about the past, the future, and the what-ifs, you project these images and the feelings that accompany them outside to the world. You become your thoughts. A false self forms. And that false self has needs. She needs constant validation. She needs life to go her way to feel safe. She needs everything outside of her to meet her safety needs so she can feel okay inside.

But when you stop identifying with those stories and that version of you and come back into the now, you remember who you really are. And in that moment of presence, the ache dissolves.

It does not need therapy. It does not need a ten-step plan. It needs you to pause. It needs breath. Stillness and space.

This is the moment the sacred shift begins when you stop seeking relief in the outside world and start feeling yourself again.

Not in an abstract way. In a grounded, cellular way. In a real, embodied, holy-hell-my-body-is-buzzing kind of way. That is not spirituality. That is aliveness.

It is what happens when you remember that presence is not passive. It is power. It is the power to shift the entire trajectory of your life by placing your awareness on what is true instead of what has been taught. And from that place, you turn on. You become magnetic. Not because you are trying to be, but because you are no longer trying to be anything else.

That is what this whole first part of the journey has been about. Sacred unlayering. Shedding the false. Undressing the performance. Disarming the survival self. And landing back inside the holy, grounded, ecstatic truth of your own presence.

But do not think you are now done. You are not done. But you are no longer where you started. You have seen the game. And now you have realised where the real answers live: inside.

Preparing to Go Deeper in Part Two

Part One laid the foundation. You began the sacred undoing. You unhooked your worth from performance, undressed the illusions, and re-met the woman (or man) beneath the roles. What comes next is not about striving harder or becoming better. It is about remembering who you already are and creating from that place.

As we move into Part Two, we step into a deeper dimension of reality. The space where creation actually begins. Not from a to-do list, but from truth. Here, we do not chase outcomes.

We amplify energy. We align with the pulse of the universe. This is where your deepest power lives, not in effort, but in embodiment.

You will begin to meet yourself in new ways. Not as the woman or man shaped by their past, titles, or timeline, but as the essence beneath it all. The you who is present, pure, and powerful beyond measure. You will explore the realm of conscious creation, where you no longer build from conditioning or urgency, but from frequency and knowing.

This is where you will tap into the universal qualities of your true self and your unique expression. Not the expression the world asked you to become, but the one deeper intelligence in you has always whispered you are. You will begin to shape a life not as a reaction, but as a remembering. You will learn to move in flow with life rather than against it. Not to control, but to co-create.

Imagine walking into a new reality. One where your relationships do not trigger collapse, where your past no longer pulls you backward, where your environment reflects who you are becoming, not who you have been. In this timeline, your inner peace is no longer negotiable. Your inspiration is no longer delayed. In this space, you do not wait for joy. You become it.

Let yourself soften. Open. Be willing to enter the unknown. This next chapter is not about expansion. It is about awakening to your truth.

The magic begins here.

PART TWO:

AWAKEN
AWAKEN
AWAKEN
AWAKEN

Remember

Chapter 9:

Penthouse of Perception

From the performance personality to Life Intelligence.

What you are looking for is where you are looking from.

— David R. Hawkins

She leaned forward, frustrated. "Look, I just want the steps. The practical stuff. I don't need any of that mystical, spiritual fluff. Just tell me what to do."

Her mentor smiled, unfazed. "Ah… you want the cheat-sheet. The checklist. The 'how-to' for enlightenment." He leaned back in his chair. "Alright. But tell me something first, if the answer was just in a set of steps, why can't you just Google it?"

She frowned, caught off guard.

"Because," he continued, "it's not just about the steps. It's about how you perceive the world. A simple shift in awareness can do more for your peace of mind than any checklist ever could. Right now, you're trying to solve your problems from the same level of thinking that created them. You're stuck seeing life through a lens of separation, scarcity, and fear, rather than understanding the deeper connected web of abundance that already exists."

She crossed her arms. "So, what am I missing?"

The mentor studied her for a moment. "You see life as though it is happening to you (or maybe even because of you). But what if life isn't happening to you or by you, but through you and for you?"

A pause. A flicker of curiosity. "Through me and for me?" she mumbled.

"Until you understand this," he said gently, "you'll always feel like something is missing. You'll keep trying to fix things with frameworks, models, or steps (using logic to control what only deeper awareness can dissolve). That's what you've overlooked."

From Here Everything Looks Different

This chapter marks the beginning of Part Two: Awaken. And I'm so glad you're here, because this is where everything changes.

If Part One was about undressing the survival strategies, the conditioning, the masks, then this next phase is where everything shifts. You've stripped back the layers that no longer fit. But now, we change gears. Because this part isn't just about what you let go of, it's about what you begin to see.

What you're about to unlock here isn't just insight, it's ignition. This is the chapter where most of my clients, readers, and even I had the holy shit moment. The one that makes you sit up straighter, breathe a little deeper, and whisper to yourself: Why did no one teach me this sooner? Because transformation doesn't only come from subtraction, it comes from expansion. This is where the shift begins: not by doing more, but by perceiving differently, and being able to hold more.

In Part One, we dismantled the patterns of a survival-based identity. In Part Two, we turn toward awakening, toward seeing life through a higher lens, where clarity replaces confusion, and flow replaces attachment and force. This chapter and this part of the journey are where your deeper self begins to exhale, where your mind starts to loosen its grip. Where you remember that you were never broken, just buried under layers of survival.

And when the layers fall away, the truth emerges: you were made for flow. Success was always in your design. You just hadn't yet stepped into alignment with the living intelligence that lives through you.

Up until now, we've focused on the undoing. Now, we move into expanding. Because the deeper truth is this: success and I'm referring to real, sustainable, aligned success, doesn't come blindly from doing more. It comes from first seeing more. And the more you see, the more success becomes your natural state, not just a pursuit.

So take a breath. Let your shoulders drop. You've undressed the noise, and now we begin to awaken to the clarity that was always beneath it. When you're operating from a lower level of awareness, life feels heavy. You react, you control, you cling to what's familiar. Everything feels personal, and you stay trapped in a loop of surviving, fixing, and striving. But at a higher level, something opens. You begin to access possibilities where before you only saw dead ends. You step out of reactivity and into conscious creation. Life becomes more fluid, more spacious, more alive.

Until now, we've explored the two most common levels of awareness: the Physical and the Mental, where your experience of life is reduced to what can be seen, measured, or rationalized.

At the Physical Level, level one, you operate from the ground-floor perspective, where life is interpreted as purely objective, governed by external circumstances and measurable events. You believe what you see is all there is. Life happens to you, and your job is to survive it.

At the Mental Level, you move up to level two, and your quality of life increases, but you are still only operating from a first-floor perspective level, where you begin to realize that perception is subjective, shaped by your thoughts, beliefs, and prior experiences. You feel more in control, but your sense of reality is still filtered through the lens of past conditioning or what you want to conquer next. Here, life happens because of you, but you're still trapped within the walls of your mind.

At both of these levels, life feels intensely personal, though a little less personal if you are driving it, as you are at level two and start to see how the world is filtered by everyone's unique perception of it. Either way, you are either being pushed by circumstances or you're the one doing the pushing (constantly strategizing, fixing, or micro-managing life). In doing so, you remain stuck in a loop of either victimhood or forcing and controlling people and outcomes.

But there is a third level. A higher floor in the building of perception, the penthouse.

This is the realm of High-Level Awareness, where the noise fades, old attachments loosen, and life opens through a more spacious, connected field of awareness. From this place, you don't just witness life differently, you become different. You shift from survival-led to living in rhythm, with the intelligence that moves through all of life.

What is High-Level Awareness?

High-Level Awareness is the state where you begin to rise above the personal and see the wider picture of life. It's like standing on the top of a mountain, watching the world below, not from detachment, but from clarity. You're no longer caught in the drama or swept up in every thought or emotion. You can still feel, but you don't fuse with it. You observe it. Witness it. Allow it.

From this elevated perspective, you begin to realize: life isn't just happening to you, or even by you, it's happening through you. You stop identifying so closely with your thoughts, emotions, or reactions. Instead of being tangled in them, you become the presence behind them. And in that shift, something incredible happens: peace arrives. When you're no longer shaking the snow globe of your mind, things settle. Your system softens. Life starts to flow.

Clients often ask me: "How do I reach that level of awareness?" And while there are many pathways, sometimes the simplest truths are the most profound. Don't poke the snake, and it won't bite you. But us humans, oh, we love to poke. We cling, prod, ruminate, even when we know it hurts. There's a strange comfort in the familiar pain, where suffering can become a layer of identity you didn't know you were wearing. Awareness breaks that cycle, not by force, but by insight.

To rise into High-Level Awareness, you must begin to notice what most people ignore: the naked energies shaping your experience. This isn't just about noticing your habits or reframing your beliefs; it's about attuning to the subtle architecture of life itself. The undercurrents. The forces moving beneath the surface that influence how you feel, what you notice, what you attract, and how you respond.

Quantum physics shows us that invisible forces are always at play. We don't need to see the quantum field to know it's real. Just like a fish doesn't see water, and a human rarely considers the air they breathe. But that doesn't mean these forces aren't constantly influencing us. In the same way, these naked energetic currents are shaping your life, whether you're aware of them or not.

Their effects are as real as gravity or wind. You don't need to see the wind to know it's moving through the trees. The same goes for these subtle forces. They're not invisible because they're absent; they're invisible because most people never learned how to perceive them. But once you begin to notice, everything changes. Patterns emerge. Life reveals itself. You start to sense the difference between pushing and aligning. You stop swimming upstream and start surfing the current.

When you attune to these naked energies, life becomes less about effort and more about flow. Less control, more congruence. This is where we begin to awaken, not by striving, but by seeing. And once you see, you can never unsee.

Flowing with Life

When you shift into High-Level Awareness, life opens its doors. You begin to see through a more expansive, intuitive, and connected lens. Where others see obstacles, you begin to see possibilities, opportunities, and synchronicities. You realize you're not just reacting to life, you're co-creating with the field beneath it. This is the moment you step beyond the limitations of the lower mind and into a space where you can observe your thoughts, rather than be ruled by them. High-Level Awareness becomes the bridge between survival and flow. Life stops feeling like a struggle and begins to unfold with more natural grace.

Picture yourself living in a glass penthouse. You look out and take in a 360-degree view of everything below. You can no longer hear the traffic. The noise of the street doesn't reach you. There's no one banging on the walls next door, disturbing your peace. You can see for miles, but there's a spaciousness between you and everything else. That space gives you clarity. It allows you to pause before responding. It loosens your attachment to the appearance of chaos in life below. You're still aware of it, but you're no longer entangled in it, as it no longer appears like drama to you anymore; it's all divine lessons, a playground for people who are yet to find their way back to connection. You don't judge, you just observe and notice that where they're at is only a reflection of their level of awareness, and that can shift for them, like it has for you.

This shift changes everything. From this higher perspective, you no longer feel the need to control what's happening outside of you. Instead, you begin listening to what's unfolding inside.. You become less fixated on the objects in the room and more attuned to the space in the room itself. And because you're not clinging to or avoiding what's in the space, your energy becomes liberated. You stop scattering it outward and begin conserving it. As a result, you become a magnet for more ease, more clarity, more flow.

The higher your awareness, the more you begin operating as your higher self, accessing a more refined mind, processing higher-quality thoughts, and cultivating higher-quality relationships. And from that elevated mind come elevated feeling states (peace, love, and joy). You feel calm yet alive. Grounded yet expansive. Because you're no longer managing the noise, you can finally hear the music.

From this place, you don't force alignment. You become it.

When you're living from this state of connected consciousness, life stops happening to you. You stop reacting to old patterns and start responding with clarity. You begin to see your thoughts, beliefs, and emotions as impermanent, and with that comes a deeper sense of responsibility for your happiness, your impact, and your peace.

As your awareness rises, so does your energy. The more you conserve your energy, the more vitality you actually have. You're no longer exhausted from bracing against life. You're responding from a rested nervous system and a regulated emotional field. Life still brings challenges, but now, you meet them with grace. You don't fight the waves. You surf them.

Here's the simplest way to describe the difference: at lower levels of consciousness, your energy is dense, like the heavy objects on the ground floor. You're weighed down, reactive, and often disconnected. You're more likely to feel fatigued, anxious, or needy. But when your awareness expands, your energy lightens. You rise. And when you're deeply connected within, everything you touch begins to resonate with that congruence.

You're no longer performing alignment as an outcome. You're embodying it as a state of being. You don't have to strive for clarity, truth, or direction; they begin to emerge through you because you're no longer obstructing the flow. You are the flow. You begin to access what's always been available: higher frequencies of thought, deeper insight, intuitive guidance, and creative vision (not because they suddenly arrive, but because your inner static is quiet enough for you to tune into them).

You start to feel less bound by the past, less fused to your current circumstances. And because you're not clinging to them, they start to loosen their grip on you. In this state, your perspective changes. Life doesn't need to shift for you to feel different. You shift, and life meets you there.

As you learn to focus less on the 'objects' in your outer reality, such as your job title, your relationships, your bank balance, and more on the spaciousness around and within you, your perception recalibrates. You begin to experience that your inner world is not just reflecting your life (it's shaping it).

This is the turning point. You stop blaming life. You stop outsourcing your peace. You stop waiting for others to change. And instead, you realize: Life is not as it is. Life is as you see it to be.

High-Level Awareness is not about reaching for something outside yourself. It's about remembering what's already within you, and finally being in the right energetic state to let it in.

Trusting In The Unseen

People tend to resist what they cannot see. And in many ways, who can blame them? The human eye can perceive only a sliver of the electromagnetic spectrum, just 0.0035% of all available light frequencies. Most of what exists around us is invisible. We can't see gamma rays, radio waves, or the full vibrational spectrum that shapes our physical reality, and yet they're all present, operating, and affecting us. The fact that we can't see them doesn't make them any less real. It just means we haven't learned how to perceive them yet.

But this limitation doesn't just apply to the physical realm; it extends to the energetic and emotional dimensions of our lives. We've been taught to trust only what's visible, measurable, and logical. If we can't quantify it or explain it with certainty, we often dismiss it. As a result, we cling to what feels solid and concrete, such as data, checklists, and outcomes. We avoid the abstract, the intuitive, the subtle. We've been conditioned to believe that only what we do creates results. But in doing so, we ignore one of the most powerful forces for change available to us: awareness.

This is why so many people resist the concept of higher awareness, not because it's too complex, but because it challenges how we've been trained to think. It feels unfamiliar. Alien, even. It's not the kind of conversation you typically hear at the office, over breakfast, or in corporate performance reviews. It doesn't come with a KPI. It doesn't guarantee instant gratification. And because we've equated intelligence with logic and progress with productivity, we've come to see awareness as something 'woo-woo' or irrelevant, when in fact, it's the quiet key that unlocks everything we seek.

We want certainty. We crave formulas and guarantees. We want a seven-step path with a predictable ROI. We want life to make sense in spreadsheets. But higher awareness doesn't operate in bullet points. It isn't linear. It's not something you achieve by force. It's something you access when you soften your grip and start to see the unseen.

Because this work isn't about doing more, it's about perceiving differently. It's about developing the kind of sight that doesn't rely solely on the eyes. The kind of wisdom that emerges when your mind quiets, your nervous system settles, and your awareness expands beyond the surface of things.

That's when you start to feel the frequency behind the conversation. The energy behind a decision. The truth behind someone's words. That's when life starts to speak to you, not just in events, but in vibrations. In nudges. In patterns. In synchronicities. And when you learn to trust what you feel, even when you can't explain it yet (you begin to move in alignment with something far more powerful than logic).

You begin to awaken to Life Intelligence.

Awakening To Life Intelligence

Life Intelligence is the invisible, intelligent energy behind all of life. It's not a concept to believe in; it's a reality you begin to feel when your awareness expands beyond the noise and shines a light on it. Some call it Universal Intelligence. Others call it God, Life, the Field, or Truth. I call it Life Intelligence: the naked, organizing principle and guiding intelligence pulsing behind every moment, every insight, every breath. It's not separate from you; it's the current you've always been swimming in, whether you knew it or not.

The more you expand into awareness, the more you begin to sense this current. It's not loud or forceful. It doesn't shout. But it speaks in subtle ways: a thought that arrives with clarity, a knowing in your body, a feeling of resonance you can't explain. The more you attune to it, the more you begin to realize it was never absent. You were just distracted.

Most of us spend our lives pushing against this current. We override our instincts, ignore the signs, and try to force outcomes with our minds. But when you begin to remember who you truly are (not a separate self scrambling for control, but a unique expression of a greater whole), something profound shifts. You stop fighting the current and start flowing with it.

This is what I call Life Intelligence. Not a formula to follow, but a frequency to feel. It's the energetic blueprint beneath the surface of things. The deeper organizing intelligence that knows where your life is meant to go, even when your mind hasn't grasped it yet. And when you begin to awaken to it, you stop trying to control every outcome and start trusting the unfolding, trusting that this is a living organizing principle of all of life that already knows your destiny.

Think of a time when something fell apart, perhaps your job, your health, or your relationship. At the time, it felt like chaos. But looking back, you can see it was this life principle re-routing you. At a higher level, it wasn't failure; you were being returned to alignment, even if it didn't feel that way at first. That's what Life Intelligence does. It carries wisdom, it moves, and it organizes so that what's truly meant for you has space to arrive and can come into form.

And the more you trust that intelligence, the more certain and peaceful your life becomes. Because you're no longer carrying the weight of having to work it all out, in fact, all you need to do is get your survival self out of the way so that you make it easier for the intelligence to move you. That's when you can let go of the clinging, fixing, and chasing (because you see that life will redirect you anyway).

When you do, you stop asking, "How do I make this happen?" and start asking, "What's already happening through me?" You're simply tuning in (moment to moment) to the deeper signal beneath the noise and following the guidance.

This is the essence of awakening, not to a better version of yourself, but to the truth that's always been beneath the noise. Life intelligence isn't something you find. It's something you tune into. And as you awaken to it, you don't just feel more connected, you are more connected.

And from that connection, your life begins to flow in ways the old you could never have orchestrated. You shift from taking everything so personally to understanding that no-thing is ever truly personal (and that there is a deeper intelligence beneath us all).

The Naked Architecture of Life

Beneath everything you experience (your thoughts, emotions, relationships, even your physical reality), there's an invisible structure, like an energetic fabric holding it all together. This is the Naked Architecture of Life.

It's not a blueprint you can hold in your hands. It's an energetic scaffolding that shapes how life moves through you. And the more aware you become of this deeper design, the more you rise, automatically, from the personal into the transpersonal, not through force, but through perception. You stop identifying as the builder of life and start becoming the observer of its construction.

This invisible architecture includes unseen energetic currents, which I call the naked energies. These are the subtle yet powerful forces influencing every moment. They're not separate from life; they are life. Just like gravity or magnetism, they operate whether you acknowledge them or not.

Your level of awareness determines how much of this structure you can perceive. It's always there; however, at the lower levels of being, all you see are the visible objects, the circumstances, emotions, people, and roles in your life. But as your awareness expands, the scaffolding behind those objects begins to reveal itself. You see patterns. You sense energy. You feel the truth.

And one of the first recognizable shifts that occurs when you glimpse this architecture… is the transition from personal to impersonal perception.

Shifting From Personal to The Impersonal to The Transpersonal

One of the most profound shifts that happens when you begin to perceive the naked architecture of life is this: you move up the ladder of consciousness from personal identification to impersonal observation to transpersonal integration. You begin to merge with life and co-create with it.

Shifting gears isn't about becoming cold or detached; it's about expanding your lens. You begin to zoom out of the tight frame of your day-to-day identity and see yourself as part of something far bigger. You no longer see life only through the eyes of the small self. You begin to experience reality through a more universal lens, one not bound by the survival self, emotion, or history. This shift happens not because you try to rise, but because once you glimpse the energetic structure holding life together, rising becomes natural.

When you transition from the personal to the impersonal to the transpersonal, it's like expanding your capacity to see. You move from a narrow, me-focused bubble into a broader understanding that we all think differently, to a universal understanding of reality. It's the moment you stop mistaking your immediate experience for the whole truth and begin seeing the deeper intelligence behind it. Suddenly, your nervous system softens as you're no longer in the drama; you're watching the unfolding of life force in others and can witness where they are on their own journey of awakening. You have to go through the journey to see through the illusion. And like you, you can't see it when you're in it, only when you have transcended it.

At the personal level, we interact with life through what we can see, touch, and measure. We trust the tangible. But as your awareness expands, you begin to perceive the energetic patterns beneath the surface (the forces you couldn't see before, but that were shaping your life all along). You move from reacting to surface-level events to recognizing the unseen currents influencing them.

This is the shift from the visible to the invisible. From the concrete to the subtle. From what's loud and logical to what's quiet and energetic. You begin to sense the field, not just the forms within it.

In simple terms, you stop seeing life as happening to you or because of you and start sensing that life is happening through you. You begin to shift from reacting or responding to life to relating with it, as if you're part of a larger system at play. One that has always been operating, whether you were aware of it or not.

It's like shifting from being the headline act to realizing there's a script guiding every word you say. You stop living like a single blood cell fighting its way down the vein (and begin realizing you're part of a much bigger circulatory system. Your problems may still be present, but they no longer consume your entire field of view. You gain perspective, humility, and freedom. You begin to notice not just the system you're in, but the systems within it. You are important, and not important, all at once. You gain distance, perspective, and mental freedom.

This shift becomes clear in moments of conflict. Take an argument: from a personal lens, it feels sharp, emotional, righteous. You want to defend, attack, or retreat. When you step into the impersonal, you realize it's not you and them. It's just two bundles of beliefs colliding, two thought storms trying to make sense of themselves. And with that, the urgency to be right dissolves. Peace enters. You see what's playing out, but it no longer pulls you out of your center. As you go deeper into this work, you realize that what you thought was real, that is, your judgments, emotions, and identifications, were never the full story. They were just projections from a narrower lens. But awareness helps you zoom out. You begin to see how past trauma, conditioned thinking, and survival strategies have been coloring your perception. What once felt like an immovable fact was actually a temporary filter.

The more impersonal your awareness becomes, the more space opens in your mind. You're no longer hijacked by every thought or belief. You don't lose care or compassion (you simply become less entangled). The world doesn't pull at you the same way. Triggers lose their charge. Your responses slow down and become deliberate. Emotion doesn't override your clarity.

You start to perceive that every thought is not your thought. Every emotion is not your identity. You are not the storm, you're the sky that holds it. This is the space where consciousness begins to lead. It's a shift from believing you are the voice in your head to realizing you are the space the voice speaks into.

This is the gift of transpersonal awareness: the ability to see the human condition more clearly, with less judgment and more curiosity. You start to understand that everyone is operating from their current level of awareness. No one is exempt. Everyone is doing their best with the story they believe. You see how much suffering could fall away if people simply knew a higher lens was available to them.

From this vantage point, life becomes less about being right and more about being real. Less about defending the self and more about becoming aware of the system. You stop being consumed by your experience and start understanding how experience is created from within. From here, something else activates: a curiosity about the energetic system that holds it all together. You begin to ask different questions. Not "What's wrong with me?" but "What energy is moving through me?" Not "Why is this happening to me?" but "What unseen force is asking to be seen right now?" You become less tangled in the story and more tuned into the structure beneath it. And that's when you start rising, not just emotionally, but energetically.

That's the moment the illusion of the false self begins to dissolve. You are no longer just the passenger of life; you become one with the creator. No longer tethered to survival scripts or personal narratives, you begin to operate from a deeper field of intelligence. From that place, you begin to create, not reactively, not forcefully, but consciously, creatively, and in harmony with the naked architecture of life.

Come with me. What lies ahead is not only a higher view, but a higher way of being. You're not just stepping back from the story; you're stepping into the very current from which the story flows.

Rising Up to the Transpersonal Level

As we rise beyond the personal and the impersonal, and step out of the familiar mental frameworks we've lived within, we're invited into an entirely new dimension of being, what I call transpersonal awareness.

"Trans" means beyond. So trans-personal simply means beyond the personal self (beyond your identity, beyond your story, beyond the small "I" you've long believed yourself to be). It's not a rejection of the self. It's a remembering of something deeper. At this level, you don't just know you're connected to something greater, you feel it. You no longer see yourself as a single drop in the ocean, but as the ocean in a drop.

If personal awareness is street level, and impersonal awareness is the mental balcony, then, as we have already alluded to, transpersonal awareness is the penthouse.

Ironically, this level, though it may feel like the peak of consciousness, is also the most foundational. It's the energetic bedrock beneath all of life. It's the awareness that was there before your personality took shape, and the one you'll return to when all identities fall away.

The transpersonal level is not just a new way of thinking. It's a different quality of being. You begin to experience life through the timeless, not the temporary. You feel rooted in something that doesn't change, even when everything around you does. You begin to sense the presence of an invisible architecture holding everything together, a framework made not of bricks or beliefs, but of conscious energy.

When exploring the transpersonal level of awareness, we need to understand its nature and rise up to it by examining the fundamental, underlying energies, their innate qualities, and the consequences of aligning with them. Consequences here refer to the powerful, often life-changing outcomes that emerge when you live in harmony with these deeper forces. Like an architect studying the integrity of a structure, we must investigate the energetic scaffolding that holds life together and understand how it shapes our own.

Because here's the truth: when you begin to live from this level, everything changes. Life softens. You experience less resistance and more synchronicity. You stop micromanaging every detail and start co-creating with a deeper intelligence. There's an inner stability that remains intact, even when the outer world trembles. Your emotional reactivity fades, replaced by grounded presence. Relationships deepen, not because you try harder, but because you're truly there. You begin to feel led, guided, even held. The exhausting belief that everything depends on you dissolves. In its place, you gain access to deeper intuition, creative insight, and a sense of connection that doesn't need to be earned. Peace stops being something you chase and becomes the state you live from.

To reach this level, we need to shift from analyzing life to observing its fundamental forces. Like an architect studying the hidden beams beneath a grand design, we start to explore the invisible energies shaping our experience, not in theory, but in practice.

In this next part of the journey, we'll explore three core energies, the naked forces that structure reality and your experience. Each is part of the transpersonal landscape. They are not abstract concepts to understand; they are living energies to attune to.

As you come to know them, you'll start to feel something extraordinary: that your experience of life is not being randomly assembled by circumstances, but intelligently shaped by your relationship with these unseen forces.

This is the naked architecture of life (a universal structure underlying beliefs, culture, or conditioning). These core energies are constant and unchanging. They are not shaped by your thoughts; your thoughts arise from them. They are not bound to your story; your story unfolds through them. They are the deep scaffolding of existence, and whether or not you're aware of them, they are shaping everything.

To live at the transpersonal level is to understand that truth doesn't change based on your perspective. What changes is how clearly you perceive it. Let's explore these naked energies (the quiet, foundational expressions that are always at play, even when we can't see them).

Understanding Naked Energetic Forces

So what exactly do I mean by naked energy?

A naked energy is a core, invisible force of life. It's not cloaked in performance, opinion, or belief; it simply is. These are the raw, foundational currents that shape how your reality gets created. You can't always see them, but you can feel their effects (just like gravity).

In physics, gravity is one of the most basic, undeniable forces shaping the world around us. You don't have to believe in it for it to work. It's happening, whether you're conscious of it or not. In the same way, naked energies like creative force, awareness, and life intelligence are always in motion. They are the energetic scaffolding of your human experience (silent, self-evident, and constant).

These are not mystical ideas. They are fundamental truths. You could call them spiritual laws, but they're more precise than that (they are energetic realities that govern your perception, your behavior, and your inner world). Whether you call it spiritual, scientific, or simply natural, these naked energies are always operating beneath the surface.

And here's what makes them naked: they are invisible to the eye, but undeniable in consequence. They're stripped of opinion, belief, or mental interpretation. You don't invent them. You realize them. Just like gravity didn't begin the moment someone named it, these forces don't need your understanding or agreement to operate; they simply are. And the moment you begin to perceive them, everything changes.

But here's the thing: even if you don't see these forces, you are still at the mercy of their effects.

Just like you don't float into the sky when you stop believing in gravity, you don't escape the energetic impact of these forces just because they're invisible. Most people go through life unknowingly working against themselves, misinterpreting thoughts, resisting or ignoring intuition, without ever realizing why life feels like a constant struggle.

It's not because the world is broken; it is because many people in it are trying to bypass the laws that are designed to help them rise.

If you jumped out of a window because you didn't "believe" in gravity, we'd call that madness. And yet energetically, most people do exactly that, every day. They dismiss the invisible framework of life and then wonder why things keep falling apart. The truth is: it's far more empowering to understand how these energetic forces work for you, so that you can flow with them, not crash against them.

This is where realizing them becomes your superpower. When you learn to sense the unseen and align with it, life begins to open. Not because the rules have changed (but because you've finally learned how to dance with them).

When you start to perceive these energetic forces, something shifts. You begin to relate to your experience differently. You stop assuming that every thought is the truth, or that every emotion needs to be acted on. You stop clinging to the surface-level events and begin feeling into the deeper architecture beneath it all.

This is where you rise into transpersonal awareness, not through effort, but through realization.

Understanding these energies isn't about adding new beliefs. It's about removing distortion. You begin to undress your perception of reality by stripping away the mental noise, leaving only the truth. And what remains is this: life is being shaped by a living field of intelligence. It's not random. It's not chaotic. It's not personal. It's patterned, precise, and always in motion.

Just as understanding gravity helps you navigate the physical world, understanding these naked energies allows you to navigate your inner world more peacefully, more powerfully, and more on purpose.

Explaining the Nature of Three Forces That Shape Your Reality

As explained with the metaphor of gravity, these forces don't require your awareness or approval to function. You don't have to believe in them for them to be real. Just like you won't float to the moon because you disbelieve gravity, these energetic forces are universal laws (unseen but always operating). Their invisibility doesn't make them irrelevant. It makes them foundational.

In earlier sections, we explored the idea of hidden scaffolding, a subtle, energetic architecture behind every human experience. The universal forces that structure your inner and outer reality, whether you're conscious of them or not.

They're naked because they are:

Invisible: they operate beneath your thoughts, emotions, and behaviors.

Unfiltered: they exist beyond belief, opinion, or interpretation.

Undeniable: their effects can be observed in every human life, just like gravity or time.

And here's the truth: You are always at the mercy of these energies. The only question is whether they're working for you or you're working against them. When you're unaware of them, you unknowingly resist life. But when you start to see how they move, and align yourself with their nature, your experience of life begins to shift (naturally, powerfully, and without force).

Together, these forces are the invisible framework, like the energetic architecture behind life. They are:

Life Intelligence: The living pattern of truth, order, and divine wisdom that organizes all of life. It is the invisible architecture that guides everything back into harmony and alignment with its highest expression.

Creative Mental Energy: The spark that arises from Life Intelligence when it is received through the mind as thought, imagination, and vision. It is the current behind every idea, possibility, and inspiration that enters your field of awareness.

Awareness: Although not an energy in the same way as life intelligence and creative mental energy. Awareness is an expression, an aspect of life intelligence. Without it, we would not notice or direct the flow of creative energy. Awareness is the ever-present light of consciousness, beneath and beyond the mind. It is the vast field in which all experience arises and dissolves, and the lamp that illuminates whatever you choose to focus on.

These aren't abstract ideas. They are living, energetic truths. They are the unseen laws that govern your internal reality and shape how you relate to the external world. And when you live in alignment with them, you begin to express a new kind of intelligence (not survival intelligence, but life intelligence).

Each force carries its own nature, expressed as a set of characteristics. And each one awakens specific qualities within you, what I call Jewels. They are the inner qualities, like divine DNA. The inbuilt, unbreakable facets of your highest nature. Like natural built-in qualities, gifts, superpowers, traits, capacities, and frequencies that become activated in your system as a result of alignment with that force.

You don't have to chase these inner jewels or force them into being. When you understand the energy, you become its expression. In a later chapter, I will help you activate these inner qualities, but for now, I'd like to explain the nature of each force so that you first gain an intellectual understanding of each one. Let's explore each of the three naked forces in depth.

The Nature of Life Intelligence

This force refers to the vital energy that sustains all living things, regardless of size, species, status, or form. It is the intelligent rhythm behind life itself, governing everything from the orbit of planets to the unfolding of petals. You could call it the cosmic architect, or the infinite breath behind biology. It is invisible, but it is everywhere.

Life Intelligence is the organizing principle of the universe, the blueprint embedded within all of life. It's the same intelligence that knows how to grow an embryo into a baby, how to mend a cut on your skin, or orchestrate the movement of the planets. It is the unseen wisdom behind balance, rhythm, and repair. It governs your body, your breath, your voice, and your becoming. You don't have to control it; it already knows what to do. But the more you align with it, the more life begins to organize itself through you.

This is the universal intelligence that organizes and orchestrates the entire web of life, an energetic matrix that connects all beings and events across time and space. Like gravity, you don't need to believe in it for it to shape your reality. It functions whether or not you are aware of it. Its nature is not personal. It is primal, foundational, and always at play.

When teaching clients, I often use the term 'web of life' because it's how I experienced it directly during a deep meditative state on a therapeutic medicine journey. In that vision, I found myself suspended in space, gazing down at the Earth. What unfolded before me was a pulsating, intricate lattice of light, an energetic web, alive and intelligent. It stretched across the globe like a spider's web spun from sunlight, connecting all creatures (bees, butterflies, cows, humans) by an unseen, golden thread. Each heartbeat is linked to every other, all tethered to the same life intelligence. As a consequence of seeing this, you no longer see yourself as a separate wave crashing through life. You begin to know yourself as the ocean moving through a temporary shape. Your form might look different to others, but the fabric of your essence is still made of the same intelligence. The same life intelligence.

This intelligence isn't passive. It is the living organizing principle force behind healing, growth, balance, and change. It guides everything from the movement of galaxies to the synchronicities that land in your inbox. It organizes, it moves with precision, yet allows for freedom. And it holds an inherent intelligence that shows up as wisdom far beyond human intellect, one that reveals itself most when you stop trying to control everything.

The more you become aware of this force, the more you begin to express it, not through effort, but through being in alignment with it. But the more you align with it, the more life begins to organize itself through you.

The more you lean into it, the more these qualities begin to show up in your life. You stop seeing yourself as the one who has to push, grind, and make everything happen, and you start realizing that life is organizing itself through you. This is what alignment really means: you become a living transmission of Life Intelligence.

Life Intelligence has inherent qualities. These are the natural attributes of the intelligence itself: order, harmony, abundance, clarity, peace. You don't manufacture them; you activate them by placing your conscious awareness on them. They are embedded within you and become activated through you the moment you return to resonance with it. The more aligned you are, the more those qualities express through your words, choices, creations, and relationships. You don't try to be wise, grounded, generous, or loving. You simply are. Because these are the embedded truths of the wisdom of life intelligence itself, and by aligning with life intelligence, you become a living transmission of it.

Importantly, this energy is not something you have to earn, summon, or construct. It is already here. It has been here all along. And as we will explore in the chapters to come, aligning with it does not require effort. It requires realization and attention.

The Nature of Creative Mental Energy

From the elevated awareness of the penthouse, realizing the nature of creative mental energy means beginning to see the survival patterns of thought, perception, and personal worldviews more clearly. It is as if, until now, you have been looking at life through your survival self. Your beliefs, memories, fears, and biases subtly color everything you see, more fear-based survival. But once you become aware of the nature of this mental energy, you notice the tint. You begin to see through it. You glimpse the veils of Maya, the illusion that distorts reality, as described in ancient spiritual traditions. This awakening allows you to move beyond personal projections and into a clearer relationship with the creative force that shapes your entire experience.

This is the raw, formless power behind thought, the electrical impulses in the brain, the intuitive nudges, the constant stream of ideas coming into your awareness. It is neutral, pure, and universal until shaped by your perception. Creative Mental Energy is not personal; it is the same energy that powers every mind on the planet. What differs is the quality of mind that receives it. When your mind is clouded, this energy becomes distorted. When your mind is clear and aligned, it gives birth to thoughts that are clear, insightful, and inspiring. It is the painter's brush, the poet's spark, the life intelligence whisper waiting to be materialized and vocalized.

Here is the thing: your mind is always creating, that's the nature of it. Whether you are conscious of it or not, this energy is constantly generating thought, like a machine that never turns off. What it creates is entirely dependent on what you are shining a light on with your awareness.

If your awareness is anchored in the survival self or mental over-identification, the system is like a computer running with malware. It still functions, but the output is distorted, noisy, and often unproductive. When you are operating from this lower level of awareness, the thoughts you produce tend to be reactive, fear-based, and repetitive. You are still creating, but unconsciously. And the energy of those thoughts shapes how you feel, what you see, and how your life unfolds.

As you shift your awareness to focus on more of the qualities of life intelligence, the quality of your thoughts naturally shifts. You do not try to think better. You simply start thinking better quality thoughts. You tap into a deeper intelligence, and the mental energy flowing through you becomes clearer and wiser. You become a channel, not just of more positive thoughts, but of higher truth.

This is the essence of creative mental energy. It is always available, always moving, and always shaping your inner and outer experience. The only variable is the level at which you are relating to it. From the ground floor, you are lost in distortion. From the first floor, you are overthinking and analyzing. From the penthouse, the transpersonal level, thought becomes crystalline, elegant, sparse, and precise. You become the creator, not the reactor.

Also, remember this: all thoughts, whether fear or insight, anxiety or inspiration, are neutral until you assign them meaning. By understanding this, you loosen the grip of your unconscious mind. You stop believing every thought. You start to discern between signal and noise. And you begin to create from a more spacious, aligned place.

The more you are attuned to the deeper intelligence of all of life, the more your thoughts reflect its qualities of order, clarity, creativity, and compassion. You become a transmitter of that same intelligence. What you think, say, and create carries the frequency of Life Intelligence.

The Nature of Pure Awareness

At the highest level of reality, there is only one awareness, one ocean of consciousness illuminating every living being. This pure awareness is not something we have; it is what we are. It is not personal, yet we live in it and it lives through each of us intimately. We are not a separate wave. We are the ocean experiencing itself as a wave, temporarily forgetting the vastness of its own being.

Awareness is the field in which all experiences arise. It is the silent witness behind your thoughts, emotions, sensations, and identity. This is the space you return to when living in a consistent state of living meditation, the part of you that can observe without judgment, that remains constant even as life changes. From a universal perspective, awareness is the shared field that connects all living beings. You may experience it as personal, but it is not limited to you. Like the ocean watching through many waves, awareness observes through each of us. The more you awaken to this realization, the more you perceive life not from separation, but from unity.

From the penthouse perspective, awareness is not just what you notice. It is the noticer, non-judging observer. It is the space in which all thought, sensation, memory, and perception arise. It is the silent observer, the witnessing presence that sees without effort and knows without grasping. This is the pure awareness behind your eyes, and behind every pair of eyes. It is Life Intelligence, watching itself, through itself, in all its forms.

Pure awareness is like a lamp; it shines a light on the very object you place your attention on.

You might think you are hiding from others, from your past, or even from yourself. But at this level, you realize you have never been hidden. You have simply been watching yourself from different angles. Awareness sees it all. It is the light that cannot be dimmed, the presence that cannot be escaped. Even your judgments, your suffering, and your longing are all part of awareness watching awareness.

Each of us is a mirror, reflecting back some facet of its infinite expression. When we meet another, we are not just encountering a different person. We are encountering another aperture of the same intelligence, the same field of awareness peering through a different lens.

This is why, from this level, separation dissolves and compassion deepens. We realize that every wave is made of the ocean. Every eye is an eye of the divine. We are not many awarenesses, we are one awareness, refracted through many forms.

And the more you live in alignment with this truth, the less you need to judge, strive, or hide. You no longer try to become something in order to be worthy of being seen. You realize you are always seen. You are always held. You are already home.

Why Knowing This Matters

When you begin to see for yourself the universal, fundamental energetic forces that underlie all human experience, you uncover the hidden architecture shaping your life. These are not abstract concepts. They are invisible forces that are always at play, whether you realize it or not.

Your current perception of reality is clothed in thought. Personal thinking acts like a veil, distorting the pure, interconnected nature of existence and creating the illusion of separation. It convinces you that your individual experiences are the whole truth when they are filtered interpretations. This misunderstanding leads you to believe that the outside world is solely responsible for how you feel, causing you to unconsciously give away your power to people, circumstances, and outcomes.

By exploring the nature of Life Intelligence, Creative Mental Energy, and Awareness, you begin to strip back these layers of belief, bias, and conditioning. What emerges is a clearer, truer experience of life that reveals how things actually work beneath the surface.

These three naked energies, though invisible, are the generative forces behind everything you think, feel, and do. They precede form. They shape thought, emotion, matter, and experience. Just like gravity, they do not require your belief or permission to operate. They simply are. Their effects are evident in every moment, even if their origins remain unseen.

When you realize their presence, something extraordinary happens. You stop mistaking the symptom for the source. You stop reacting to life as if it were random. You begin to perceive the deeper patterns and principles running the show.

You also start to recognize the interconnectedness of all things, not as a spiritual idea but as your felt living truth. You see that your experiences are not isolated or accidental, but shaped by energetic laws that transcend your personal mind.

As you align more deeply with these truths, you naturally return to your truest self. You begin to think more clearly, feel more grounded, and act from a place of authenticity. The more attuned you are to these energetic foundations, the more you express the wisdom, creativity, and intelligence of life itself. Understanding these universal truths allows you to navigate life with greater clarity on where to place your focus and time and with more creative power. Instead of working against the current, you move with it. Instead of chasing fulfillment, you begin to live from it. You see through the illusion of trying to control every aspect of your life and remember the deeper intelligence of life guiding everything.

In essence, by undressing the illusion of what you think is creating your experience, you gain access to the real forces shaping it. And with that awareness, you can move through life not as a survivor or a reactor, but as a sovereign, a co-creator, and a conscious participant in your own becoming.

Wisdom Through the Ages

The universal forces that shape human experience are not new discoveries. They carry the same truths that Saints, Sages, and Gurus in India have been pointing to for thousands of years, truths encoded in ancient texts like the Vedas, dating as far as 1500 BCE. These teachings were designed to help us live in alignment with the deeper forces of life.

Yet much of this wisdom, often expressed in poetic Sanskrit or symbolic verse, can be difficult to fully grasp, especially through the lens of modern, Westernized, and often scientifically favoured thinking. For many, the esoteric nature of these teachings has made them feel unattainable, impracticable, or inaccessible.

That is why this chapter has been written to make these timeless truths experiential and applicable. You do not need to adopt a new religion, master ancient texts, or renounce your life to access them. You simply need to be willing to recognize that there is more to your experience than what seemingly is met by the physical eyes. Today, more and more people are rediscovering this wisdom not through doctrine, but through direct experience. Through insight, through reflection, and through that undeniable feeling when something clicks into place deep within you and you know, without a doubt, it is true.

You may want to revisit this chapter more than once. Each reading will likely reveal something new, because the deeper your awareness, the more you will see. The next chapter will guide you further into this territory. You will begin observing these energies in real time, noticing how they interact, influence, and shape your lived experience.

You will also learn how to align with these invisible forces, not by controlling them, but by attuning to their nature. By understanding how they work, you can begin to move with them rather than against them. This is where life starts to feel less like a struggle and more like a dance.

Remember, this is not about overnight enlightenment. It is about subtle realizations, quiet shifts, and new ways of seeing. The fact that you are still here, reading, means you have already begun this process. Let your curiosity do the work. You do not need to force anything.

Truth does not shout. It reveals itself in stillness. The more you see, the more visible these forces will become.

In the next chapter, we will bring this awareness down from the penthouse and into the present, into the conversations, decisions, and patterns of your daily life. You will begin to recognize the movement of these energies in real time. Not in theory. In truth. And once you do, something powerful happens: you stop seeking transformation and start living it.

Awakening Realizations

What hits when you glimpse the naked architecture of life:

You are not the story you have been living in. You are the energy that precedes it. You have been wrapped in narrative, but the deeper truth is that you are not the character; you are the current.

There is no such thing as a negative or wrong thought. Thought is a neutral, creative force. It only becomes personal when you dress it up in identity and meaning.

Your mind is always creating, but it is only as clear as the level of awareness it is plugged into. Most people are generating thoughts from a glitching system and wondering why they feel broken.

You do not become peaceful by controlling your life. You become peaceful by aligning with Life intelligence. There is a natural rhythm underneath everything. Fighting it is optional, but so is peace.

The more you become aware of Life intelligence, the more of the energy of Life intelligence expresses itself through you. You do not need to try to become wise, loving, or intuitive. It is built into the blueprint. You just need to stop blocking the signal.

You are not the voice in your head. You are the awareness it echoes into. Until you know this, you will mistake the voice of this echo chamber for truth.

Every experience comes from within, no matter how real the outside world looks. You have been blaming the mirror, but the reflection starts behind your eyes.

There is only one awareness, one deeper intelligence, watching itself through billions of eyes. We are not separate. We are waves forgetting we are an ocean. Flames, thinking we are not part of the fire.

You have never been disconnected. You have just been distracted. The wisdom of Life intelligence has always been speaking to you. You just were not tuned to the right frequency.

What looks like chaos is often just misalignment with universal order. It is not that life is cruel. It is that most people are fighting gravity without knowing it exists.

Mirror Moments

Where in my life am I still living inside a story rather than sensing the energy beneath it? (What roles, identities, or meanings have I wrapped myself in that might not be true?)

What thoughts do I currently take personally that could simply be seen as neutral energy? (Which thoughts am I feeding with meaning that may not serve me?)

What is the current quality of the thoughts I am generating, and what does that reveal about the level of awareness I am operating from? (Am I plugged into fear? Control? Or Clarity and Source?)

Embodied Practice — Living from the Penthouse

This week, live as though you are already in the penthouse.

Take three minutes each morning to pause before the day begins. Imagine looking out from the top floor of your inner awareness, above the noise, above the roles, above the chaos.

Ask: "What is really creating my experience today?" "What energy is moving through me now?"

Then, throughout the day, use these three mini invitations to integrate what you have remembered:

Observe without reacting: When a trigger arises, pause. Step back. Do not label it good or bad. Just notice the energy moving. Can you see it before you become it?

De-personalize the moment: In moments of conflict or self-doubt, ask: What if this is not about me? What if it is just a thought storm passing through?

Return to the observer: Before sleep, reflect on one moment where you felt disconnected. Gently ask, Who was watching that moment? Who was still aware, even when I was lost in it?

Now, let's go a little deeper.

Chapter 10:

Getting Turned On

Realizing The Forces That Have Been Guiding You All Along

"The real change begins the moment you realize you were never broken—only disconnected from the energy that made you whole."

– Yung Pueblo

There comes a moment on the awakening path where intellectual understanding is no longer enough. You've read the books. You've heard the terms. Maybe you've even glimpsed the bigger picture. But something deeper is asking to be felt, not just known.

Because, unless you begin to realize, not just understand, the deeper architecture of life (the energetic forces that animate every moment), you'll continue to chase happiness like a moving target, believing it exists somewhere outside you, hoping it will finally bring peace. But peace doesn't come through rearranging the outside. It comes when you wake up to the truth: you were never cut off from it, only blind to the life intelligence that was there all along.

In the last chapter, we explored the three core energetic forces behind all experience: Life Intelligence, Creative Mental Energy, and Awareness Itself. These aren't abstract spiritual ideas. They are the invisible blueprint beneath your reality.

They operate like gravity; silent, consistent, impersonal, and always at work. You don't have to believe in them for them to be true. But once you start to recognize their presence, your relationship with life begins to shift in profound ways.

This chapter marks a turning point. Up until now, you've been gathering knowledge. But knowledge alone doesn't awaken you. Direct experience does.

Realization begins when these truths stop being something you read about and start becoming something you feel moving through your cells. This isn't about memorizing concepts or becoming a better thinker. It's about becoming a more open channel that can tune into the subtle energies that have been guiding you all along. The more you attune to these frequencies, the more life begins to flow, not because the world changes (but because your relationship to the world does).

Realization isn't just a lightbulb moment in the mind. It's a full-body remembering. A cellular recognition. You start to feel life in a different way. More vivid. More alive. More electric. And eventually, you realize that life is not something happening to you; it's something happening through you.

This is where we shift from theory into truth. From ideas into embodiment. From external striving to internal attunement. In this chapter, you'll begin to realize the three core forces shaping your experience. And in doing so, you'll begin to remember a truth so simple and so profound that you are Life Intelligence realizing itself through your physical body, your voice, your mind.

If the word awakening still feels mysterious or out of reach, that's okay. Awakening doesn't require perfection or years of practice. It requires one thing: your presence. Your willingness to drop into the now and feel what's real beneath the noise.

If the word awakening feels unfamiliar or unclear, let me paint a picture of what it actually feels like, because awakening isn't a concept. It's an experience.

I often describe awakening as the moment you first realize the invisible architecture behind all life. It is like waking up to it. Or turning on from the inside. As if someone has just hit the switch that lights up your true nature.

But this is not just an intellectual awakening. No. This is a full-body takeover, the kind that ignites something deep within you. It is that electric, orgasmic pulse running through your system, a high-voltage buzz of energy that makes your skin tingle and your mind expand, as if you have finally plugged into the main artery of life itself, the channel through which everything flows.

And let's be real, it feels a lot like your best orgasm. That "holy fuck" moment when you realize your body has the capacity to feel that good… and you think, Why did no one ever tell me this was possible?

This is where the magic happens. When you activate the pleasure center within, it is like lighting up your own internal fireworks. We are talking about an awakening that makes you feel so good, so alive, that the external world starts to look a little less appealing. Because once you are tapped into the juicy energy coursing through your body, you begin to see that nothing outside of you can compare.

It is like unlocking the vault of your most divine self, and no one else has the key but you.

This inner awakening is often referred to as kundalini rising, when the dormant energy at the base of your spine uncoils like a serpent and begins its journey upward, activating energy centers (chakras) as it moves. When this rising energy reaches the pineal gland, your so-called third eye, it is as if the universe flips the switch to maximum pleasure. You begin to taste the ecstasy of cosmic bliss, where your mind, body, and spirit are all vibrating in perfect harmony.

I like to imagine the pineal gland as your internal pleasure DJ, spinning tracks so good they make you feel like you are floating in space. When activated, it becomes a gateway to higher states of consciousness, states where life feels like a sensual, vibrant, interconnected dance. You start to feel turned on by life itself. Every moment becomes charged with this delicious, electric presence. It is a state of pure flow, like moving through the world with a cosmic beat in your step.

If you have seen The Matrix (and if you have not, add it to your must-watch list), then you know the moment I am pointing to. That scene where Neo takes the red pill and everything he believed to be real begins to crumble. He wakes up from the artificial world that had been controlling him, only to discover that reality is far deeper, stranger, and more powerful than he ever imagined. That is what it is like when you awaken to the deeper truths of existence.

You begin to break free from the illusions that were keeping you stuck. And suddenly, everything looks different, because you are different.

This awakening has been described across cultures and scriptures for centuries. In the Bible, Paul writes: "...the eyes of your heart may be enlightened…," (Ephesians 1:18). That is spiritual code for: "Wake up. There is more to life than what your physical eyes can see."

In the Bhagavad Gita, Lord Krishna gives Arjuna divine sight, saying, "But you cannot see my cosmic form with these physical eyes of yours. Therefore, I grant you divine vision." (Bhagavad Gita 11:8 (Translation)). With that vision, Arjuna sees reality as it truly is, cosmic, infinite, alive. A moment that changes everything.

And of course, we cannot forget the Buddha, who sat beneath the Bodhi tree and experienced his moment of enlightenment, seeing through the illusions of the material world and awakening to the interconnectedness of all things.

These are not just stories. They are maps, pointing to a level of perception that transcends the five senses.

In my own journey, I first began to awaken when I realized there was something, some force, powering, shaping, and illuminating my experience of life beyond the material. I began to see that behind every thought, emotion, and action, deeper energies were at play. That realization allowed me to align with those energies and activate the innate qualities of the inner intelligence that was always there. It deepened my relationships, clarified my purpose, and reminded me that I am the co-creator of my reality.

It was not until much later that I began to consciously play with these pleasure centers. Once I understood how the human experience actually works behind the scenes, and how to turn myself on from within, life shifted. It became a playground.

I used to think life was something that happened to me. But now I know my hands are purely holding the paintbrush, but the strokes are guided by the intelligence within. And that changes everything. The deeper I went, the more I began tapping into something far beyond intellectual understanding. I started activating the body's internal energy centers. And suddenly, life was a full-body light show.

Maybe you have just had your first taste of awakening. Maybe you are a total beginner to this type of language. Or maybe you have been riding this wave for years, getting new upgrades every full moon. Wherever you are, just know: sometimes awakening happens suddenly. Other times, it unfolds slowly, in waves, as we surrender more and more of the survival self's grip.

One thing I know from my own experiences is that awakening does not happen in a straight line. It spirals, revisits old habits, and then expands you. And that is why this chapter is here. Whether this is your initiation into direct experience or a powerful reminder of what you already know, this is an invitation to realize the more you remember, the more you align with life intelligence.

In the rest of this chapter, we will go deeper into the nature of energy itself. We will explore each of the three naked energies individually. You will come to see how they shape not just your thinking, but your biology, your behavior, your relationships, and your entire reality.

What is Energy

To truly understand the energetic forces behind your human experience, we must begin with a foundational truth: everything in the universe, at its core, is energy.

The word energy comes from the Greek energeia, meaning activity or operation. It is the essential, animating force that powers all life, matter, and movement. In both science and spirituality, energy is recognized as the unifying essence that permeates all existence. Everything you see, touch, think, or feel is a manifestation of energy expressed in different forms.

From the smallest subatomic particles to the vastness of galaxies, energy is the thread that connects the entire universe.

You may remember this from physics class: energy is defined as the ability to do work or cause change. It appears as kinetic energy (motion), thermal energy (heat), or potential energy (stored energy). But what does this have to do with you?

You Are an Energy System

Your body is not just flesh and bone. It is a living energy system. Your heart beats with an electrical rhythm. Your brain fires through bioelectrical impulses. Every cell in your body vibrates, carrying coded instructions for life (whether to contract a muscle, digest food, or repair tissue). This subtle energy is the invisible engine driving every biological function.

You've probably felt it. That post-yoga buzz. The grounded stillness after meditation. The lift of energy after a deep breath in nature. That is your internal energy shifting states. Energy is not just something you "have." It is what you are made up of. Every aspect of your being is shaped by how energy flows through you, how it is expressed, and how it is blocked or enhanced.

The Building Blocks of Energy

It is easy to question and even challenge the claim that "everything is energy," especially when you think of solid objects, such as your kitchen table. You might be thinking, "This table feels solid. It is not vibrating. I can knock on it." But at the atomic level, everything, including that table, is mostly empty space and vibrating energy.

All matter is made of atoms, the smallest building blocks of the material world. An atom is composed of protons and neutrons in the nucleus, and electrons that orbit the nucleus. These subatomic particles are held together by powerful, energetic forces.

That sense of solidity you feel when you touch a table is an illusion. It feels solid. But it's not really.

Allow me to geek you out for a brief moment. That sense of solidity you feel when you touch a table is an illusion. What feels firm beneath your hand is, in truth, mostly empty space, that is, atoms held together by invisible forces that your senses translate as form. When you press your palm against it, the negative electrons in your skin are repelled by the negative electrons in the table. That invisible resistance is what you experience as pressure or solidity. You're not really touching a solid object; you're meeting a field of energy that pushes back. Just knowing this blew my mind. But then our nervous system detects that resistance, sends signals to our brain, and our brain translates it into the familiar language of touch. So, on the surface, the table is solid; you can rest your coffee on it. But at the deepest level, it's mostly empty space and electromagnetic energy, a necessary illusion so your body can move through the world and call it real.

And it goes even deeper. Within atoms are smaller particles, quarks bound by gluons, and electrons moving through fields of energy. Even light itself is made of photons, tiny packets of energy. I'm no scientist, so I'll stop here. All I'll add is that what we call "matter" is simply energy taking form, vibrating in patterns dense enough for our senses to perceive as real.

Vibration and Frequency

Vibration is the natural movement or oscillation of particles. Every physical object, from a rock to your own body, is made of atoms in constant motion. Frequency refers to the speed or rhythm of that vibration, measured by how many oscillations occur each second.

In denser objects such as a rock or a table, atoms vibrate within tight, structured bonds, which gives the sensation of solidity. In lighter substances such as air or water, those atoms move more freely, creating a sense of flow and fluidity. Your body vibrates too, not in a mystical way, but in a very real physiological sense. Every heartbeat, every neural impulse, and every breath creates measurable energetic patterns. These patterns shift with your state of being. Calm, joy, tension, and fear each leave their own signature on your nervous system and electromagnetic field, the subtle electrical and magnetic activity generated by your heart and brain.

Energy does not stop at the edge of the physical. Thoughts and emotions are energetic as well, expressed through electrical activity in the brain, hormonal signals in the body, and subtle electromagnetic changes in the heart. When you feel gratitude, your system becomes more coherent and open. When you feel fear or guilt, it tightens and contracts. The difference is not moral; it is vibrational coherence versus dissonance.

You experience this every day. Certain music lifts you instantly. A place or person can either soothe or agitate you. That is resonance: frequencies meeting, syncing, or clashing. You are constantly exchanging subtle energy with the world around you, receiving, transmitting, and shaping reality through the vibration you carry.

Thoughts and Emotions as Vibration

The concept of vibration extends beyond physics. Your inner world, your thoughts, feelings, and beliefs, are energy in motion. Each thought sparks electrical activity in the brain, and each emotion creates measurable changes in the body. Thoughts themselves are neutral, but the meaning you attach to them shapes how your body responds.

You have felt it before: walking into a room thick with tension, or meeting someone whose calm presence immediately settles you. That is energy, nervous systems, and emotional fields interacting and resonating.

The empowering truth is that you can influence your internal state. When you interpret experience through awareness, compassion, or gratitude, your system becomes more coherent and open. When you interpret it through fear, comparison, or threat, your system contracts. It is not about good or bad thoughts; it is about the energetic effect of the meaning you assign them.

And that state is fluid. Through intention, movement, music, breath, environment, and words, you can recalibrate your internal rhythm and reclaim what might be called vibrational sovereignty: the ability to choose the quality of energy you bring to each moment.

The Law of Attraction: Like Attracts Like

This brings us to a concept that is often misunderstood: the Law of Attraction. At its core, it speaks to resonance. Like attracts like. The energy you express through thought, emotion, and behaviour shapes how you experience the world. What you focus on expands in your awareness. What you believe, you tend to act upon and reinforce.

If your dominant inner state is fear, frustration, or a sense of lack, you will naturally notice and recreate more of it. If your state is rooted in appreciation, openness, or joy, your perceptions and actions begin to align with those qualities.

This is not about forced positivity. It is about alignment. Positive thinking alone does not change your life, but a regulated, coherent inner state does influence how you show up and what you notice. The shift happens not because the universe rearranges itself around you, but because you become attuned to what already matches your state.

Energy Is Constantly Transforming

One of the most essential laws of energy is this: energy cannot be created or destroyed. It only transforms. This law, expressed in Einstein's famous equation E = mc2, shows that energy and mass are interchangeable. What looks like solid matter is simply energy in form. That same energy is always moving, shifting, recycling.

Think about it:

The food you eat becomes fuel. Sunlight becomes sugar in plants. Grief can become wisdom. Stillness can become clarity. Thoughts can become actions.

Everything is in motion, including you. So, when you understand that you are energy, and that your energy is malleable, you stop seeing yourself as fixed or broken. You realize that you are in a constant state of becoming, of transforming. You're in motion. Always.

Summary on The Essentials of Energy

Let's recap the key truths from this section.

Everything is energy. Your body, your thoughts, your emotions, and your experiences all express energy in different forms.

Vibration is the rate at which something moves. Frequency is how fast it vibrates.

Your inner state, the emotions, and meanings you carry, influence the quality of your experience. When your energy is coherent and open, you perceive and create from clarity. When it is contracted, you repeat familiar patterns.

The principle, often called the Law of Attraction, reflects the idea that like attracts like. You tend to notice and recreate experiences that match your internal state.

Energy is always transforming. Nothing in you is fixed. You are never stuck; you are always in motion.

How Universal Energetic Forces Work Together To Create Your Reality

Now that we've explored the scientific foundation of energy, let's turn back to the three energetic forces. In the last chapter, we explained the nature of each of these forces, and now we want to go one step deeper to help you to realize how these invisible forces are working together to actively shape your moment-to-moment experience.

These three forces: Life Intelligence, Creative Mental Energy, and Awareness, are not separate. They form an inseparable trinity, a dynamic dance that mirrors your level of consciousness in every moment. Life Intelligence holds the structure, the sacred geometry that ensures order, direction, and evolution. Creative Mental Energy flows into your system as wisdom, thought, and possibility. Awareness shines the light on the very thought that it gives attention to. Let's make this more real. Think of your mind and experience like a television set. The electricity that powers the TV, the invisible force that allows everything to function, is Life Intelligence. Without it, nothing would work. Then, the actual images on the screen (the colors, characters, dialogue, and movement) are creative Mental Energy. It's the content being expressed, shaped, and experienced. And finally, the TV screen itself, the stable, silent background that even allows you to see what's playing, is Awareness Itself. Without the screen, you couldn't witness the show at all.

Now imagine you're watching your favorite episode of Friends. The characters, the plot, the emotions, that's the mental energy of thought in motion. But none of it would be possible without the power running behind the scenes, or the screen making the images visible. You need all three: the power (Life Intelligence), the pictures (Creative Mental Energy), and the screen (Awareness). When these forces work together, experience becomes possible. When you understand their interplay, you start to realize you're not just the viewer, you're the one holding the remote.

In this chapter, I just want you to grasp these three forces and how they interact with each other. In a later chapter, we will go deeper to explore the invisible inner qualities of these forces, how you can experience them, and how they show up.

These energies are not abstract; they are highly practical. When you think of Life Intelligence, the wisdom comes through the Creative Mental Energy. Your ability to notice and shift those thoughts comes through Awareness. And the direction your life naturally wants to move in, toward healing, truth, and alignment, is the whisper of Life Intelligence. Whether or not you're conscious of them, these energies are always in motion and become your expression of how you think, feel, speak, and act.

The moment you begin to see them operating within your own mind, your body, and your relationships, a great softening happens. You stop fighting what is. You begin collaborating with the flow of life. You start living from alignment with this deep intelligence rather than from effort.

The energetic nature of these three forces is not merely philosophical. They influence your state of mind, your body and breath, your voice, your physical health, your sense of connection to others, and even what you choose to invest your time in. As you begin to realize their existence, not just understand them conceptually, you'll experience greater energy coherence, clarity, and calm. You'll start to live from the inside to the outside, responding from a depth within, rather than reacting from the shallow end of survival.

Let's pause here for a moment. I'm aware that what you've received on these energies is knowledge. But knowledge is not the same as knowing. Knowing comes through direct experience. Now it's time to turn your attention inward and experience these energies for yourself.

Realizing the Energies Shaping Your Reality

The most powerful way to understand the forces behind your reality is not by reading about them, but by realizing them. When I work with clients, I often guide them through simple experiments to test these truths in their own bodies and lives. It is not theory; it is direct experience. In science, this would be called gathering empirical evidence. With my clients, I call it awakening.

In my live work, this process usually unfolds over at least three days. During immersive retreats, I set up a series of small, practical experiments that allow each person to notice these energies for themselves and share what they discover. It takes that time for the body to slow down, for the mind to soften, and for awareness to open. My role is to guide, reflect, and help them interpret what they are seeing and feeling, almost like a tool guide for consciousness, as they awaken to the qualities and implications of the three energies themselves.

This short guided activation is designed to give you a glimpse of that experience. It will not replace the depth of a live retreat or the steady unfolding of a longer course, but it will offer you a doorway, a moment to begin noticing how these energies are moving through you and directing your experience.

For the audio activation, head across to my website and download the free companion Playbook: https://www.gemdentith.com/playbook

A Fundamental Shift in How You See the World

The paradigm shift that changes everything.

There comes a moment in every awakening journey when something inside you clicks (and everything shifts). You begin to realize that the way you've been experiencing life wasn't the full picture. You were only seeing from the ground floor, through the filters of thought, emotion, conditioning, and personal stories. But when you begin to see the invisible architecture underneath all of that creative energy, consciousness, and a higher organizing intelligence, you ascend to a higher floor, and the view is radically different.

This shift isn't something you force. It happens naturally through realization. You start to see that life isn't a series of random external events. But that life is being shaped from within you. The energy you're emitting, your state of being, your beliefs, and your level of awareness are actively shaping how you interpret, respond to, and even attract what unfolds around you.

For many of my clients, this realization is both humbling and liberating. There's often a moment of disbelief. How did I not see this before? It's as if they've been playing a game without knowing the rules, and now the rules are finally visible. It brings not only a new understanding but a deep, cellular permission to exhale. They no longer feel they have to fight for control, approval, or outcomes. They begin to operate from a different energy altogether.

Here are the core realizations and the natural shifts in consciousness they ignite.

Life Is Created from the Inside Out

The moment you realize that life is happening through you (not to you) is the moment you reclaim your power.

We've been conditioned to scan, monitor, and analyze the outside world as if it were the control panel of our lives: looking for signs, reacting to circumstances, searching for validation. But when you realize that the quality of your life is being shaped from within, a new level of authorship arises. The world no longer feels like a series of threats or puzzles. It becomes a mirror, reflecting your inner state back to you in real time.

From this, a new value emerges: self-awareness, not as a burden or a demand to do better, but as a quiet liberation. You are no longer just the product of what has happened to you; you are a conscious participant in what unfolds next. The space between stimulus and response becomes a living moment of creation. In that space, you remember that you can choose, not out of duty, but from presence. And from that choice, your entire life begins to shift.

Thoughts Are Creative Forces

At some point, you begin to see that thoughts are not just ideas floating around in your mind. They are energetic impulses. Creative forces. And like any force, they have an effect. Thoughts are neutral until you assign meaning to them, but once you do, they start shaping your emotional state, your actions, and your perception of the world around you.

This realization often comes with a deep pause. You begin to notice how much power you've been giving to outdated, fear-based, or simply not true. But now you start choosing differently. You recognize that not every thought deserves your attention. You become a curator of your inner world, focusing on ideas and beliefs that raise your vibe and honor your truth. This alone can shift the trajectory of your life.

Emotions Follow Your Thinking

Emotions are not random. They are direct feedback. They follow the vibrational frequency of your thoughts. When you understand this, you no longer feel at the mercy of your emotions. You start to read them like signals. If you're feeling low, anxious, or overwhelmed, trace it back to the thought or perception fueling that state, and adjust from the inside.

This is a radically different way of living. You stop trying to manipulate your environment to feel okay. Instead, you tend to your inner ecosystem. You regulate your own energy. You shift from reactivity to conscious presence, using your emotional guidance system to return to alignment. Over time, this cultivates not only emotional intelligence but emotional sovereignty.

Your Experience Is Subjective

One of the most powerful shifts is the realization that your experience of life is not objective; it's entirely shaped by your state of consciousness, your beliefs, and your energetic frequency. You begin to understand that everyone is living in their own uniquely constructed reality, based on the same invisible principles of energy, thought, and awareness.

This creates a deep sense of compassion. Instead of assuming others should see the world as you do, you begin to honor the diversity of perception. You approach conversations with curiosity, not judgment. You let go of being "right," and instead, seek to be real. This softens conflict and deepens connection, both within yourself and with others.

The Present Moment Is All There Is

There is no true power outside of the now. The past is memory. The future is projection. Only the present moment offers the raw material of reality (energy, attention, choice). When you understand this, you stop living in delay. You stop waiting for better circumstances to feel peace or joy. You access your power now.

From this space of presence, you become more intentional with your energy. You respond rather than react. You create rather than cope or consume. Life becomes more vivid and more meaningful because you are fully in it, not drifting through thought loops or survival scripts.

Together They Express Your True Nature

Eventually, you come to see that beyond the swirl of thought and emotion, there is something steadier. Something is always watching. Always aware. That something is you. Not the personality, not the performance, but the field of awareness behind it all. This is your true nature.

When you experience yourself as pure consciousness, the identity you once clung to becomes more flexible. You stop defining yourself by past stories or future goals. You start to live from the spaciousness of being, where nothing needs to be added or fixed for you to feel whole. This isn't a concept, it's a felt experience. And it's available the moment you turn inward and rest in the awareness that never leaves.

You Are Supported By a Higher Intelligence

Finally, you begin to trust that there is an organizing intelligence running through everything. It is what breathes your lungs, heals your wounds, and delivers insights seemingly from nowhere. This intelligence is not separate from you. You are part of it. It flows through you and is available to guide you, if you choose to listen.

This realization allows you to soften your grip on control. You begin to trust life again. Not blindly, but deeply. You collaborate with life, rather than wrestle with it. You learn to feel your way forward, honoring the quiet wisdom that lives beneath the noise. This creates a life of flow, rather than friction.

Embracing the Shift

As this chapter draws to a close, you may begin to notice a subtle but profound shift taking place within you. That shift is the awakening (not just to new information, but to a new way of seeing, feeling, and experiencing life). This isn't about learning something new; it's about remembering something ancient, something that has always been guiding you from within.

The moment you begin to realize that the forces shaping your life are not external, random, or punishing, but intelligent, benevolent, and vibrational, you stop grasping for control. You stop outsourcing your peace to the world outside you. And instead, you begin to attune to the flow of life as it moves through you. That's what awakening really is. It's not a destination. It's a recalibration. A return to the rhythm that's been playing underneath the noise all along.

Awakening to the energetic nature of reality isn't just a change in perspective; it's a complete shift in how you move through life. What once felt confusing becomes clearer, and life feels a lot lighter. It's not because the world around you has changed. It's because your relationship to it has.

You begin to soften. Not because you've become passive, but because you no longer need to fight the current. You stop bracing against life and start dancing with it. You begin to live from a place of resonance rather than resistance. Your thoughts become more intentional. Your emotions become teachers. Your presence becomes a superpower.

This is not about becoming someone new. It's about remembering who you've always been before the world told you otherwise. A being of energy, of awareness, of intelligence far beyond what you were taught in school. You're not here to control life (you're here to co-create with it). You're not here to chase safety, you're here to remember you've always been held.

And the beauty of this shift is that you don't have to force it. The more you relax into what's true, the more truth reveals itself to you. The more you let go of needing to figure everything out, the more clarity arises from within. This is the paradox of awakening: it doesn't ask you to climb a mountain; it asks you to remember you are the mountain.

You start to experience what it feels like to be in harmony with the universe (not separate from it). You feel the spaciousness that comes with inner clarity. You realize that happiness isn't something to achieve; it's something you activate when you're aligned.

You are no longer who you were. And yet, you begin to feel more you than you've ever been. In the next chapter, we will dive into this topic of the real you in much more detail, but before then, I'd like to invite you to get out your journal and conclude this chapter with a few mirror moments.

Mirror Moments

What if the thing I've been searching for has been breathing me all along? Where have I mistaken disconnection for absence, when the truth was I was never separate?

When did I last feel the pulse of life moving through me (not from effort, but from alignment)? What was present in that moment? What was I no longer trying to control?

If I'm not my thoughts, not my feelings, not even my story (then who is the one watching it all unfold)? And what would it mean to live from that place instead?

If you've made it this far, you might feel a little exposed, and maybe even a bit disoriented. That's not a bad thing, trust me. In fact, it's a sign that the old stories are loosening their grip. You're beginning to undress from the layers of illusion that once defined you. And yes, it might feel vulnerable, raw, or even confusing. That too is all part of the process as you're breaking open.

In the next chapter, where we're headed next is deeper still. This is where we begin the inner work of reclaiming your true self. The one you were born as before the world told or taught you who you needed to be.

Seeking your true self is the universal human quest, the core, unresolved problem people face. To know who we really are, so that we can live and love from this place, is what everyone is quietly seeking. I hope that this next chapter serves as a stepping stone closer to your quest to realize your true self.

Chapter 11:

Jewelled

The Self Beneath It All

What lies before us and what lies behind us are small matters compared to what lies within us. And when we bring what is within us out into the world, miracles happen.

– Henry David Thoreau

Up until now, we have been looking at the big picture: the universal architecture that shapes life itself and the energetic forces that create your experience moment by moment. We have explored the benefits of understanding this at a general level.

And now you might be thinking, "So what? What does this actually mean for me?"

That was exactly my question, too, when I first began exploring these energies.

Here is where it becomes more personal. Here is what I discovered as I went deeper. If it is true that each universal force has its own nature and characteristics, then it must also be true that it carries its own distinct qualities. And those qualities naturally create their own expressions in the world.

This is where it gets interesting. If each of these forces is part of us, if they are naturally shaping our experience, then it must be true that we carry their inner qualities too. These are not random traits. They are naturally occurring capacities built into the very DNA of these energies. If that is what we are made of, then we are also made of those qualities.

So my next inquiry became: how do I undress, drill down, and excavate within myself to recognize and experience these inner qualities, these "inner gems," like gemstones hidden in a cave? How can I reclaim what has always been mine so I can live from my natural identity? And how can I help others do the same, so they too can benefit from their inherent nature and express it fully in their lives?

This is where we are going next. Because this is true for you, too. If we are all made of these universal forces, if they are the fabric of our human experience on this planet, then the same qualities that live within those forces live within you.

My first inquiry into this began when I was thirty-two, during yoga teacher training. A visiting philosophy lecturer stood in front of our group one morning and asked a deceptively simple question: "Who are you?"

Not who you are in terms of your job, age, relationship status, or even your personality. Who are you really? Fundamentally. Beneath it all.

That's the question most of us spend a lifetime seeking, and if you realize it, a short time actually living as it.

I shot back the first answer that came to mind. "I'm a trainee yoga teacher," I said proudly.

A resounding "No" came back at me like a boomerang.

I tried again, running through job titles and roles I'd worn: consultant, yogini, helper, healer. Still, every answer was met with the same firm response. No.

"Okay, well… if I'm not what I do, and I'm not my sex, not my thoughts, and not my body, then what am I?" I pushed back, irritation rising. The question felt maddeningly illogical at the time.

For a moment, I zoned out in class, imagining a meditation I could write, based on the topic of not being this or that, and looking back now, it was probably the seed of this book, Undressed. In my mind, I was imagining stripping away layer after layer of identity (our image, our roles, our achievements, our status, everything I had been stacking up for the past thirty years), and seeing if I could uncover what remained. But this lecture felt like a game: the teacher knowing the answer but refusing to give it, teasing us the way my older sibling used to when I was little.

"Look more deeply," he said.

I scanned my classmates' faces. They looked as confused as I felt. My analytical mind switched on. I started visualizing blood, veins, and organs (a throwback to my days as an ambulance technician, when the body was just mechanics and matter).

Finally, the teacher relented. "There is a part of you that has always been with you. It has observed every single experience you've ever had. It has never aged. And when it knows itself, it only knows love, because that is what it is made of."

He sounded like he was reciting a riddle from the Bhagavad Gita. I loved that book, an ancient sacred poem. But every verse felt like a puzzle I couldn't quite solve. And yet, something in his words landed differently that day. Something stirred.

That question stayed with me. Who are you? Not as an idea, but as a lived inquiry. And over time, through meditation, stillness, and the willingness to look beneath every label I'd ever worn, I began to glimpse the answer. Not in words, but in feeling. In presence. In the spaciousness that remained when everything else fell away.

This is one of the most powerful chapters of the whole book. This is where you begin to realize your inner qualities. You have learned about the nature of these forces. Now I am going to explain their characteristics and their inherent qualities, which are also your inherent qualities.

And here is the key: because they are built in, you do not have to apply them like a new skill. You do not have to study or earn them. You simply have to become naked enough, undressed enough, so the real you, a collection of all these inbuilt qualities, can shine through the coverings that have been blocking you from seeing what is already true and available within you.

The only thing blocking you is not a lack of worth or capacity. It is the stories you have been telling yourself and the conversations running in your head. Beneath that noise is a still presence that allows all of these qualities to be known and expressed.

In other words, if these universal forces are the very fabric of life itself, and if they carry qualities, then those same qualities must live within you. If you are made of the same stuff, by aligning with them, by seeing and activating them more clearly in yourself, you can live and express those qualities in the world.

Getting Naked and Jewelled

Embarking on the journey of self-revelation isn't about stacking on more tools or adding more layers of self-improvement. It's about peeling them off. Stripping away the masks, the armor, the identities you built just to survive. This undressing is not cosmetic. It's the difference between living in performance and living in presence, between running on survival programs and living as an expression of infinite Life Intelligence.

As Deepak Chopra reminds us, "In the process of letting go, you will lose many things from the past, but you will find yourself."

That's the work here: letting go of the hardened identities you've been wearing so that the original self, the one built of Life Intelligence, can step forward. Getting naked isn't about loss. It's about activation. Reclaiming the inner gems, the fundamental qualities of who you are, and upgrading your identity so it runs on truth.

As you let go, what emerges is the essence of your being, the pure current of energy that carries your uniqueness, quirks, psychology, and form, while also plugging you back into the infinite source that orchestrates everything.

And here's the key: this essence isn't empty. It's encoded. You are born jewelled. These are the original imprints of your divine nature, the jewels of your being. They are your divine DNA, the qualities through which Life Intelligence expresses itself through you.

When you activate your in-built jewels, it's like your whole system gets an upgrade. You stop running on outdated survival programs and start running on the truth of who you really are.

And here's where language matters. These qualities don't need to be applied like techniques. They are implications, expressions that naturally flow out of you once the jewel is active. You don't have to force compassion, clarity, or presence. You simply embody them. You live them. They are the implications of alignment.

That's what we are about to do together now.

Awakening Your Hidden Jewels

I want to show you how that same universal, fundamental architecture lives inside of you. You are not a blank slate. You are built of living forces, each with its own nature and its own set of jewels; the qualities already encoded within you, waiting to shine. And when these qualities are activated, they don't just shift how you feel inside; they ripple outward as real changes in how you live, love, and lead. I know this because I've lived it.

So here's how we'll explore them. Each force carries its own nature (the essence of what it is). From that nature flow certain characteristics (how you would describe them to others). Then we'll look at the qualities, or jewels, which are how those forces live inside of you, the inner gifts already coded into your being. Finally, we'll look at the implications: those qualities naturally express themselves in your life when they are activated.

You don't have to "apply" these jewels like tools. They are not techniques to add on top of who you are. They are implications (natural expressions of alignment). The more you awaken them, the more they express themselves without effort.

Next, we'll look at each of the three forces individually: Awareness, Life Intelligence, and Creative Mental Energy. For each, I'll recap its nature, name its characteristics, name the qualities (jewels) it holds, and show you the outer expressions those jewels bring into your life. And then, we'll move into an activation to bring them forward in your own being.

This is where it gets juicy. Here we go.

Awareness
Nature

Awareness is the Seer. It is the silent witness of your life; unchanging, ageless, untouched by circumstance. It is the spacious field in which every thought, feeling, and experience arises, and it quietly illuminates all of it without clinging or condemning. Awareness is constant, even when you forget it. It is like the sky behind every weather system: clear, vast, and steady, no matter what storms pass through.

Its essential characteristics are:

Unchanging: thoughts, emotions, and circumstances come and go, but awareness stays.

Ageless: beyond time, beyond birth and death, awareness simply is.

Untouched: no trauma, opinion, or failure can wound it.

Unbreakable: your core essence cannot be shattered.

Continuous: like a river that never stops flowing, it's always here.

Neutral: it doesn't judge or cling, it simply observes.

Illuminating: wherever your awareness rests, it brings things into light.

When Awareness begins to recognise itself through you, its qualities reveal themselves like jewels, each one reflecting a different facet of your true nature.

Jewels of Awareness

These are the innate qualities of Awareness that you already carry:

Worth

The recognition of your inherent value, untouched by achievement or failure.Expression: For years, my sense of worth was outsourced. I stacked up certificates like trophies, as if each piece of paper proved my value. It was exhausting. Think of a diamond: does its worth change depending on whether it comes with a certificate? Of course not. A diamond is a diamond, whether or not it's been stamped and graded. But most of us live as if we need that stamp. True worth is the realization that you are already valuable, certificate or not.

Connection

The felt sense that you belong, that you are part of something larger, woven into the fabric of life. Expression: I used to think connection meant being chosen, fitting in, or pleasing others so I wouldn't be left out. But a real connection is different. It's not conditional. It's the deep knowing that you already belong, simply because you exist. When I began to live from this place, my relationships transformed. I stopped trying to earn connection and simply started being present with people.

Presence

The jewel of simply being here, deeply and fully in the moment. Expression: Presence is what slows life down. It's what gives you that sense of peace in the middle of chaos, or that safety when you're sitting alone and not reaching for a distraction. In relationships, it's the ability to look someone in the eye and actually see them. Peace is the fruit of this jewel. It's not something you force; it's what naturally radiates when you're anchored in Presence.

Sovereignty

The jewel of wholeness and emotional independence. It's what rises when you no longer cling or collapse into others for validation. Expression: Sovereignty shows up as freedom from neediness. You stop begging to be chosen because you already know you're whole. You stop clinging in relationships because you no longer believe someone else is the source of your safety or fulfillment. Sovereignty isn't about building walls; it's about knowing you can stand on your own, anchored in your own being, and choose from truth rather than fear.

As you start to recognize the jewels of Awareness worth, something shifts. You begin to see that awareness itself is steady, but what flows through it has its own rhythm and organizing power. That's where Life Intelligence comes in. If Awareness is the witness, Life Intelligence is the architect, arranging all of life into harmony.

Life Intelligence
Nature

Life Intelligence is the organizing principle of life, the blueprint that arranges all things into harmony. It is the same intelligence that knows how to turn an embryo into a baby, how to repair a cut on your skin, or how to orchestrate the movement of galaxies. It's the invisible rhythm behind healing, balance, and repair.

This intelligence is not passive. It is active, self-organizing, and endlessly creative. It knows how to mend, evolve, and adapt. You don't have to control it. You don't have to manage it. The more you align with it, the more life begins to organize itself through you.

Its essential characteristics are:

Limitless: boundless and immeasurable, always expanding.

Self-organizing: continually arranging and harmonizing.

Healing: always tending toward repair and balance.

Purposeful: always moving toward evolution and meaning.

Creative: birthing new possibilities, endlessly adaptive.

Abundant: expressing itself as overflow, generosity, flourishing.

Jewels of Life Intelligence

Intuition

Direct knowing beyond logic. Expression: I used to ignore my gut feelings because they didn't seem "rational." I'd overthink, weigh pros and cons, and make decisions that looked good on paper but left me empty. Intuition changes that. It's not dramatic or loud. It's a quiet compass that whispers the truth before your mind catches up. Trusting it has guided me into work, relationships, and decisions that no spreadsheet could have justified (but they turned out to be exactly right).

Resilience

The strength to bend without breaking. Expression: I thought resilience meant "keep pushing" (another word for endurance). But true resilience is softer. It's the ability to stretch, to bend, to be knocked down and rise again, not because you forced yourself but because something unbreakable within you cannot collapse. This jewel shines most in life's storms, when you discover a strength you didn't know you had.

Vitality

The life force that animates you. Expression: Burnout stole my vitality. I was running on fumes, disconnected from my body. But vitality is not about doing more; it's about feeling alive in your body. It's the spark that makes you want to move, dance, create, and love. When this jewel is active, you don't have to "push" yourself into life (you're pulled into it by joy and energy).

Self-Organizing

Trust in divine order, the ability to see how life arranges itself when you allow it. Expression: For years, I thought I had to force everything (relationships, work, outcomes). If I wasn't hustling, I thought life would fall apart. But the truth is, life has its own rhythm. When this jewel is alive, synchronicities begin to appear. You think of someone, and they call. You miss one opportunity, and a better one lands in your lap. It's not a coincidence. It's Life Intelligence organizing the pieces. The more I trust this, the lighter life feels.

Purpose

The deeper direction that pulls you toward meaning and contribution. Expression: Purpose is the jewel that won't leave you alone. It whispers in the background, reminding you that you are here for more. When I ignored it, I felt restless and unfulfilled, even when I was "successful." But when I leaned in, life stopped feeling like a treadmill and became a mission. Purpose makes everything count.

Abundance

The overflow of life when you live in harmony with Source. Expression: For years, I thought abundance was money. I hustled harder, thinking that if I just earned more, I'd feel secure. But abundance is bigger than that. It's the richness of love, opportunities, beauty, and experiences that flow when you are aligned. When this jewel is shining, money is part of the picture, but never the whole thing. Abundance feels like overflow.

When the organizing principle of Life Intelligence is alive in you, it naturally starts to shape the way your mind receives and expresses reality. This is where Creative Mental Energy comes into play. If Awareness is the field and Life Intelligence is the blueprint, then Creative Mental Energy is the spark that brings it all into form through thought, vision, and imagination.

Creative Mental Energy
Nature

Creative Mental Energy is the spark of imagination and vision. It's Life Intelligence moving through the mind, coloring and shaping your experience like sunlight refracted through a prism. It's the raw, formless current behind every thought, idea, or intuitive nudge that drops into your awareness.

Its essential characteristics are:

Neutral: not personal; it flows through every mind.

Constant: like electricity, it's always on.

Shapeshifting: it takes on the form of whatever your awareness is focused on.

Illuminating: when clear, it produces thoughts that bring truth and insight.

Creative: it turns the unseen into form, giving birth to new ideas, art, and solutions.

Jewels of Creative Mental Energy

Clarity

The capacity to see truth clearly, cutting through distortion. Expression: Without clarity, I used to spiral into overthinking. I'd make endless pros-and-cons lists, ask ten people for advice, and still feel stuck. When clarity shines, it's like a diamond cutting through fog. Suddenly, the next step is obvious. You don't waste energy debating yourself (you just know).

Creativity

The pulse of expression, the artistry of life moving through you. Expression: For a long time, I thought creativity was only for "artists." I told myself I wasn't creative because I didn't paint or sing. But creativity is everywhere. It's in how you solve a problem at work, how you comfort your child, how you style your clothes, and how you write a sentence. When this jewel shines, life feels playful. Ideas bubble up. Inspiration finds you instead of you chasing it.

In my own experience of realizing these qualities as part of my fundamental nature, two key things stand out. First, I've been given what I can only describe as new eyes. New eyes to see, new eyes to understand. It has been a complete paradigm shift. Life just looks different now.

With these new eyes, the ordinary has become extraordinary. Everyday moments that once felt plain are now alive with depth and meaning. I see the invisible architecture behind every person's experience in every moment. And with that, I can't help but notice how much untapped potential lives inside people. So many of these qualities sit dormant or under-expressed in the majority of people I meet.

That pains me, but it also excites me. Because I know that, given the right support and the right amount of time and presence, anyone can uncover these jewels within themselves. And when they do, what emerges is breathtaking. That untapped aliveness waiting in every one of you is just waiting to shine into existence. That, for me, is real transformation.

Real transformation is not about adding something new. It's about bringing the unseen into the now. It's about excavating those hidden gems (those inner jewels, those qualities that have always been there) and making them known. My job, my purpose, is to shine my light on those gems within you so that you can activate them and see them for yourself.

I see them in me. They are activated in me, which is why I can see them in you. My life's work is to help you see these things as true within yourself. And once you see them in you, you will also begin to see them in others. That's when the ripple effect begins. You'll help others see what's true in them, because you've recognized what's true in you. That is the beauty of transformation at scale.

And forgive me for slipping into my change management language for a second, but this really is transformation in its truest form. It's a universal transformation, a shift into a new paradigm where we learn to see and unleash the untapped potential in everyone around us.

As you integrate these implications into your daily life, something subtle but profound happens. You begin to radiate the qualities of these forces in ways that are effortless. The more you embody them, the more you realize they were never something to strive for. They were always yours, waiting to be activated.

The purpose of this chapter has been to offer you a glimpse into the extraordinary nature of your true essence and how these qualities express themselves through you as natural expressions of the infinite universal forces.

Activating Your Inner Jewels

Now, I want to take you on a journey. A guided meditation. An activation. Something that allows you to actually experience these inner qualities coming alive in you. Once each one is activated, what you'll find is that they express themselves in a way that is uniquely yours. I can share with you how these qualities show up for me, but it's your job, your journey, to discover how they want to express through you.

So first, we'll enter an activation to awaken each jewel within you. Then, in the second activation, you'll explore the unique ways your inner gems want to be expressed.

To listen to the full guided activation, go to: https://www.gemdentith.com/playbook

Reclaiming your inherent qualities is another step on the journey. As you honor them, the bond to your true essence grows stronger. You begin to live not from borrowed roles or borrowed rules, but from the pulse of your original design. This is where authenticity is no longer something you chase, but something you embody.

And as these qualities come online, something remarkable happens: they ripple outward. They begin to color your relationships, your work, your presence in the world. What was once hidden now becomes a force for connection, healing, and transformation (not only for you, but for everyone you touch).

The question now becomes: how do these universal characteristics and qualities choose to express themselves uniquely through you?

That is where we go next.

Universal Qualities, Unique Manifestations

Now that you've touched the essence of your true self, it's time to explore how these qualities actually move through you. Awareness itself is universal, yet the way it is expressed is entirely personal. Your body, mind, and personality are not obstacles to your full expression (they are the very channels through which life gets to experience life as you).

This is the meeting place of the universal and the personal: where Source finds a voice, a shape, a presence that can only ever be yours. No one else on this planet can replicate it. That is the jewel of you.

Activation: Your Unique Expression

Each quality has a universal essence, but its expression through you is utterly unique. What you might notice is that you feel drawn to one jewel more than the others (almost like it's calling you into deeper alignment so it can shine more fully in your life). Or you may find yourself working with a handful of jewels at once, weaving them together into your own creative expression. There is no right or wrong way.

Here's what I do in my own practice: every so often, I revisit the natures and characteristics of the forces and conduct a personal "audit." I check in on the quality of my life (relationships, work, health, creativity) and ask myself which jewel wants more of my awareness right now. Then I consciously align with that quality and let it move through me in daily life.

My suggestion: choose one to three jewels. Sit with them. Ask: How do you want to come alive through me right now? Then notice how life responds.

We go deeper into this when I work with my clients, but for now, let's begin with a guided activation designed to help you sense how these jewels want to express themselves through you.

For this activation and exploration, go to: https://www.gemdentith.com/playbook

Awakening Realizations

In this chapter, you have journeyed beneath the surface layers of identity to the essence of universal energies, the ground of your being. You have seen that these energies themselves are universal, and they carry timeless characteristics.

Yet their expression is uniquely yours. For one person, a quality may express itself in one way, but for another, another facet may be expressed. Therefore, each quality is a jewel, already alive within you, waiting to be remembered and expressed in your own way. These qualities are not something you need to chase or acquire. They are your birthright. They have been with you all along.

This is the transformational truth. As you align with your true self, you awaken to its universal nature.

Embodied Practice

Choose one of the qualities that felt most alive during the meditation. It may have been love, peace, clarity, or resilience. For the next twenty-four hours, allow that quality to guide your thoughts, decisions, and interactions. Let it move through you as if it were the organizing principle of your life.

Notice how it changes the way you see yourself. Notice how it changes the way others respond to you. This is how you begin to live undressed, not only in stillness or meditation, but in the everyday moments where your true self is called to shine.

Chapter 12:

The Threshold

Your New Life Will Cost You Your Old One

"Letting go of the false self is like shedding layers of an old skin. In the transition, we emerge as the true self, a radiant soul awakened to its divine essence."

– Ramana Maharshi

Now it is time to face the raw truth of transformation. Awakening is not only about recognizing your higher self, it is also about realizing that becoming her will cost you the version you have been living as.

What I share with my clients, from lived experience, is this: there are two of you inhabiting this body. The false self and the true self. The lower self and the higher self. The survival self and the aligned self. The old self, and the new one that is already waiting for you.

This is the threshold. This is the pause. You stand between two worlds, no longer who you once were and not yet fully who you are becoming.

In this space, you may question everything. Do you want the new version enough to let the old one die? Or will you retreat into the safety of what is familiar, even if it means continuing to carry the ache of disconnection and suffering?

The pause is not a weakness. It is an initiation. It is the sacred moment every person must face before they can cross into a life aligned with truth.

In this chapter, we will explore that sacred pause: the in-between space where you are no longer who you once were and not yet who you are becoming. This threshold moment asks you to face the cost of awakening and decide whether you will let the old self fall away or retreat into the comfort of what is familiar.

We will uncover why letting go feels terrifying, how hidden payoffs keep us stuck, and why grief, fear, and hesitation are not signs of weakness but doorways into initiation. You will learn how to recognize the false self and the true self, dismantle outdated identities, and bag up any of the stubborn old clothes of habits, personas, and conditioning that no longer serve the higher you.

Through story, reflection, and practice, you will see that leveling up is not glitter and bliss but a gritty and beautiful process of dissolving the survival self so the aligned self can finally lead. And you will discover that once you awaken, there is no turning back. Dark moments, grief, and even fear become the openings that lead you home to your most authentic life.

The Threshold Choice

When you realize there is both a higher, authentic self and a lower, false self, you also realize you have a choice. Which self will you live from?

Let's recap the decision you need to make.

At the physical and mental levels of awareness, life feels heavy. You either live as a victim of circumstance or you fight to control and manipulate it. This is where most of life's suffering happens.

But when you shift perspective and begin to see how life actually works, your level of awareness rises. Your view expands. As your consciousness shifts, you begin to see more than you ever did before.

From this new vantage point, you can look back at your old self. You see how she lived at the ground level of life, always protecting, coping, fighting, controlling, surviving. It is like looking at last year's fashion. You can no longer identify with that style, let alone wear those clothes again.

Later came the mental level. A new wardrobe. A new look. You discovered positive thinking and mindset tools, and for a while, it felt like you had cracked the happiness code. If you could not control others, at least you could control your thoughts. You worked tirelessly at managing your mind. But eventually, even this felt exhausting. It was still you against the world, just dressed in different clothes.

Choosing to show up as your higher self is what allows these old versions to shed naturally. You no longer have to force it. The clothes fall away on their own. And what remains is who you have always been, the real you, the aligned self, uncovered from beneath the layers that life and expectation placed upon you.

And yet, if living from this self is so liberating, so expansive, so full of creativity, clarity, and peace, why is it not the default choice for everyone? Why do so many of us hesitate? Why do we retreat, even when the higher self is calling?

The answer is simple and complex at the same time. There are forces still running in the background (subconscious stories, inherited beliefs, protective patterns) that keep us bound to the old identity. It is like hidden malware in your inner operating system, a code you never chose, but which quietly drives your behavior until you see it.

This is where we return to the undressing process. To fully step into your higher self, you must bring those hidden codes into the light, strip away what no longer belongs, and face the fears and hidden payoffs that keep you clinging to the old self.

The Hidden Payoff

If choosing your higher self is so obvious, why do so many of us hesitate? Why do we hold on to identities and behaviors that only bring suffering, when freedom and expansion are right in front of us?

The answer lies in what I call the hidden payoff. Even when we say we want change, there is often an unconscious benefit to staying the same. We may not even realize it, but some part of us clings to the struggle because it feels safer than what lies beyond it.

For me, this showed up for years around speaking. I wanted nothing more than to share my voice on stage. I longed for what I had to say to reach people and land in their hearts. And yet, whenever an opportunity came, I shrank. I told myself I was too busy. I made excuses. I stayed small.

The hidden payoff was that by avoiding the stage, I could protect my invisibility. I could stay safe in the shadows. But underneath that was a deeper fear. The truth is, I feared the very thing I desired most: being seen, being heard, being known. As much as I wanted it, I also feared rejection, dismissal, or ridicule. So I chose the safety of staying invisible, even as I craved expansion.

This is the strange paradox of transformation. Often, the hidden payoff is freedom from the risk you foresee it bringing. Sometimes it is invisibility. Sometimes it is the ability to avoid responsibility, pressure, or change. Whatever form it takes, it keeps us dressed in clothes that no longer fit.

Let me turn this back to you. What is the payoff you might be getting from staying exactly as you are? Does holding on to the old self give you safety, predictability, or familiarity? Does it give you the comfort of knowing what to expect, even if that comfort feels like low-grade suffering?

What about your relationships? Is there a payoff in staying in the same partnership, even if it does not truly serve you? Is there a payoff in staying at the same job, even if your innate nature has outgrown it? Is there a payoff in staying the same body weight, carrying the same unhealthy habits, even when you know they are not aligned with your true self?

Human nature is wired to avoid pain. So if you are not changing, there must be a hidden benefit in staying the same. Maybe the current discomfort is still manageable. Maybe it costs less, for now, than the fear of stepping into the unknown.

Here is where the invisible code comes in. These hidden payoffs are like old programs running in the background. Many of them are the survival habits we first met in the Happiness Whore chapter. They are patterns of seeking approval, protecting yourself, performing for others, or chasing conditional happiness. Until you name them, they continue to operate like malware in your system, quietly keeping you tethered to the false self.

So let me ask you plainly. What is the hidden payoff that keeps you clinging to an identity you no longer want? What fear sits beneath the desire you keep postponing? What story convinces you that it is safer to stay small, even when the intelligence of life is asking for expansion?

Because once you see it, you can undress it. And when you

do, the higher self you have been craving will finally have the space to enter.

I've created a guided process for this called The Final Undressing. You'll find it in your Undressed Playbook, at https://www.gemdentith.com/playbook

Set aside at least twenty minutes to walk through it fully. It will take you deeper than words on a page ever could.

Do not skip this. It is one of the most potent threshold practices I can offer you.

Bagging Up Old Clothes

Once you bring the hidden payoff into the light, you see it for what it really is. And the moment you stop feeding it with your energy, the old identity begins to weaken. This is where the process of bagging up your old clothes begins.

By aligning your thoughts, emotions, and actions with your true, higher, awakened self, there is no space for your old, false self, and certainly no room for all those outdated clothes. When you no longer give energy to the old patterns and stories that kept your false personality alive, they naturally start to break down. You find yourself motivated to bag up those old clothes and drop the suitcases at the charity shop, or toss them into the nearest skip.

The breaking down of the old personality and the dismantling of its protective walls allow your true, original self to shine forth. In the process, habits that once defined you begin to dissolve, making way for a healed, renewed, and authentic you to emerge. The unclothing and shedding of these layers is not forced (it happens as a natural consequence of awakening to your true nature).

When you rise up from and move beyond the false survival

self, this is called self-transcendence and self-transformation. You shift from the old conditioned you to the real you, and a beautiful transformation takes place. The chains that once bound you to habitual patterns and beliefs begin to dissolve, freeing you from their grip. Like taking off clothes that no longer fit or reflect your style, you let go of what you no longer identify with, creating space for what truly belongs.

As you awaken to your true self, you become a witness to your old conditioning. With clarity and detachment, you observe the thoughts, beliefs, and emotions that once defined you. You realize that these are merely layers that can be taken off, just like clothes that no longer serve you. And as each layer falls, your authentic self is revealed.

For me, being liberated from the confines of conditioning felt less like slipping off an old jumper and more like tearing off a heavy straitjacket (the kind used in psychiatric wards to restrain a person). I had been held in by it for years, and suddenly it was gone.

For the first time in my life, I realized the mental freedom that the Gurus were pointing to when they spoke of the true self.

Leveling Up Is Not All Glitter

There is a preconception that leveling up in awareness means living in a permanent state of bliss, floating around like yogis at a festival, covered in sequins and fairy dust. Awakening does make it easier to access peace, creativity, and joy, and you will bounce back from challenges faster than before. But it does not mean you will be in a constant state of happiness.

I am not here to tell you that taking off your old clothes is all glitter, stars, and rainbows. It isn't. But do not let that put you off.

So why bother then, your mind might ask? Because what you

gain far outweighs what you lose. Greater clarity. Untapped creativity and wisdom. Limitless power. Deep connection and love. An unlimited supply of energy. Less wasted time on people and places that drain you. More focus on what matters and what makes the biggest impact in your life. That is why.

Awakening is not a fantasy. It is like plugging into a living well of awareness and power. But you must be prepared. There is no going back. Once you know, you know. Once you see the truth, you cannot unsee it. Here is your first warning. No one told me this before I stepped further down the path, but I will tell you now.

From this point on, you do not really have a choice. You may think you do. You can try to slip back into your old clothes, but they will not fit the same. The seams have already split. You can force yourself into them for a while, but you will feel uncomfortable, restricted, and false. At some point, you have to admit the truth. Those clothes belong to a person you are not anymore.

Spiritually, it is no different. Once you awaken, you cannot return to the smallness you once lived in. The new reality is this: you can only move forward.

Even if you pretend you do not know the truth, even if you try to slip back into the illusion, the fit will never be the same. You have outgrown it. It is like trying to squeeze into your size six jeans from your twenties (you can wriggle your much larger, beautiful butt in as much as you like, but the seams are already split). At some point, you need to stop lying to yourself and upgrade to a new pair.

Once you have expanded your awareness and awakened to the truth of your being, there is no going back. The veil has lifted. You now see the world and yourself with new eyes. This expanded awareness brings profound implications for your life. You cannot settle for the old; you cannot retreat into the limited perspective you once held.

With this clarity, you see through illusions and masks that once clouded your perception. You see through the superficiality of societal expectations and the falsehoods you used to swallow whole. You begin to discern truth from illusion, the authentic from the fake, and you live in alignment with your deepest essence.

And here is the real initiation. Expanded awareness is not just liberation. It is a responsibility. Once you have seen, you cannot unsee. You are called to live in alignment with this truth and embody the wisdom that has been revealed to you. That requires conscious choice and deliberate action. It is empowering, but it will also test you.

Some will try to turn their back on what they know, because the familiar feels easier. But remember this: if you go back, you go back into a state of suffering with the rest. Why would you return to a life of suffering once you know the way out? Unless you secretly enjoy suffering (which, let's be honest, nobody does).

When you know better, you have a responsibility to live better. And often, that means leading from the front, even if you walk alone for a while until others catch up.

Grieving Your Old Life

As you let go of the layers that no longer serve you, you may experience a sense of loss, grief, and discomfort. It is natural to mourn the parts of yourself that you are leaving behind, the people who no longer match your new energy, and the places you have outgrown.

In this phase, it is important to embrace the process of grief and allow yourself to feel the emotions that arise. It may be necessary to confront and release shame, resentment, guilt, or regrets that have been resisting, that still reside within you. By acknowledging and accepting these emotions, you create space for them to be fully felt and processed. This involves experiencing the emotions without resistance, allowing them to flow through your body and mind until they dissipate. In doing so, you clear emotional blockages, making room for healing and growth.

Forgiveness plays a crucial role in this process. It is not only about forgiving others but also forgiving yourself for the roles you played in perpetuating the conditioning and habits that you are now releasing. Forgiveness does not mean agreeing that someone's actions were acceptable. Their behavior may never be acceptable. Instead, forgiveness recognizes their ignorance (that they were operating at a lower level of awareness, acting from survival, and doing the best they could with what they knew).

Forgiveness for how others have acted is for you more than for them. When you forgive, the memories and hurts that once held power over you begin to dissolve. You free yourself from the weight of the past and reclaim your energy to live fully in the present. You do not have to speak to the other person, nor do you need their acknowledgement. Forgiveness can be a quiet, private act of release.

Here is a simple forgiveness poem to use if you wish to practice this in your own time. Find a quiet place, bring to mind someone whose actions still weigh on you, and repeat these words three times:

I forgive you, I forgive me. I release stored memories and stories of you. I call back my energy. I wish you well. May we both be set free.

Forgiveness is a powerful act of self-compassion and liberation. When you let go of the past, you free yourself to move forward with grace.

This is the work of the sacred pause. It is not about rushing ahead, bypassing, or denying what still hurts. It is about honoring what you are leaving behind, grieving what has been, and forgiving yourself and others so that the path ahead is clear. Every garment you lay down, every story you release, every old self you grieve creates space for the aligned self to rise.

As you step forward, lighter and freer, you carry only what is true and meant for you.

Chapter 13:

Being Naked

Finding Peace And Power In Simply Being

"In the space between the death of the old identity and the emergence of the new self, lies the fertile ground of transformation, where the seeds of our true potential silently take root and prepare to bloom."

— Mooji

In this chapter, you have quietly chosen to align with the true, original version of you. I invite you to explore how, as you undress from your old life and stand in the raw nakedness of your true radiant being, before your new life has materialized, you might feel a little bit exposed and a bit too naked.

Previously, in my position as a change management consultant in the corporate world, this state is known as the transitional state. It's the messy middle.

The new, original version of you has not yet manifested itself into reality.

Embracing nakedness symbolizes the vulnerability and openness to be your true self, naked and free from the need for external approval, acceptance, or validation. This phase is the period where you stop doing and are "simply being."

Another way to describe this state of simply being is as "Simply Source." When we are stripped of pretenses and the masks we wear, and we fully embrace our divine nakedness, a profound sense of liberation emerges. We liberate ourselves from the burdens of conformity and self-imposed limitations. Our focus shifts from the activities of seeking external validation to submitting to the present moment, where we feel alive, peaceful, and fully accepting of all that is happening.

Feeling liberated in our nakedness means surrendering to how the creative energy of universal life intelligence wishes to use our body vessel to manifest itself through us as a combination of codes, qualities, quirks, and passions. It is about submitting ourselves to this divine energy so it can be expressed authentically and fearlessly. Universal intelligence and divine conscious awareness have no need to people-please and are without the fear of judgment, rejection, or abandonment. In a state of pure liberation, we express fully and experience a deep sense of freedom and joy as we connect with the true essence of our being. By submitting to our nakedness, we open a space of full acceptance and non-judgment for ourselves and others. From this place, we encourage others to unclothe from their own masks and surrender to the flow of life, so there is no fear in stepping out or stepping away from things that are no longer in alignment with the deeper intelligence that wants to be known through you.

Throughout this chapter, we explore practical ways to surrender to universal Life Intelligence and its divine codes and qualities so we can embrace our nakedness and cultivate a sense of liberation without needing to act just yet. Through self-reflection, self-acceptance, and self-expression, we discover the beauty and strength that come from standing fully present, fully healed, and fully liberated in our nakedness.

The stage of simply being in our nakedness can last for a

day, a week, a month, a year, or even a few years. In my experience, it lasted a few years. Let's explore what this means in a bit more detail now.

Entering a Period of Nakedness and Simply Being

When you first begin to undress the layers of your old personality, you enter a period of uncertainty and unfamiliarity. In this state, you may no longer know quite how to be yourself, unsure of what qualities are to manifest through you. This is because it's not you who makes the choice; it's the universe that decides. Just as a bee cannot choose its role, being inherently programmed by its DNA, you, too, have a function to fulfill (a purpose), but it's not yours to determine. The more you surrender and submit to divine energies, allowing them to guide you, the closer you will come to activating your original blueprint, your true purpose. Until then, you remain in a period of stillness, true nakedness, united with the divine essence of the present moment.

Nakedness represents the transition from the old to the new. You realize that your previous way of navigating the world, built on illusions and false identities, can no longer continue. However, your new self is still in the process of forming, like a seed waiting to grow and bear fruit. This in-between phase is a time when you may not know exactly what to do or how to be. You let go of old activities and behaviors that no longer resonate with your true self, stripping away external layers and returning to the bare essence of your natural self.

During this time, you may find that your preferences and desires regarding activities and appearance begin to shift. The activities that once brought you joy or fulfillment may no longer hold the same appeal. Your sense of style and fashion may change, and you might no longer feel the need to dress or present yourself as you did before. For example, you may no longer feel the desire to wear makeup (what my grandad Mike would call "warpaint") or spend hours on elaborate hairstyling or other practices that were part of creating your old identity. Instead, you may feel a natural inclination to strip away these external layers and embrace your body in its bare, natural state.

This shift in preferences reflects the inner transformation taking place. As you align with your true self, the external trappings of your old identity lose their significance. Your focus shifts from outward appearances to inner authenticity and self-acceptance. Letting go of societal expectations and embracing your body in its purest form is a powerful act of liberation.

By stripping away these external layers, you create space for your true essence to shine through. You allow your authentic self to be seen and to fully experience life, free from the constraints of old identities and external validations. This stage is both empowering and transformative, honoring your divine nature.

As you continue to embrace your nakedness, shedding the layers of your old self, you begin to experience the profound state of standing fully present and abundant, where the essence of your true self emerges with clarity and peace.

Standing Fully Present and Abundant

When you realize the nature of your true self for the first time and the old, false self falls away, there's a period where it feels as if you are standing naked. You are totally free from all old conditioning yet feel full of the inherent qualities of your true self, fully present in the now, not wanting or needing anything, experiencing a sense of complete abundance where all your needs have been met.

This feeling of abundance can only happen when you come

into contact with the present moment. When your mind is still and you feel a sense of inner calm throughout your entire body, you know you are fully present in your awareness. It is in this present moment that you experience a space opening up in you and all around you, as if you have unlocked a doorway or an opening to a dimension that is infinite and boundless. A depth that cannot be described with words but only known by the deepest essence of your being.

Imagine a small two-inch-by-two-inch trapdoor on the pavement that you could easily miss and walk straight over, but once you realize it's there and open the door, it leads to a space millions of miles wide and trillions of miles deep. It is here in this vast space that all the qualities, gems, and potential we discussed in Chapter 11 are just waiting to be owned. This depth is often referred to as a gateway into the Kingdom of Heaven, because when you are in this expanding space of the present moment, there's a heavenly quality to it. The world around you may not have changed, but through discovering your true nature and its inherent qualities, the light of consciousness shines forth upon the world and illuminates its inherent qualities back at you (giving the world a heavenly glow).

Let me share a short story of when I first had the profound feeling of presence and abundance. It was not long after my big burnout, during which I was studying a book called A Course In Miracles (ACIM), while on maternity leave with my second daughter. Each morning, I would perform my lesson tasks and then take my baby for a walk around the town of Hemel Hempstead, where we were living at the time. We would normally walk about ten thousand steps on the way to the gym while listening to the audiobook that accompanied the ACIM course.

If you're not familiar with Hemel, it is a very industrial, built-up town with concrete streets, containing many twenty-plus-floor blocks of flats. Up until this point, my then partner and

I had been desperate to leave this town, as it didn't have a very good reputation and could be very ugly to the human eye. But something happened to me on my journey of self-discovery (as my old self started to fall away, I was left for a period with no identity, no role to play, nothing to achieve, but I felt totally and truly at peace with myself and content with my life). Everything around me had a certain beautiful shine to it (even the ugly town of Hemel).

I remember walking down a very busy road, surrounded by lots of traffic and tall buildings, but not being bothered by it. I remember walking past the mums rushing their kids to school and just looking at them with a loving smile, honoring their inner beauty shining through them. I remember looking up at the sky in awe of the birds flying together in a group, just watching how there is always one bird leading the way while the others follow, and how the leader changes every few wing flaps. I marveled at the beauty of the streets, appreciating the sunlight shining down on the towering skyscrapers that provided shelter and joy to the people who called them home. Even the cracked and weathered pavement, though imperfect, seemed to have been perfectly smoothed for my daughter's stroller. Rather than trying to change the external appearances, I cultivated deep acceptance of how things were. In that acceptance, I found contentment, a profound sense of peace, serenity, and a deep appreciation for everything and everyone around me.

At the time, I didn't have the words to describe this experience of presence and abundance, let alone give it a name. I now refer to it as my true nature, my essence, my essential self. I just remember feeling totally full of all the inherent qualities that were available to me in that moment.

As you experience this state of profound presence and abundance, you can deepen this connection through gratitude. Let's do an activation designed to activate appreciation for all experiences.

For the guided activation, visit https://www.gemdentith.com/playbook

Having activated gratitude and appreciation for the present moment, you naturally open yourself to the vulnerability required to fully embrace your true self. Let's explore how this is an essential step in aligning with life energy.

Reframing Vulnerability

Embracing vulnerability is an essential step towards authenticity and submitting to life energy. You may have grown up believing that vulnerability is a weakness, but this is only a conditioning of the old self. In the context of living more authentically as your true, unlimited divine creative expression, vulnerability fades because allowing yourself to be fully seen is the only way you can fully serve.

Society often encourages you to present a polished and perfect image, but true authenticity lies in your willingness to show up (nothing more, nothing less). Just show up as you are, ready to serve whatever the moment needs.

Like being seen and heard, being vulnerable in public can be scary as hell if you are operating from your wounded child's former self, who, like me, needed to be seen as perfect. But perfection is a game that the survival self plays on you (perfection doesn't connect with people, because people automatically know it's not real). And when something is not real, it creates a sense of unease and distrust in what you are saying and sharing. Vulnerability, on the other hand, connects with the hearts of the listener; it touches them more deeply and opens up a gateway of connection. When you embrace vulnerability, you open yourself to deeper connections with others.

By embracing vulnerability and showing both your divine expression and your more human imperfections, you create a space for genuine connection and understanding. It is through your willingness to show your true self, including displaying the fears, insecurities, and imperfections of your more human self, that you invite others to do the same.

Embracing vulnerability is not only a pathway to authenticity but also a fundamental aspect of submitting to life energy. Now, let's explore some practical ways to incorporate this submission into your daily life.

Practical Ways to Submit to Life

Submitting to life and where life wants to take you means allowing universal energies to guide your everyday interactions and decisions. Here are some simple, practical ways to do this:

Daily Surrender Practice: Begin each day with a moment of surrender. Take a few deep breaths and silently affirm, "I release control and trust the guidance of universal energy today." Allow yourself to be open to whatever unfolds, trusting that life's intelligence is leading you where you need to go.

Listening to Inner Guidance: Throughout the day, take time to pause and tune into your inner voice. When faced with decisions, ask yourself, "What is life guiding me to do?" Listen to your intuition and follow the gentle nudges you receive, even if they seem small or insignificant.

Going with the Flow: Practice going with the flow in your daily life. Instead of resisting or forcing outcomes, allow events to unfold naturally. Trust that you are being led by life energy, and embrace the idea that things are happening for your highest good, even if they don't seem to align with your initial plans.

Letting Go of Control: Recognize areas in your life where you tend to control or micromanage outcomes. Make a conscious effort to let go and allow life energy to take the lead. Whether it's in relationships, at work, or with personal goals, practice releasing your grip and trusting in the divine plan.

Acts of Kindness: Submit to life by acting from a place of love and compassion. Engage in small acts of kindness without expecting anything in return. These actions align you with the flow of universal energy, reinforcing your connection to life.

Gratitude as a Form of Submission: Cultivate gratitude as a way to submit to life. By appreciating what you have and the experiences you encounter, you acknowledge the flow of divine energy in your life. Take time each day to express gratitude for both the big and small things, trusting that all is happening as it should.

Trusting the Unknown: When faced with uncertainty, instead of seeking immediate answers, practice sitting with the unknown. Trust that life energy will provide clarity in its own time. Embrace the mystery and be patient with the process, knowing that divine timing is at work.

Mindful Movement: Engage in mindful movement practices such as yoga, tai chi, or simply taking a walk in nature. As you move, focus on being fully present and allow your body to be guided by the flow of life energy. This helps you align with the universe's natural rhythms.

Connecting with Nature: Spend time in nature to reconnect with life energy. Observe the effortless way in which the natural world operates, and allow it to remind you of the ease and flow that comes with submitting to life. Whether it's a walk in the park, sitting by a river, or simply admiring a tree, let nature guide you back to your true essence.

Saying Yes to Opportunities: When opportunities arise, even if they take you out of your comfort zone, consider them invitations from life energy. Say yes to new experiences that feel aligned with your inner guidance, trusting that they are part of your divine path.

As you integrate these practical ways of submitting to life energy into your daily life, you will find yourself more aligned with your true purpose. This alignment naturally leads to being truly seen and heard, as you express your authentic self without fear or reservation.

Vulnerability is not about striving for perfection or avoiding discomfort. It's about allowing your authentic self to express creatively and letting others see you as you truly are (without fear). Understand that nothing can ultimately harm your true self, which is the observer, untouched and unaffected by external circumstances. It is only the survival self (the false self) that feels attacked or insecure in response to external appearances.

By engaging in this inner work and consciously reframing vulnerability, over time, you will begin to notice that as you step into life energy and allow it to flow through you, your body becomes a vessel for manifesting divine creativity in the physical world. The more you submit to this energy, the more you will feel drawn to serve the divine force within you.

Being Truly Seen and Heard

If you have always hidden your true self underneath a baggy t-shirt or a stiff suit out of fear of rejection, abandonment, or humiliation, you have likely been denying yourself the opportunity to be fully seen and heard. This is your moment to surrender to what wants to reveal itself through you, from the core of your being.

It might be intimidating to be seen and heard if you have learned to keep yourself hidden to make others feel comfortable or to maintain peace. But now, it's not the small, survival-self version of you who's doing the talking (you are being talked by the divine who wants to express itself through you).

Likewise, it's no longer about the small, survival self-traumatized version of you being seen; it's about you embracing the function that the universal life energy has bestowed upon you. This purpose is usually about serving others, so when you come from a place of service, you feel safe to be seen and heard. The more you surrender to the universal intelligence that flows through you and submit to your function in the world, the more you will inspire others with confidence and joy, knowing you are operating from a place of true alignment with the intelligence of life. You were not brought into this world to play small. You are here to light up the world like Oprah Winfrey, inspiring millions with your authenticity.

By submitting to the naked energies and allowing them to flow through you, you will naturally start to share your words of wisdom with others in a way that deeply impacts them to their core.

To be truly seen and heard, it's essential to first cultivate an inner foundation of stillness and surrender. Let's engage in another activation, "Activating Stillness and Submitted to Source." Get the Playbook at: https://www.gemdentith.com/playbook

designed to deepen your connection with this inner stillness.

This activation is intended to help you fully embrace a period of stillness so you can surrender to divine guidance, allowing it to emerge as your true essence and give you instruction on what to do next, without the need to rush into action.

Knowing When to Step Into Doing

Through stillness and surrender, you gain clarity of your true self through alignment with life energy. This clarity naturally leads to an understanding of when the time is right to transition from being to doing. At this juncture, you are ready to immerse yourself in both states. But first, let us recap the journey you have been on so far.

You have realized the illusory nature of your old "Happiness Whore" personality is a construct that has caused you pain and suffering your whole life. With this realization, you've also gained an understanding of reality, the nature of experience, and your true self. Shedding the old layers of your former personality, you've embraced the transitional state of presence, where you simply exist and align with life's intelligence to understand how your authentic self is to be manifested in the physical world. This journey of transformation is profound.

As you spend time in this state of being, a natural desire to take action will begin to arise. This is a clear indication that you are ready to move on to the next phase: operating in the world with your newfound realizations, becoming a unique expression of universal intelligence, and manifesting as your authentic self.

Recognizing when to step into doing is crucial. The desire to move from a state of being to a more deliberate approach with what the universe wants you to create in your lifetime signifies that you are ready to manifest your true self, express your unique qualities, and contribute meaningfully to the world around you.

A Personal Story

During my own journey of transformation and awakening,

I discovered that support for those who have awakened to their true nature is often lacking. In many teachings, reaching this point seems to be the end goal. But after spending a few years in this state of simply being, I found myself feeling somewhat adrift.

One of my mentors told me, "Now that you know the secrets of the universe, the nature of your experience, and your true self, now you live."

"Simply live?" I would ask. "But how do I manage the practicalities (pay the bills, feed the kids)? Surely there's more to do now that I've reached this level of awareness?"

"No," he said. "Go back to your life and live it fully. Embrace it with your newfound realizations. Living at this level of awareness will have profound impacts on those around you. This alone is enough."

I tried living this way for a few years, experiencing an awakened bliss, but I still felt a pull, a knowing that I was meant to do more with the knowledge and internal shifts I had gained.

Uncertain about how to navigate these insights and dissatisfied with my mentor's response, I sat with this feeling for a while. I came to realize that true enlightenment does not require forsaking the material world. It's possible to surround yourself with beautiful things that enhance your experience without being attached to them.

Once you realize you are whole and complete, your relationship with objects naturally shifts. You learn to love the beauty of the creative process. Yes, this might mean you still enjoy expensive art, watches, or designer items, but now you appreciate them for the creativity and craftsmanship behind them (not as symbols of identity or worth). You are in awe of how things come into being and how the divine manifests through creativity in the physical world.

From this understanding, I realized that you don't have to choose between the spiritual and material worlds. You can live in both, fully and balanced. You become more creative, not for personal gratification, but for the upliftment and benefit of all beings.

I also came to understand why some who awaken choose to sell everything and pursue a minimalist lifestyle (like becoming a monk or joining a convent). Others might join an eco-village where awakened individuals gather to simply be. However, I also recognized the potential drawbacks of these choices. It often felt like they were hiding from life, creating a divide between those who know and those who are still in the dark.

We need a different approach. We need to guide others to awaken to their true selves, but not stop there. We must then help them discover their original blueprint (their purpose, their reason for being). The world doesn't need more people sitting around in bliss. It needs awakened individuals who are living their true purpose and contributing positively to the world at large.

So, my friends, this is how Part Three of this book came to be.

Awakening Realizations

Chapter 13, Being Naked, is an invitation to see vulnerability not as weakness, but as the foundation of authentic power. Having stripped away old identities and external expectations in previous chapters, this chapter focuses on the concept of "nakedness", the state in which you stand in your raw, unfiltered self. Real power is not about controlling outcomes or seeking validation, but about surrendering to your true essence.

By submitting to this "naked" state, you tap into an energy that is pure and unencumbered by societal conditioning or past roles. No longer needing to hide behind masks, you can trust the process of simply being (letting the universe work through you). As you stand in this vulnerable space, you allow creativity, flow, and the powerful forces of the universe to move through you effortlessly.

As you reflect on this chapter and your own journey, consider the following.

Mirror Moments

Alignment with Your True Self: How do you currently align with your true self in your daily life? Are there aspects of your life where you feel disconnected from this alignment?

Your Unique Expression: What unique qualities do you feel called to express in the world? How might these qualities contribute to the upliftment of others and the world at large?

Navigating the Material World: How do you relate to the material world now that you have gained deeper insights into your true nature? What role do material objects and experiences play in your life today?

Take some time to journal your responses to these questions. They may provide valuable insights into the next steps on your journey, helping you navigate the transition from being to doing with clarity and purpose.

Embodied Practice

Surrender to Vulnerability: Set aside time to explore vulnerability in your life. Whether it's through a conversation where you share openly or a moment of personal reflection, allow yourself to be seen without needing to control or protect.

Embrace Stillness: Spend time each day in stillness, without the need to accomplish anything. This is where you can tap into your authentic power (by simply being present in your nakedness).

Authentic Expression: Commit to expressing yourself authentically in one area of your life. It could be in your work, relationships, or creative pursuits. Let go of the fear of judgment and allow your true self to shine through.

Chapter 14:

Surrender to Flow

The Art Of Surrendering To The Journey

"True wisdom comes to each of us when we realize how little we understand about life, ourselves, and the world around us."

– Socrates

As we near the end of Part Two of this book, let's reflect on the journey so far and the wisdom encapsulated in Socrates' words. The more we explore ourselves and the world around us, the more we realize how much we don't know. This humbling truth opens us to a deeper wisdom, a wisdom that comes from surrendering to life's unpredictability, embracing the unknown, and allowing ourselves to evolve beyond the need for control or external validation.

To reach this point in the journey, you've come a long way. You've stripped away the false self, awakened to deeper truths, and begun to glimpse the invisible energies shaping your experience. But right now, you may still feel like you're standing in the in-between, no longer living from the old survival self, but not yet fully sure how to build from your true essence.

This is the naked stage. Maybe feeling a bit lost. But wide open and wide awake. It's here that the art of surrender becomes essential. Because if you rush to rebuild too quickly, you risk recreating the same patterns you've just worked so hard to release.

In this chapter, I want to show you how to stay steady in this space of not-knowing. We'll explore what it means to live in flow, to trust the deeper intelligence of life, and to begin orienting toward what I call your "highest timeline" and "original blueprint." Don't worry if these terms feel new. We'll dive into them in greater depth in Part Three, where you'll learn how to activate your purpose, values, and aligned action. For now, think of them as glimpses of the path ahead and a reminder that a truer, more authentic expression of you is waiting to unfold.

Being okay with not having everything figured out just yet is something that you may struggle with initially, or at least swing between, needing to know exact outcomes and then being okay with going with the flow. What we often forget when we are learning to surrender to the flow of life is that life will always contain uncertainty, and no matter how much we plan or prepare, unexpected events will occur. Plans will shift. People will surprise you. Markets will turn. True success is not about controlling the uncontrollable. It is about staying anchored and grounded in yourself, while the world changes around you.

Awakening to your true self does not guarantee a smooth road. It guarantees a true one. The path still includes obstacles, pivots, and choices. What changes is how you meet them. Approach this truth with a beginner's mind and in each moment remember your attention is your contribution and your presence is your power.

This chapter is about surrendering to the current of life, trusting that the unfolding itself is part of your alignment. In this chapter, you will learn how to cultivate the resilience, humility, and presence you'll need as you prepare to step into the work of alignment in the next part of the book.

Why Surrender Matters in This Phase

When you first awaken, there is often an urgency to burn down your current life and rebuild. You have glimpsed a deeper truth, felt the pulse of something more real, and suddenly the old life no longer fits. The temptation is to rush ahead, to create new plans, new structures, new identities, and to prove to yourself and others that you are now different.

But here is the truth most people skip over: if you rush into rebuilding too soon, you will simply reconstruct the same house you just tore down, only with shinier walls. You will take the same patterns, the same wounds, the same survival strategies, and dress them up in new colors. On the outside, it may look different, but underneath it is still driven by the same unconscious need to perform, prove, or belong.

This is why surrender is the medicine of this phase. Surrender is the pause that prevents you from reattaching to the false self. It is the sacred space between who you were and who you are becoming. It is the soil where new seeds can take root without being choked by old weeds.

To surrender is not to give up. It is to soften. It is to stop gripping at the reins and allow life to reveal itself through you. In surrender, you learn to breathe again. You learn to trust what is moving through your body, your heart, your awareness. You begin to experience that you are not separate from life but part of a larger rhythm.

When you surrender, you are no longer forcing timelines to appear, no longer hustling for signs, no longer manipulating outcomes to make yourself feel safe. Instead, you are listening. You are watching. You are attuning to the whispers of life and allowing yourself to be moved by them.

This is why so many mystics and sages have described

surrender as a form of wisdom. Socrates called it humility, the realization of how little we know. Spiritual teachers call it faith, the willingness to trust the unknown. In truth, it is both. Surrender is the portal through which your awakening deepens into embodiment.

Only when you let go of your need to control life can you begin to truly receive it.

Your Highest Timeline, As a Glimpse

At this point in your journey, you may not yet know what your original blueprint looks like. You may not have words for your highest timeline, and that is exactly as it should be. This is not the phase where you need the map. This is the phase where you begin to sense that a higher path exists.

Think of it like standing at dawn. You cannot yet see the full landscape, but you can feel the light rising. You can feel the potential of a day yet to unfold. That feeling is enough. It is not your job right now to force the sun to rise faster. It is simply your job to stay awake long enough to notice when the light changes.

This is why surrender is so essential here. If you try to define your highest timeline too soon, you will likely describe it through the lens of old desires and borrowed beliefs. You will project survival goals onto a life blueprint and call it purpose. But purpose is not born from pressure. It emerges through patience. It reveals itself when you are quiet enough to notice what keeps pulling at your heart and lighting you up from within.

So for now, allow yourself to live in the in-between. You are no longer the old self, and you are not yet fully inhabiting the new. You are suspended in the sacred gap. This gap is not a mistake. It is an initiation. It is the place where you learn to live without clinging, without rushing, without demanding clarity before you are ready to receive it.

Your highest timeline will come into focus later, as we move into the next part of this book. For now, let it remain a glimpse, not a map. Trust that the seeds of it are already alive in you, waiting for the right conditions to sprout.

Common Obstacles in the In-Between

When you are in this in-between space, no longer who you were, but not yet fully anchored in who you are becoming, the journey can feel both liberating and destabilizing. You have glimpsed what's possible, but you don't yet have the full picture. You feel lighter in some ways, but untethered in others. This is where many people falter: the survival self wants certainty, while life asks for surrender.

Here are some of the most common obstacles that tend to arise in this phase of awakening:

1. Falling back into old patterns.

The pull of the familiar can feel irresistible. Old habits, distractions, and coping strategies may resurface. You may find yourself scrolling, overworking, over-pleasing, or chasing validation again. This doesn't mean you've failed (it simply means your nervous system is seeking safety).

2. The urge to change others.

When you wake up, you want everyone else to wake up, too. It can be frustrating to watch loved ones live in the patterns you're beginning to shed. But trying to pull others onto your path usually creates resistance, not connection. Your transformation will speak more loudly than your persuasion ever could.

3. Feeling disconnected from others.

As your awareness shifts, you may notice a divide between yourself and the people around you. Conversations that once excited you may feel shallow. Activities that once felt fun may feel draining. This can bring loneliness, but it's also a sign that your frequency is shifting. In time, new relationships aligned with your truth will emerge.

4. Pressure to define your purpose too soon.

You may feel an anxious push to name your purpose, write your vision, or "figure it all out." But rushing to define purpose from a half-dissolved identity can pull you off course. Trust that clarity will come. Right now, it's enough to notice what feels true, alive, and nourishing.

5. Resistance from those who knew the old you.

Not everyone will celebrate your changes. Some may want you to stay as you were, because your growth challenges their comfort. Others may pull on old versions of you, unconsciously trying to bring you back into a role that no longer fits. This is not a sign to shrink. It's an invitation to hold steady in your new awareness.

6. Avoiding the world.

It can be tempting to withdraw from people or situations that feel misaligned. While solitude is powerful, complete avoidance can keep you from embodying your awakening in the real world. The invitation here is to find balance, honoring your need for space, while still practicing how to hold your truth in the presence of others.

The important thing to remember is this: obstacles in the in-between are not signs you're off path. They are part of the path. Each challenge is an initiation, asking you to stay awake, to choose awareness over autopilot, and to anchor more deeply in the qualities of your true self.

Navigating the Obstacles

Now that we have named the common obstacles of the in-between, let's talk about how to meet them. These challenges are not here to block you; they are here to refine you. Think of them as the resistance that strengthens your muscle of awareness. Every time you meet an obstacle consciously, you weave yourself more deeply into alignment.

1. When you fall back into old patterns

Pause before you spiral into shame. Falling back does not mean failure; it means you are human. Instead of asking, "Why am I back here again?" ask, "What is this showing me now?" "And what is the correction?" Use breathwork, journaling, or one of the meditations in this book to bring yourself back into presence. Each return is a victory.

2. When you feel the urge to change others

Breathe. Remember that awakening is invitational, not instructional. Others do not need your fixing; they need your embodiment. Live your truth with integrity, and let curiosity draw others in when the time is right.

3. When you feel disconnected from others

Notice the ache without rushing to fill it. This disconnection is proof that your resonance is shifting. Trust that space is being created for new relationships, communities, and opportunities to enter. In the meantime, practice meeting people where they are without needing to abandon yourself.

4. When you feel pressured to define your purpose

Soften the grip. Purpose does not need to be declared at once; it is discovered through lived experience. For now, follow what feels nourishing, truthful, and alive. Let your purpose emerge from the inside out, rather than trying to construct it out of the fear of not knowing.

5. When others want the old you back

Ground yourself in compassion. Remember that their resistance is not about you; it is about their own comfort zones. You do not need to fight or defend; simply stand in your truth. Over time, those who cannot meet the new you will naturally drift, and those who are aligned will rise to meet you.

6. When you want to avoid the world

Give yourself rest when you need it, but also practice re-entering the spaces that once drained you. Notice how you can hold your frequency differently now. Each encounter becomes a rehearsal for living your awakening in the world, not just on the meditation cushion.

The key is this: every obstacle becomes medicine when you meet it consciously. Each is an invitation to return to your breath, your body, your awareness. Notice that even when you feel thrown off, your deeper self is never lost.

Anchor Tools: Staying Steady in the In-Between

Recognize that obstacles are a natural part of any journey. Take time to anticipate potential challenges that may arise along the way and remind yourself that to overcome them, you just need to meet them with conscious awareness. Then, in these moments, you will connect with your authentic self, where wisdom will naturally flow from you.

In a world filled with distractions and uncertainties, setting boundaries is crucial for staying focused. One practical tool is time-blocking, where you allocate specific times of the day for activities that help you align with your values (whether it's deep work, meditation, or simply resting). By setting clear boundaries around your focus, you prevent external chaos from pulling you off track.

I remember a time when I was juggling multiple client projects, running two companies, managing personal commitments, and unexpected family issues (a divorce). Everything felt overwhelming, and I could feel my attention scattering in multiple directions. It wasn't until I committed to a daily practice of anchoring, through breathwork and a strict morning routine, that I began to feel clarity return. Every morning reminded myself of my purpose, life map, core values, and goals, which helped me block out unnecessary distractions and stay focused on what truly mattered.

So, when life feels uncertain, what you need most is not a grand solution but an anchor. An anchor holds you steady when the winds change direction. It keeps you grounded when everything else feels in flux. The more intentional you are about building your anchor tools, the easier it becomes to return to presence, clarity, and truth.

1. Your Anchor Plan

An anchor plan is a set of simple, repeatable practices you can turn to when life feels overwhelming. This is not about perfection; it is about reliability. Think of it as your personal safety net. For me, it has been a combination of morning breathwork, meditation, and a strict daily routine of writing down my purpose and values. For you, it might look like stepping outside for five minutes, repeating a mantra, or opening your journal. The key is consistency. When chaos pulls you in, your anchor plan is what brings you back.

2. Time-Blocking for Presence

One of the most practical anchors you can create is time-blocking. This means carving out protected space for what truly matters: deep work, rest, or simply being. By scheduling these blocks as non-negotiable, you prevent external demands from eroding your focus. Even one uninterrupted hour can reset your nervous system and remind you of what you stand for.

3. Daily Micro-Practices

Anchoring does not only happen in big rituals. It happens in tiny pauses sprinkled throughout your day. Three conscious breaths before opening your laptop. A two-minute body scan after a meeting. A moment of stillness before you respond to a text. These micro-practices are small, but over time, they train your system to return to presence without effort.

4. Journaling for Integration

Your journal is not just a record of your thoughts; it is a mirror of your becoming. By writing down your insights, obstacles, and realizations, you create a dialogue with your deeper self. Journaling helps you catch patterns you might otherwise miss, and it integrates your inner work into daily life. Later in this chapter, I will share a simple daily journaling structure that you can adopt as a lifelong anchor.

5. Finding Your People

Anchors are not only practices; they are people. Who you surround yourself with matters. Seek out those who see the real you, who support your growth without needing you to shrink. Whether it is a women's circle, a trusted mentor, or an aligned friend, these relationships remind you that you are not walking alone. They anchor you in belonging.

6. Returning to Your Breath

When all else fails, your breath is the most reliable anchor you will ever have. It is always with you, always accessible, always able to bring you back to now. A single deep inhale and slow exhale can shift your physiology and remind you of the simplicity beneath the noise.

Anchors are not about avoiding the storm. They are about remembering that you can stand in it without being swept away. Each anchor you cultivate strengthens your ability to meet life's uncertainties with steadiness, clarity, and trust.

Journaling Habit and Inner Guidance

One of the most powerful anchors you can carry into your daily life is journaling. Throughout this book, I've given you many journaling prompts, and hopefully by now, journaling your insights and thoughts has become a habit.

Continuing your daily journaling practice brings numerous benefits, including integration and growth, increased self-awareness, and expanded perspectives. By reflecting on your realizations and making intentional adjustments, you continue to evolve and align your actions with your values.

At first, it might feel simple, but the act of putting pen to paper each day becomes a profound mirror of your growth. Your journal is where insights crystallize, where patterns reveal themselves, and where your inner guidance finds a clear channel.

Think of journaling as a conversation between your conscious mind and your deeper self. In the rush of daily life, thoughts can feel scattered, looping, or overwhelming. But once they are written down, something changes. The page does not judge. The page does not interrupt. The page receives everything and, in return, reflects clarity back to you.

Consistency is what transforms journaling from an occasional practice into a lifelong anchor. A few minutes each morning to set intentions, and a few minutes each evening to reflect, are enough to create a rhythm of self-awareness. Over time, you will notice your entries shifting from confusion to clarity, from frustration to wisdom, from reaction to response.

Here is a simple daily practice you can adopt:

Morning Intention

When you wake up, before reaching for your phone, open your journal. Write down your intentions for the day. Ask yourself:

How can I show up as my truest self today? What energy do I need to embody and carry throughout the day? What would alignment look like in action?

This sets the tone and reminds you of who you are becoming.

Evening Reflection

At the close of the day, return to your journal. Reflect on what unfolded. Ask yourself:

What went well? What challenged me? What did I learn? Where did I feel most like my real self? Where and in what situations did I forget?

Capture your realizations without judgment. End with gratitude by writing down three moments or people you are thankful for. Gratitude is a frequency that aligns you with abundance and opens you to receive more of it.

Adjustments and Insights

Use your journal to note any shifts you want to make tomorrow. Perhaps you noticed an old pattern resurfacing, or a moment where you could have paused instead of reacting. These are not failures. They are data. By recording them, you build a map of your growth and a reference point for your alignment.

Journaling in this way becomes less about keeping a diary and more about cultivating dialogue with your inner guidance. The more you practice, the clearer your intuition becomes. You begin to trust the subtle nudges that arise from within. You notice synchronicities. You feel more guided, less lost. Journaling turns your inner whispers into written truths, and those truths become a compass for your daily choices.

When I look back through my own journals, I see the arc of my transformation written in real time. Pages filled with confusion eventually gave way to clarity. Entries filled with searching became entries filled with knowing. What once felt like chaos slowly revealed itself as a map. This is the gift of journaling: it does not just record your journey, it reveals it.

The Real Meaning of Yoga

If you have reached this point in the book, then you have already been practicing yoga. Not the kind measured by whether you can touch your toes or hold a headstand, but the deeper kind, the yoga of awareness.

"Yoga is the journey of the self, through the self, to the self."
– Bhagavad Gita

Yoga, at its essence, means union. Union with your Source. Union with your true self. Union with life itself. If, as you've read these chapters, you have begun to feel a stronger connection to something deeper than your mind, if you've tasted even a moment of intelligence moving through you, then you are already living yoga.

Yoga, in its truest sense, is not about touching your toes or perfecting a posture. The word itself, from the Sanskrit root yuj, means "to yoke" or "to unite." It points to something far deeper than physical flexibility. Yoga is union. Union with your breath. Union with your body. Union with the universal mind, source, and Life Intelligence.

In the West, yoga has often been reduced to asanas, the physical postures, and pranayama, the control of breath. These are powerful practices, but they are only doorways. The ultimate state of yoga is to experience union with the deeper forces of life. To know yourself not as separate, but as part of the vast fabric of intelligence that animates everything.

When you live in this awareness, yoga is no longer something you "do." It becomes a state of being. Every step becomes a practice. Every breath becomes sacred. Every moment is an opportunity to align yourself with the life intelligence that is already flowing through you.

So take a moment to recognize that. To honor yourself. You have been walking the path of yoga without even stepping onto a mat, yet. The stretching and postures can come later. Yes, in the next part of the book, I will introduce some physical practices to help you keep a clear body and a clear mind. But right now, the fact that you are more awake to yourself, more connected to life intelligence, more open to life, that is the real practice. Let's seal this with a guided meditation, Union with the Whole. Visit https://www.gemdentith.com/playbook

Whenever you feel disconnected or overwhelmed, use this meditation to reconnect with the deeper truth of your existence. You are not separate from the world around you but an integral part of the intricate web of life. Let this awareness shape how you show up grounded, clear, and intentional in your actions and interactions.

Awaking Realizations

In a world full of unpredictability, surrendering is not about controlling every situation, but about allowing flow. By centering yourself on what truly matters, you cut through distractions and remain anchored in yourself and your purpose.

The tools you've explored so far (meditation, journaling, and the inner work of undressing are not just practices, but disciplines that keep you aligned with your highest, truest self. The more you develop your capacity to stay present, the more resilient and adaptable you become. You have everything within you to navigate the unknown with clarity and confidence.

Now is the time to embrace your journey with conviction, trusting that no matter what life brings, you are capable of thriving.

From Surrender to Self-Care

Well, my loves, you've nearly made it to the end of the magic of Part Two. Before we move into Part Three, where we explore your highest blueprint and purpose, I've written an extra chapter for you. Why? Because awakening is not enough on its own. You also need a body and mind strong enough to hold it.

This next chapter is about attuning your system so you can stay in flow with your destiny. It is about keeping your energy clear, your body nourished, and your mind steady so that you don't just awaken for a moment, but live from that awakened state.

Have you ever noticed how your "fit friend" seems to glow? Whether single or in a relationship, they're outgoing, thoughtful, and start new projects or adventures with ease. Here's the secret: they practice self-care. And self-care, in its truest form, is not indulgence. It is attunement. A healthy body and mind are not just functional (they are instruments in harmony with the universe).

That is where we go next: self-care as an awakening and alignment practice, not as vanity but as sacred practices that allow you to sustain your awakening and keep your energy expanded.

Chapter 15:

Sacred Self-Care

Aligning Body, Mind, And Spirit With Life Intelligence

"The body is your temple. Keep it pure and clean for the soul to reside in."

– B.K.S. Iyengar

When most people think of self-care, they picture the basics: eating better, squeezing in a workout, maybe getting a good night's sleep. At best, it's seen as maintenance, the minimum required to keep going. At worst, it becomes another box to tick, something you'll get around to when life feels less overwhelming.

But sacred self-care is different. It's not about surface-level maintenance; it's about remembering that your body, mind, and spirit are a vessel for Life Intelligence energy. It's about attuning yourself to the universal current that flows through everything. When your vessel is clear, nourished, and balanced, you don't just function better, you vibrate higher. You become a living channel for wisdom, vitality, and purpose.

This is the perspective shift I want to offer you here. Self-care isn't indulgence. It isn't even optional. It is devotion. It is how you honor the temple that allows life intelligence to express itself through you.

In this chapter, I'll share a new way of seeing self-care (not as a chore, but as a sacred practice of alignment). We'll explore how nourishment, movement, breath, water, nature, and sleep can become portals for higher connection, grounding, and clarity. You'll learn how to treat your body as a vessel that can hold and transmit more energy, creativity, and joy.

By the end of this chapter, I want you to see self-care not as something you "have to do," but as something you get to do. A sacred responsibility that keeps you in flow with your awakened self and aligned with the intelligence of the universe.

A New Perspective of Self-Care

Throughout this book, we have explored the concept of self from different perspectives. We began by defining the fictitious self, the "Happiness Whore," driven by the survival self and external validation. From there, we undressed the layers to reconnect with the original self, the deeper, truer version of you. And then we expanded even further into the universal self, the interconnected self that exists within you, in others, and in all of life.

True self-care is not just about tending to the small self, the physical body, or the survival self. It is about nurturing the big Self, the supreme, omnipresent awareness that you are part of. When your body and mind are clear, they become a vessel that can hold and circulate more Source energy. The healthier and more balanced you are, the easier it becomes for universal intelligence to move through you.

To really labor the point, self-care is not merely about maintaining fitness or keeping up appearances. It is a holistic practice of attuning and aligning with the universal self, the higher intelligence. It is about maintaining a clear connection to Source so that your physical and energetic vessel becomes a channel for universal energy to flow through. When seen this way, self-care takes on a whole new level of meaning.

In many Eastern traditions, this flow of energy is described through energy centers known as chakras. The word chakra comes from Sanskrit, meaning "wheel." These centers represent key points in the body where energy collects and circulates, from the root at the base of the spine, which represents grounding and survival, to the crown at the top of the head, which represents consciousness and connection to the divine. You do not need to memorize the system here. What matters is understanding that practices like yoga, meditation, breathwork, nourishing food, cold water immersion, time in nature, deep rest, and even digital detoxes all support the clearing and balancing of these centers. They help you maintain equilibrium in body and mind, while also keeping your connection to Source alive and strong.

This is the perspective of self-care I want you to hold. It is not just routines or rituals for your body; it is acts of alignment that sustain your entire being. When you live from this perspective, self-care is no longer a chore. It becomes a sacred act of remembrance.

Now, let us explore the specific practices that help keep your vessel, your body, both physical and energetic, in balance.

Cultivating Balance in Your Physical and Energetic Vessel

When I talk about nurturing your physical and energetic vessel, I mean creating balance. Balance in your cells. Balance in your organs. Balance in your thoughts, emotions, and breath. From my time as a fitness instructor, emergency services technician, breath work facilitator, naturopathic health coach, chef, and yoga teacher (and through my own personal health crises), I've come to understand one core truth: balance is what cultivates real health.

When your body and mind are in harmony, when everything inside is operating in sync, it sets the stage for overall well-being. It is simple: when there is balance within, there is balance without.

Balance is not just about keeping yourself alive; it is about unlocking your body's highest energetic potential. When you create conditions of ease and flow, you begin to notice more than just "health management." Sometimes you witness true vitality. Sometimes you even witness spontaneous healing. I have seen people shift illnesses, dissolve chronic tension, or regain joy, not through medication alone, but through alignment with their true self and with universal intelligence.

When you are in sync with who you really are, your body responds. Your health improves. You feel more alive. With energy flowing, life itself feels brighter, lighter, and more fulfilling.

On the other hand, dis-ease (literally "lack of ease") arises when balance is disrupted and energy is low. One system out of sync can throw everything else into disharmony. And while it is possible to live in alignment with your true self even when the body is unwell, disease becomes an interference if you identify too closely with it. When you define yourself by the imbalance, it takes root. But where there is ease, balance is restored. Where there is balance, there is harmony. And where there is harmony, there is health.

The way I see it, your energy centers are like tuning pegs on a musical instrument. When one is out, the whole song feels off. But with care and regular tuning, the instrument can produce its clearest, most resonant sound. In the same way, practices like yoga, breathwork, meditation, sound, nourishing food, rest, and time in nature act as tuning tools. They help you restore harmony to your system so that life force flows freely and you experience alignment in body, mind, and spirit.

Self-care in this deeper sense is a daily act of tuning, like tuning an instrument so it can play its purest song.

Before you dive into this section, I've recorded a Mini Activation called "Balancing Your Energy System. Head to https://www.gemdentith.com/playbook download the Playbook, and listen to it for free.

Conscious Consumption: Nourishing the Body and Mind

What you feed your mind is just as important as what you feed your body and how you treat your body.

Most of us are aware that our diet and physical activities directly impact how we feel, our energy levels, and our overall well-being. But what about the mental "diet" we're consuming daily? When we unconsciously consume processed, nutritionally poor foods and binge on junk TV, while leading a sedentary lifestyle, we're left feeling drained, agitated, and discontented. Often, mindless eating becomes a way to escape boredom or avoid uncomfortable emotions. Foods that lack life force sap our energy, dragging us into a state of overthinking and negativity, which clouds our true essence. This imbalance creates an environment ripe for drama, victimhood, and lower levels of existence.

In contrast, nourishing our bodies with vibrant, energizing foods elevates our vitality and zest for life. When we choose to embark on a conscious health journey by swapping out nutritionally empty foods for nutrient-rich options and increasing physical movement, we feel more vibrant, joyful, and alive. This inner vitality naturally reflects outwardly.

Conscious consumption extends beyond just food and exercise (it permeates every aspect of our lives). By becoming mindful of what we put into our bodies and how we care for them, we invite a higher level of awareness into our everyday activities. This shift in consciousness leads to better decisions about what we eat, who we spend time with, and how we interact with the world around us. Ultimately, this fosters a smoother, more aligned flow in life.

High Vibrational Practices

The term *high-vibrational* is often used to describe an elevated state of energy, vitality, and coherence within the body and mind. In holistic spiritual language, it reflects how certain choices and environments support balance and well-being. Nourishing foods, positive thought patterns, and mindful daily practices naturally enhance energy levels, mood, and overall resilience. Conversely, processed foods, toxic environments, and chronic stress or negativity can deplete the system, creating imbalance and disconnection.

Adopting high-vibrational practices does not mean becoming a health or fitness fanatic. It means making conscious, intentional choices that support and elevate your energy rather than drain you and freeing your body and mind from unnecessary toxins, tension, and noise. These practices support optimal physical, mental, and emotional health, allowing your natural clarity and vitality to flourish.

Stillness and Rest

I want to begin our exploration of high-vibrational practices with stillness and rest, because without them, everything else you try to implement becomes diluted. Think of rest as the soil. If the soil is depleted, no matter how many seeds you plant (nutrition, movement, practices, ideas), they will not take root as they are meant to. Stillness is what replenishes that soil, creating fertile ground for your energy to flourish.

We live in a culture that glorifies constant motion. We push, strive, and perform, often ignoring the signals our bodies are sending us. Yet if you watch animals in the wild, you'll notice something different: they move with purpose, and then they stop. They rest before they hunt. They conserve energy until it's needed. They don't burn themselves out by staying in a state of perpetual motion. This is a rhythm that high performers in human life often forget. The best athletes train hard, but they also prioritize recovery. Without rest, performance collapses.

The same principle applies to you. Rest is not laziness. It is a high-vibrational practice that restores your nervous system, recalibrates your energy, and allows your body the chance to heal. Stillness creates space for integration; all the insights, awakenings, and shifts you've experienced on this journey so far need quiet to settle into your system. Without that pause, you risk rushing forward without truly embodying what you've learned.

Stillness and rest are also deeply spiritual. In stillness, you remember who you are beyond the noise of your mind. In rest, you surrender the illusion of control and allow Source to do what it does best: restore balance, harmony, and clarity. Just as the breath has an inhale and an exhale, your life has seasons of activity and seasons of renewal. Honor both.

This is why we begin here. Before we explore food, movement, breath, or any other practice, we must return to the most natural rhythm of all: action and rest, expansion and stillness.

Practices for Stillness and Rest

Here are some simple but powerful ways to honor stillness and rest in your daily life:

Micro Pauses

Take a few minutes between activities to simply stop. No scrolling, no planning, no doing. Sit quietly, breathe deeply, and allow your body to reset. Even two minutes of stillness can shift your nervous system from stress into calm.

Power Naps

A nap in the early afternoon, for ten to twenty minutes, is enough to refresh your system without making you groggy. Research shows that these short rests improve focus, memory, and energy, acting as a reset button for both body and mind.

Digital Silence

Choose a window each day to disconnect completely from technology. It may be the first hour after waking or the last hour before bed. Allow your mind to rest from the constant influx of information and noise.

Mindful Stillness Practice

Dedicate a few minutes each day to sit in silence. You don't need to "meditate" in the formal sense if that feels overwhelming. Simply close your eyes, focus on your breath, and observe. Notice the stillness beneath the noise. That space is your true nature.

Fasting as Rest

Fasting is about giving your digestive system a break so your body can redirect its energy to repair and restore. Start simple: a twelve to fourteen-hour overnight fast, finishing dinner earlier and breaking your fast later in the morning, can create more clarity and vitality.

The next thing I want to talk to you about in terms of high-vibrational activities is the role that diet plays in your life. But I don't want to focus on the word "diet" because, for many people, it carries a lot of baggage. When you hear "diet," you might think it means you need to give things up and that it becomes restrictive. So, I want to shift your perspective towards enjoying healthy food and, more importantly, viewing food as a way to nourish the body and mind and to have greater alignment with universal intelligence.

Nourishment

If you see your body as a vessel that allows you to connect more deeply with universal intelligence, you need to ask, How can you optimize your body, your human vessel, so it's in the best state to connect more deeply? It's not about giving up foods; it's about nourishing your body so your mind-body is in tune with the energy around you. And food plays a huge role in that. You should ask: how can I feed it? What role does food play in this process?

Let me share a bit of my own story. I've always had a complicated relationship with food. When I was a teenager, I suffered from anorexia, which really affected how I thought about eating. Food wasn't enjoyable for me at that time. I associated it with discomfort and control over me. I got so bad that I was unable to walk and unable to think. I couldn't even write a single sentence. It was like a five-year-old had taken over my brain. However, after the threat of hospitalization loomed over me, and being force-fed was even more terrifying than the concept of eating, I slowly began to eat. But my food choices were for a different purpose; I'd changed the way I viewed food. I started to see it as nourishment, as medicine for my body. After living with anorexia nervosa and bulimia, I had depleted my body so much that I had to find a way to nourish it again. I wanted to reverse the damage I'd done to myself and start feeling better. And this shift in perspective (from seeing food as something negative to something that could heal me) completely changed my life.

At the age of sixteen, I started my healing journey. I spent hours on the weekends in health food shops, buying vitamins and minerals, and studying how they worked. I began to see food as medicine (a way to help heal the trauma I had put my body through). I've carried this approach with me my whole adult life, and then finally, at the age of thirty-nine, I studied to become a naturopathic chef and health coach with the College of Naturopathic Medicine in London to understand the science of food and its healing properties.

This shift in perspective is what I invite you to consider: to look at food as a source of nourishment, and to see it as a way to care for your mind and body. If nutrition is new to you, you might want to work with a naturopathic professional to help you adjust your food choices, but the goal is to have a food plan aligned with your body's needs, rather than something that leads you down a restrictive path.

So, I invite you to think of food as medicine for your body. Ask yourself whether your food choices are nourishing your body, bringing you back into balance. And whether they are helping you be the best version of yourself and harnessing your connection with life's intelligence?

I now hope that, when it comes to nourishment, not just using the word 'diet' is helpful, but also reframing how you see it and why paying attention to what you consume is so important. Not only for physical health but as a way to align with universal intelligence (so we can be more in tune and online), allowing for greater connection with the universe.

There is some truth in the statement, "you are what you eat." I tend to think that you wear what you eat, like you wear your food on the outside too. I can always tell if someone has lots of nourishment by the quality of their skin and hair, and other physical telltale signs.

Just as we choose clothes to suit the occasion, we should also choose our food to suit our lifestyle, stage of life, and the nourishment our body needs to stay in balance. This is what I call targeted nutrition. It means eating in alignment with your individual health needs, energy output, hormonal cycle, and your body's age. The requirements of a growing, sporty teenager are very different from those of a middle-aged man or woman managing an autoimmune condition at a desk job, or from the needs of an eighty-year-old whose body requires gentler support.

With my naturopathic chef and health coach hat on, I've learned that there is no one-size-fits-all approach to what you should eat. However, what I deeply align with is the principle of targeted nutrition, rooted in naturopathic principles: eating in alignment with what nourishment your body needs to maintain its inner harmony. I'd like to share some simple, core principles that everyone can benefit from, guiding you toward healthier food choices. The goal is to help your body achieve balance, providing it with the right vitamins and minerals while minimizing exposure to toxins.

Here are a few core principles using the word

CLOTHES (which means dressing your body with the right nutrition for health):

Colorful Foods – The more colorful your plate, the wider the variety of nutrients you're getting.

Living Foods – Include fresh fruits, vegetables, and sprouts, which are packed with enzymes and life force energy.

Organic – Whenever possible, choose organic to avoid harmful pesticides and chemicals.

True Fats – Prioritize natural sources of fats like avocados, nuts, seeds, and olive oil, which support overall health.

Hydration – Keep your body well-hydrated with plenty of water to support digestion, energy, and detoxification.

Eat Whole Foods – Focus on foods that are nutritionally dense and minimally processed.

Stay Balanced – Nourish your body with variety and intention to support its natural healing and vitality.

By integrating these principles into your daily routine, you'll create a foundation of nourishment and vitality that supports your body's natural healing and well-being. Remember, food is more than just fuel (it's nourishment for your body, mind, and life intelligence). Choose foods that reflect your intention to live a vibrant, balanced life.

Just as nourishing your body with the right food is essential, caring for your physical and energetic well-being through movement is equally important. This is where dance and the practice of asana (the physical postures of yoga) come in.

Movement

Just as nourishing your body with the right food is essential, caring for your physical and energetic well-being through movement is equally important. This is where dance and the practice of asana (the physical postures of yoga) come in. Movement is a way to access deeper layers of yourself, and for me, nothing does this quite like dance and asana practice.

However, I also highly recommend other powerful movement practices, such as Qigong and Tai Chi. These ancient disciplines help cultivate energy flow, enhance mindfulness, and balance both body and mind. They're deeply beneficial for grounding and aligning your internal energy.

Personally, I love to combine the intuitive freedom of dance with the structured flow of yoga. Together, these practices create a harmonious blend of movement that helps release stagnant energy, elevate your vibration, and connect you with your true essence.

Dance

When I dance intuitively (when I just let go and move with the music without any structure), it becomes a powerful release.

You know that phrase, dance as though no one's watching? Well, when I truly embody that, whether I'm in my living room or any other space, I feel my energy shift. The stagnant energy within me loosens up and dissolves. It's as though the movement, in tune with the music, allows the energy to flow again.

Intuitive dance is my go-to for this. It's not about following a routine or specific steps (it's about tuning into the music and letting my body respond to it). The music itself plays a big role here because sound carries frequency, and that frequency impacts your energy. So, I'm always very intentional with the music I choose. I use high-vibration music to support the feeling state I want to cultivate. The sound becomes part of me, and I move with it.

So, when you feel stuck or disconnected, dance intuitively. Let the music guide you, move with it, and allow it to shift your energy. This practice has been one of the most effective ways for me to realign and feel vibrant in the moment. It's not just movement (it's a way of unlocking something deeper inside yourself, allowing your energy to rise and flow freely).

So the next time you're feeling a bit low, and by that I mean if your mood is off, if you're feeling heavy, demotivated, or just flat in general, I highly encourage you to try something simple: get up, put on one of your favorite songs, and just move.

Now, I wouldn't recommend anything too heavy (probably not the heavy metal or intense rock music like thrash metal). Instead, choose something that makes you feel good when you hear it, music that lifts your spirit or brings a smile to your face.

Once you've got that song playing, stand up, get off your chair, and start moving your body. Begin slowly (there's no rush). Close your eyes, too. When you close your eyes and just let yourself move, you let go of any self-consciousness. You'll notice something beautiful happens: the body naturally wants to move. Maybe your hips will start to sway on their own, or your arms will begin to flow. The body knows what to do (it's the mind that often holds it back). So, with your eyes closed and the music as your guide, just follow what feels right. Move in whatever way your body wants, no rules, no choreography (just pure, intuitive movement).

And if you're feeling brave, once you're comfortable with this practice, why not take it a step further? You can join one of the many sober raves or conscious dance gatherings happening around the world. There's something so powerful about moving alongside others who are also tapping into this high-vibe, intentional energy. It creates a collective rhythm and energy that amplifies the experience. There are a few near my city, London, and it's an amazing way to dance in community, feeling that shared vibration with others.

So when you feel ready, when the courage is there, I invite you to take that step (to move beyond your own space and experience this joy with others). And most importantly, remember to have fun. This is about releasing, letting go, and enjoying the process.

Asana

The next high-vibrational practice is Asana, and I deliberately say Asana rather than yoga because people often, especially in the West, associate Asana (the physical postures of yoga) with the entire practice of yoga. However, yoga is much broader than that. The term "yoga" means union; it's the practice of aligning the small self with the big Self, or, as this book explores, connecting with your true self and aligning with a supreme consciousness. In this book, we refer to this energy as Life Intelligence.

In its truest sense, as covered in the previous chapter, yoga is about the union of the individual with the divine. This whole book, in essence, is a form of yoga (guiding you to discover your true self and aligning with a greater consciousness). As you move through these teachings, you're engaging in a process that, at its core, reflects the ancient practice of yoga.

The physical postures, or asanas, are a powerful tool for aligning the body. Each asana is a means of slowing down the mind and creating space for clarity of thought. While you may not be seated in a traditional meditation posture, such as Lotus pose, or Padmasana, each asana offers an opportunity for mindfulness and connection to Life Intelligence.

Every posture, no matter how simple or complex, is an invitation for you to be fully conscious in that moment. It's not just about moving your body; it's about attuning your body to the present and using that awareness to connect with Source. This shift in focus makes asana practice a vital aspect of your journey toward self-discovery.

The real purpose of Asana is to attune the body so it can tune in with Source. That's why I've included Asana in this section as a high-vibrational practice (one that allows you to elevate both your physical and energetic state). On this path of self-discovery, asana is not just about building strength, flexibility, or detoxing the body; it's also about balancing your energy and preparing your body and mind to receive guidance from the divine.

By incorporating Asana into your daily life, you're not only benefiting physically, but you're also creating space for your mind to slow down and find clarity, ultimately opening yourself to deeper levels of spiritual awareness. The physical postures of yoga serve as a bridge, connecting your small self to the greater, universal Self, unlocking gifts that only become apparent when this connection is fully realized.

Tips for Trying Asana

I understand that for some, stepping into an Asana practice for the first time might feel daunting (especially after seeing influencers on Instagram bending their bodies like circus contortionists). Let me assure you: Asana is not about twisting yourself into impossible shapes or about perfecting a pose. Yoga is an inner practice (a way of aligning your consciousness with universal consciousness).

In my early thirties, I qualified as a yoga teacher, and while I became known for teaching challenging classes, one thing I always emphasized to my students was this: anyone can practice Asana. It's not about the flexibility you start with, but how you use the practice to better align your body, mind, and spirit.

If you're considering trying Asana for the first time, here are a few tips to help you get started:

Find the Right Class for You: There are many types of asana classes, from the slow, grounding Hatha yoga to the more dynamic Vinyasa flow. Don't be afraid to try a few different styles to see what feels best for you. You don't need to start with a challenging class (sometimes the gentler practices help you build the foundation you need). I would suggest going slow is the best approach.

Release Expectations: Yoga is not about achieving the "perfect" pose. It's about connecting with your breath, your body, and your deeper self. Whether you can touch your toes or not doesn't matter (what matters is how you feel as you move through each posture).

Stay Consistent: Like any practice, asana requires consistency to experience the deeper benefits. Even if you start with just a few minutes a day, over time you'll notice your body becomes more aligned and your mind clearer.

Listen to Your Body: Your body is your greatest guide. In a class, always listen to how your body feels and don't push beyond your limits. Yoga is about creating space, not causing strain. Remember, it's about how your practice brings you closer to balance and alignment.

The best way to view yoga is that Yoga is a personal journey from the self to the self, and asana is one way to help you on that path. Asana is not about trying to pretzel your body into the same shape as an Instagram influencer. It's a deeply personal exploration. Forget how it looks to the outside world; instead, focus on deepening your own practice by using the body and breath as tools for inner exploration and connecting with the divine. With this way of looking at it, you don't have to be an expert to start or already be a gymnast. It's never too late to begin, and you're never too old to start.

If you're new to asana practice, I've added some simple asanas to your Undressed Playbook to get you started.

I've chosen these few as they offer a balance of strength, flexibility, alignment, mental clarity, and energetic flow, while each asana serves as a seat of meditation and an opportunity to consciously connect with universal life energy:

Each pose serves not only to enhance physical well-being but also to align your consciousness with universal intelligence, offering a transformative experience on the mat that you can carry with you throughout the rest of your day.

A central part of Asana is the breath, and as you flow through each pose, you are also practicing slow diaphragmatic breathing, where your ribs expand to the side. Many of my students struggled with the concept of linking an asana with a breath, and they often either held their breath or breathed so rapidly that the class became more of an aerobic exercise for them. Where, in fact, the slow, belly synchronized breath is probably the most important aspect of the entire practice. This is why I have an entire section on it. Let's now move to our next high-vibrational practice, breathwork.

Breathwork

Breathwork is so often misunderstood. When I first started teaching and promoting it, I frequently got comments from people who didn't fully grasp its benefits. They'd say things like, "I already breathe, so why do I need to spend sixty minutes in a class just breathing? What's the point?" But here's the thing: it's not just about breathing; it's about breathing correctly. When you breathe as you should, it becomes truly transformational.

Breathwork is the foundation for everything. And when I say everything, I mean it quite literally. Your breath impacts your physical health, your mental health, and your performance (everything). The way you breathe influences how well you speak, how effectively you communicate, and how you manage stress. If you're a speaker, a dancer, or an athlete (whether you're a swimmer, runner, or any type of performer), your breath is at the core of your performance. It's not something to be overlooked, yet it's so often taken for granted.

I can't tell you how many times I've talked to people about the power of breathwork, only to be met with, "I automatically breathe, so why should I spend time on it?" Ironically, these same people are often highly stressed or anxious, and as soon as I observe their breathing patterns, I can see exactly where they're going wrong and how much they'd benefit from even a small adjustment.

What I'm really getting at here is (don't underestimate the importance of breathwork). This next section will dive into the practice in a way that can make a profound impact on your life. You'll learn how the breath can ground you, help you manage emotions, and improve your overall well-being. So stay open to the possibilities that come from learning to truly breathe, not just automatically, but intentionally. Let's get into it.

Breathwork is one of the most powerful high-vibrational practices for realigning with your higher self and releasing what no longer serves you. As a practice, you can actually visualize stripping away layers of conditioning, fear, and pain, guiding you toward a truer version of yourself. Breathwork isn't just about release (it's about creating space for clarity and stepping into a higher state of being).

At its core, breath is life. Understanding it more fully allows us to regulate the mind and body, release deeply held traumas, and shift our energetic state, moving us closer to our alignment. The Latin word spiritus means both "breath" and "spirit," reflecting the ancient belief that breath connects us to something greater (the universal life force).

By consciously controlling the breath, you can invoke positive mental, emotional, and physical benefits. There are techniques ranging from gentle, meditative practices found in yoga, Tai Chi, and Qi Gong to deeper, more intense forms like Conscious Connected Breathwork, designed to release trauma and emotional blockages.

The effects on the mind-body depend on how you are activating the nervous system. In yoga asana practice, we often activate the parasympathetic nervous system by engaging the vagus nerve through slow, deep breathing.

This type of breathwork, characterized by long inhalations and extended exhalations, soothes the nervous system, activating the body's natural relaxation response to promote healing and balance. This gentle practice helps ground you, bringing peace and balance while aligning your body and energy with Source.

To experience the calming benefits of breathwork, try this simple exercise:

Find a comfortable position: Sit or lie down in a peaceful space. Close your eyes and take a few deep breaths, inhaling through your nose and exhaling through your mouth, imagining releasing muscle tension with each exhale..

Focus on your breath: Inhale slowly and deeply, filling your belly and ribcage. As you exhale, imagine softening the attachment to any anxious thoughts, allowing them to dissolve more and more with each breath.

Lengthen your exhalation: Gradually make your exhalation slightly longer than your inhalation. This extended exhalation helps activate the vagus nerve and further calms your nervous system.

Visualize relaxation: Imagine a wave of relaxation flowing through your body with each breath, washing away tension and stress.

Stay present: Continue this rhythmic breathing for several minutes, allowing yourself to become grounded in the present moment.

In contrast, Conscious Connected Breathwork is a more intense practice that activates the sympathetic nervous system, leading to heightened awareness and deep emotional cleansing. Originally developed by Leonard Orr in the 1970s, as part of the Rebirthing Breathwork movement, this form of breathwork facilitates the release of suppressed emotions and trauma, enabling individuals to process and integrate unresolved feelings. By engaging the body and mind in this continuous, connected breathing pattern, participants have been known to experience profound emotional breakthroughs and healing.

Bare Breathwork: Undressing Your True Self Through Breath

I've developed my own breathwork method called Bare Breathwork (a transformative practice designed to help you strip away layers of emotional and energetic blockages that prevent you from living in alignment with your true essence). This practice combines the calming effects of slow, mindful breathing with the deep-healing power of conscious connected breathwork.

The term bare reflects the essence of the practice (undressing layers of trauma, pain, and conditioned beliefs to reveal your authentic self). I designed it specifically to help you "undress" emotionally and energetically, stripping away the layers of conditioning, trauma, and limiting beliefs that have accumulated over time. It reconnects you with your true essence, realigning you with universal consciousness and helping you step into deeper self-awareness and clarity.

This breathwork offers a unique combination of slow, mindful breathing (designed to activate the parasympathetic nervous system and calm the body) and conscious connected breathwork, which induces a powerful emotional release and reawakens your true self.

Key techniques of Bare Breathwork include:

Circular Breathing Rhythm: A continuous, circular breathing pattern where the inhale flows directly into the exhale without pause. By maintaining an unbroken rhythm in your breath,

Bare Breathwork bypasses the analytical mind, allowing you to connect with deeper emotional layers and release blockages. This technique helps release stored trauma and suppressed emotions.

Deep Diaphragmatic Breathing: Breathing deeply into the diaphragm ensures full oxygenation of the body, calming the nervous system, and helping release stored emotions.

Body Awareness and Scanning: Throughout the session, focus on different areas of the body to identify tension or emotional holding, directing your breath to release these blockages.

The benefits of Bare Breathwork include:

Emotional Healing: Releases suppressed emotions and past traumas, healing emotional wounds that may have been stored for years.

Mental Clarity: By shedding emotional layers, you clear the mental fog that clouds your thinking, allowing for heightened focus and insight.

Spiritual Alignment: Reconnecting with your higher self and universal intelligence, deepening your sense of purpose and connection to Source energy.

Stress Reduction: Activating the parasympathetic nervous system to promote relaxation and reduce stress and anxiety.

Physical Vitality: Releasing emotional blockages and improving your body's energy flow, promoting physical healing, and boosting vitality.

How Bare Breathwork Helps with Emotional Release

Bare Breathwork creates a powerful space for emotional

release by tapping into deeply held traumas and suppressed emotions. The continuous, connected breath pattern activates the body's natural healing response, helping you release the weight of these emotions in a safe and controlled way. You may experience a wave of relief, clarity, or even laughter or tears as these emotions are expressed and cleared.

How Bare Breathwork Releases Trauma

Through continuous circular breathing, Bare Breathwork accesses the subconscious mind, where traumas are stored. The breath bypasses the mind's defenses, allowing suppressed memories and emotions to surface and be fully released. The process is deeply cathartic, offering relief and allowing you to move forward without being weighed down by past emotional baggage.

How Bare Breathwork Resets the Mind

Bare Breathwork interrupts habitual thought patterns and shifts you out of the analytical mind, bringing you into a state of presence. By calming the nervous system and clearing emotional blockages, it creates a mental "reset," allowing you to approach life with renewed clarity, focus, and peace.

How Is Bare Breathwork Different from Other Methods?

Bare Breathwork stands out for its focus on "undressing" emotional layers, trauma, and conditioning to reveal your authentic self. While many breathwork methods focus solely on emotional release or relaxation, Bare Breathwork integrates both slow, mindful breathing and a circular breathing rhythm, offering a holistic approach that balances emotional release, spiritual alignment, and physical healing. The process is personalized to each individual, ensuring that the breathwork addresses your specific emotional and energetic needs.

By incorporating any method of breathwork into your life, you create a powerful tool for self-transformation (helping you release what no longer serves you and reconnect with your highest potential).

Practicing Bare Breathwork

There are two main ways to incorporate Bare Breathwork into your routine: a daily practice for maintenance and balance, and deeper, more intense sessions for emotional release and healing. I usually guide clients through a deeper session first, followed by teaching them a daily practice to help maintain balance and emotional well-being.

Daily Bare Breathwork Practice

Intention Setting: Every session starts with setting an intention. Whether you want to release tension, gain clarity, or reconnect with Source, having a clear focus helps guide your practice and ensures you're targeting specific aspects of your well-being.

Types of Bare Breathwork Sessions

Deeper, Intense Sessions: These sessions are designed for deep emotional release or trauma processing. Done either in person or online, these sessions are intense and are typically practiced less frequently (perhaps once or twice a week). Because these sessions can be physically and emotionally draining, it's crucial to allow time for integration and recovery afterward.

Short, Gentle Sessions: For daily practice, a short, gentle session lasting ten to fifteen minutes can be highly effective for maintaining emotional balance, reducing stress, and staying aligned with your authentic self. These sessions focus on calming the nervous system and grounding yourself through circular breathing.

How to Incorporate Bare Breathwork Into Your Routine

Preparation: Ground yourself and set a clear intention for the session. This could be emotional release, gaining clarity, or simply reconnecting with your body and mind.

Mindful Breath Awareness: Start with slow, mindful breathing to tune into your body and prepare for deeper work.

Circular Connected Breathing: Engage in continuous, connected breathing without pauses to create a flow of breath. This technique helps initiate emotional and energetic release.

Emotional Release: As emotions begin to surface, allow yourself to fully experience them. Stay present with your breath, and let the emotions flow without resistance.

Integration and Grounding: Conclude with slower, mindful breaths, and focus on grounding exercises to restore balance and integrate any emotional shifts or releases.

The benefits of a daily Bare Breathwork practice include:

Emotional Balance: Regular practice helps release daily stress and emotional buildup before they become bigger issues.

Mental Clarity: A short daily session can serve as a mental reset, improving focus and helping you stay calm throughout your day.

Alignment with Higher Self: Consistent breathwork keeps you aligned with your higher purpose and connected to your true essence and universal intelligence.

Stress Reduction: By regularly activating the parasympathetic nervous system through gentle breathwork, you maintain a state of calm, significantly reducing overall stress and anxiety.

Listening to Your Body

While Bare Breathwork is a powerful daily practice, it's essential to balance intensity with your body's needs. As you tune into your breath and gradually deepen your practice, you'll build resilience and a deeper connection to your body. But for those looking to take it a step further and truly level up, we now enter into the transformative world of hot and cold water therapy.

Hot and Cold Water Therapy

Harnessing the extremes of heat and cold can have profound effects on both the body and mind. These two contrasting practices (saunas and cold water immersion) work together to cleanse, revitalize, and balance your entire system. Let's begin with the heat.

Sauna

One of the key components of maintaining a high vibrational state is keeping your body (your physical vessel) as clear and clean as possible. When your body is weighed down by toxins from everyday life, it becomes harder to channel the energies you need to live in alignment with your highest self. This is where the power of saunas comes in.

Saunas, whether traditional coal saunas with hot stones or infrared saunas, offer a simple yet effective way to help your body release toxins and reset energetically. Sweating is one of the body's natural detoxification processes, and using a sauna encourages deeper and more efficient cleansing through the skin, which is your body's largest detoxification organ.

We are exposed to toxins daily (from the air we breathe to the products we use and even the foods we eat). Over time, these toxins can build up in the body, disrupting our natural energy flow and weighing down our system. Regular sauna use can help relieve this burden by stimulating deep sweat, clearing out impurities, and improving circulation.

Traditional saunas heat the body quickly, allowing for an intense sweat session in just a few minutes, while infrared saunas work at lower temperatures but offer a longer, gentler detox. Both types are equally effective for keeping the body clear, vibrant, and ready to channel higher frequencies of energy.

Incorporating sauna sessions into your routine helps to ensure that your physical vessel is operating at its best, ready to handle the higher vibrational energies that flow through you. As always, remember to hydrate and replace lost electrolytes to support your body through the detox process.

Next, we'll dive into the benefits of cold water therapy and how it complements sauna use to further cleanse, balance, and elevate your physical and energetic body.

Cold Water Immersion

Just as saunas help cleanse the body and mind, cold water immersion offers another powerful way to elevate your physical and mental state. Cold water immersion, also known as cold water therapy, involves intentionally exposing your body to cold water for a set time period. This practice, much like breathwork, has been shown to positively impact both your physical and mental health by stimulating the nervous system, improving circulation, and enhancing mental resilience. I started cold water therapy quite late, in my forties, but it's been a wonderful complement to the other practices.

One thing I've learned from my own cold water immersion practice (whether it's taking cold showers or ice baths) is that consistency is key. No matter where you are on your cold-water immersion journey, just be consistent with it. Some research suggests that around eleven minutes per week is the sweet spot for reaping maximum benefits, and naturally, one of the most common questions I get is, "How long do I need to do it for?" and "How cold does it need to be?"

In my opinion, it simply needs to be cold, but the more important factor is to listen to your body. A good starting point is to immerse yourself for thirty seconds to two minutes, and gradually increase that time. What really matters is doing it regularly and using what you already have at home (no need for fancy ice baths unless you want to). I didn't have an ice bath at home when I started, so I just used what I had on hand. A regular bath filled with cold water or a shower works perfectly. At the end of my daily shower, I simply turn the water to the coldest setting and let it run on me from the neck down. Over time, I worked my way up from thirty seconds to two minutes at the end of each shower.

This consistency was essential in helping me adjust and benefit from the practice. And here's something interesting (while the first few sessions were challenging and I really disliked the cold, something shifted). Over time, the initial discomfort turned into something almost pleasurable. I believe that's the endorphin release kicking in, transforming the cold into a refreshing, energizing experience.

Now, there are clear scientific benefits to this practice that tie into my experience. Cold water immersion can:

Improve Circulation: The cold constricts your blood vessels, and when you warm back up, they dilate, improving circulation. This can support cardiovascular health.

Reduce Inflammation: The cold helps reduce muscle

inflammation, which supports post-exercise recovery. I often felt this benefit for myself after a workout.

Enhance Immune Function: Some studies suggest cold exposure stimulates the immune system, helping to ward off illnesses.

Boost Mental Resilience: The mental strength required to stay in cold water translates into greater resilience in everyday life.

Release Endorphins: As I mentioned earlier, after consistently practicing, I began to feel a euphoric rush during my cold showers. This is the body's natural endorphins at work, reducing pain and boosting mood.

Incorporating Cold Water Immersion into Daily Life

Consistency is key, but so is being creative with how you get your cold exposure. If you enjoy hot saunas, consider combining hot and cold exposure, alternating between heat and cold. This combination is well-known in Scandinavian cultures, where saunas and cold plunges are a part of life.

Here in the UK, we're just catching up to the benefits of cold water therapy. Sauna culture has been around for a while, but the idea of cold exposure is still relatively new. In countries like Finland, alternating between the heat of a sauna and the cold of a plunge pool is a normal practice, promoting circulation, detoxification, and resilience.

In my experience, once I got past the initial resistance, cold water immersion became one of the highlights of my day. It's a practice that not only refreshes your body but also elevates your mental and emotional state. So, whether you're starting with thirty seconds or you're already doing longer sessions, just keep it consistent, and over time, you'll feel the shift from discomfort to deep benefit. There are various opinions on how long you should expose yourself to cold water, but it's essential to listen to your body and be mindful of how it feels and what it needs, gradually acclimating to the cold temperatures.

You don't even need a fancy ice bath if you don't have the means or space (you can use a shower, or even wild swimming in lakes, rivers, or the sea if you have safe access). Which nicely segues into the next high-vibrational practice: nature!

Nature Immersion

Nature, though not traditionally thought of as a practice, has earned its place on my list of high-vibrational practices precisely because of its abundance and accessibility. It's not something we need to "do" but something we need to be in. In today's modern world, with our fast-paced lives and technology-driven distractions, we've grown distant from the natural world (despite it being the most grounding, nourishing, and balancing force available to us).

Nature offers us the perfect opportunity to reconnect with our true selves and the divine system of which we are inherently a part. It reminds us of our place in the grand design and helps restore balance to our bodies and minds. The practice, then, is simply about making a conscious effort to regularly immerse ourselves in nature, giving ourselves permission to step away from our busy lives, and basking in the healing power of the natural world.

For me, personally, nature conjures up visions of forests and the sea (two opposing yet complementary environments that hold immense power to center and ground me). On one hand, I'm drawn to the damp, leafy freshness of a forest just after the rain, where the air is clean, and the scent of wet earth is thick. On the other hand, I picture the vastness of the ocean, its infinite power stretching to the horizon. Both of these landscapes, whether it's the green of the mountains or the deep blue of the sea, transport me to a place of deep calm and clarity.

When we immerse ourselves in nature, we naturally come back into alignment with our true selves. This state of calm and balance allows us to connect more deeply with our gifts, intuition, and the divine guidance that is always available to us. In this state, we are better able to access the clarity and wisdom that are often clouded by the chaos of daily life.

Forest Bathing

One simple way to experience this connection with nature is through the practice of forest bathing, which is not a literal bath but a mindful immersion in the forest's sights, sounds, and smells. Imagine the sense of peace you feel when soaking in a warm, aromatic bath (how your body relaxes and your mind quiets). Forest bathing is similar in that it involves fully immersing yourself in the environment (the forest), allowing nature to wash over you and cleanse your energy from the day.

It's a meditative experience, and unlike other activities that might involve a goal or purpose, the key to forest bathing is doing nothing (just being in the presence of nature). The simple act of wandering through the trees, feeling the earth underfoot, and breathing in the fresh air can have profound effects on your mental, emotional, and spiritual well-being.

Earthing

Another way to connect with nature's healing energy is through earthing, which involves walking barefoot on natural surfaces like grass, soil, or sand. This simple act of direct physical contact with the earth allows you to absorb the earth's natural vibrations, which can help restore balance to your body and mind. There's even science behind it (studies have shown that connecting to the earth in this way can help reduce inflammation, improve sleep, and regulate the nervous system).

When you're walking barefoot, you're not just connecting to the physical earth; you're tuning into its energetic field, grounding yourself, and releasing built-up stress. It's an effective way to return to your center and realign with the natural rhythms of life.

More Than Simply Being Outdoors

Both of these practices, forest bathing and earthing, are about more than simply being outdoors (they're about tapping into the ancient wisdom that nature holds). These experiences remind us that we are part of a greater system, one that always supports and helps us find our way back to balance.

If you're new to these practices, start simple. Take a walk in a nearby park or spend a few minutes barefoot in your garden. Leave your devices behind, quiet your mind, and let nature do the rest. The more you make time for these high-vibrational practices, the more connected you'll feel (to yourself, to the world around you, and to the divine).

I've been experimenting with nature in a really simple yet powerful way: within the first thirty minutes of waking up, I spend time outdoors. I've made it a habit to start my day with a morning walk, and the effects have been remarkable. This simple act of getting outdoors, moving my body, and being exposed to natural light has had an incredible impact on my sleep.

Before implementing this, I struggled with both falling asleep and staying asleep. But after adding this outdoor walk to my morning routine, my sleep dramatically improved. It's fascinating how something as simple as a walk outside can reset your body's natural rhythms and help you get your sleep back on track.

Many years ago, I had a lot going on in my life, and I wasn't meditating or practicing any of the methods I now recommend. This was before I fully understood how interconnected these practices are and the incredible impact they have on not just your physical health, but also your overall well-being, emotional balance, and creativity.

Now that I've trained in these techniques and experienced them firsthand, I'm a firm believer in the power of integrating them into a daily routine. They help me feel more grounded, more in tune with myself. And if you do the same, I promise you they will benefit you too.

Now that we've explored the power of nature, it's time to dive into another high-vibrational practice that's absolutely fundamental for your health and well-being: sleep.

Like breathing and nature, we tend to take sleeping for granted - consistent, quality sleep,

Sleep Optimization

In this final section, I want to focus on the importance of sleep as a high-vibrational practice. While I'm no expert in sleep science, I can speak from personal experience about the profound impact that poor-quality sleep has had on my life. From clouding my thinking and diminishing my focus and performance to affecting my overall health and mental well-being, a lack of sleep has always shown up in my life as a negative force.

We all know the general rule that adults should aim for seven to eight hours of sleep each night. The importance of this can't be overstated, though individual needs may vary; children and teenagers, for example, need more sleep than adults. But as an adult, that range, of seven to eight hours, is generally recommended for optimal functioning.

Sleep is a basic human need, just like eating or breathing, yet it's often the first thing we sacrifice when life gets busy. However, as I've learned, neglecting your sleep is one of the quickest ways to derail your health and well-being.

I once gave a presentation on the importance of sleep to a room full of busy personal assistants, and when preparing for it, I remember being struck by the sheer volume of research out there on how poor sleep can negatively affect nearly every aspect of your life (from cognitive function to physical health). You don't need to be a sleep expert to know this: when you don't get enough sleep, your mind, body, and the way you look pay the price.

Beauty Sleep Is a Real Thing

There's also truth to the idea of "beauty sleep." When your body has time to rest and repair itself during sleep, it shows on the outside. Your skin, hair, and overall appearance benefit when your body can carry out its natural restorative processes without disruption. So, yes (when you prioritize sleep, you do tend to look and feel better).

Circadian Rhythms and Sleep Patterns

Everyone has a natural circadian rhythm, an internal clock that regulates when you feel alert and when you feel sleepy. This rhythm governs your sleep-wake cycle and can vary from person to person. Some of us are morning people, while others are night owls, but understanding your own rhythm can help you optimize your sleep routine.

There are simple online tests you can take to identify your circadian archetype, which can help you better understand when you should be going to sleep for maximum benefit.

Tips for Better Sleep

Here are some of the practices that have personally helped me improve the quality of my sleep:

Consistency is Key: Going to bed and waking up at the same time each day helps regulate your internal clock. When you're consistent, your body knows when to expect sleep and when to wake up.

Bedtime Routine: I've found it incredibly helpful to have one. This might include winding down with a book, dimming the lights, journaling, meditating, or doing some light stretching to signal to my body that it's time to rest.

Limit Screen Time: I make a conscious effort to avoid screens at least an hour before bed. The blue light from phones and computers can trick your brain into thinking it's still daytime, which disrupts your ability to fall asleep.

Caffeine Cutoff: No caffeine after 2:00 pm. This ensures it's out of my system before bedtime.

Create a Sleep-Conducive Environment: I like my room to be dark, cool, and quiet. I've also invested in a high-quality mattress and pillow, which have made a huge difference in how I feel when I wake up. If your sleeping environment isn't comfortable, you're not setting yourself up for restorative sleep.

Morning Light Exposure: As I've already said, I've found that going for a walk shortly after waking up has helped regulate my sleep. Something about that early exposure to natural light helps reset your circadian rhythm and improves your ability to fall asleep later in the day.

Learning from Nature

If you need inspiration for improving your sleep, observe animals. My cats, for instance, have always been my "sleep mentors." They take naps throughout the day, conserving energy and resting whenever they feel the need. While we tend to think of sleep as happening at night, the reality is that rest can take many forms, and sometimes, a short power nap during the day can help restore your energy.

In summary, sleep made it into the six high-vibrational practices I wanted to include in this chapter because it's been such a foundational pillar of my own health and well-being. Whether through maintaining a consistent bedtime routine or making small changes like limiting caffeine intake and exposing myself to natural light, the quality of your sleep directly impacts the quality of your life (and I know from experience that it will be the same for you, too). Prioritizing restful, restorative sleep can transform not only your physical health but also your mental and emotional balance.

Choosing Your Path

With so many practices available, you might be wondering, Where do I even begin? Do I need all of them? The answer is simple: you don't.

Self-care is not about ticking every box or perfecting a routine. It's about choosing the practices that resonate with you right now, in this season of your life. Think of the practices in this chapter as invitations. Some will feel immediately natural. Others you may return to later.

If you are a complete beginner, start small. Choose one practice that feels accessible and enjoyable, maybe a morning walk in nature, a five-minute breath practice, or adding more colorful foods to your plate. Let it become a part of your rhythm. Once it feels natural, add another. Over time, you will build your own constellation of practices that support your energy and align with your truth.

What matters most is consistency, not perfection. One simple daily practice can shift your energy more than a scattered attempt at doing everything. Start where you are. Begin gently and let your body guide you, because it always knows what it needs.

Your Self-Care Practice Map

If you're a beginner, start small. Choose one practice that feels light and doable. This could be:

- A ten-minute morning walk in nature.
- Adding a green smoothie to your day.
- Three deep breaths before you go to sleep.

Your only goal is consistency. One small practice done daily will shift more than trying to do everything at once.

If you're ready for more, layer in balance. Once you feel steady with one practice, choose one from a different category to balance your system. For example:

- Pair movement (yoga, dance, or a workout) with stillness (meditation or rest).
- Pair nourishment (tailored nutrition) with expansion (cold water therapy or breathwork).

Balance is the key, not quantity.

If you're advanced, create a ritual ecosystem. As you deepen, you may find you naturally weave multiple practices into your life. This is not about having a rigid routine but creating a rhythm that feels nourishing and expansive. For example:

- Morning: movement + breathwork.

- Midday: conscious meal + short walk.

- Evening: digital detox + meditation or journaling.

Your practices become less of a "to-do" and more of a way of living (an ecosystem that sustains your energy and keeps you aligned).

You don't need to do everything at once. Start small. Build consistency. Let one practice root you in balance and presence. Over time, you'll find your practices weaving together into a life that feels harmonious, vibrant, and aligned.

With this foundation in place, you are ready for the next stage of your journey.

Closing Part Two: Awakening to Your True Self

You've traveled far in this section of the book. Together, we've undressed the roles, illusions, and survival patterns that once shaped your life. You've awakened to deeper truths, that you are not just the story you've been living, but the energy that precedes it. You've regained your connection to life's intelligence, felt what it means to surrender, and begun to experience life through a clearer, more authentic lens.

In this final chapter of Part Two, you discovered that self-care is more than tending to the surface of your life. It is a sacred act of alignment, that is, keeping your body, mind, and spirit clear enough to hold the frequency of who you truly are. Whether you choose one simple practice or create a full rhythm of daily rituals, the invitation is the same: care for your vessel so it can channel the intelligence and vitality of Source.

Where do you go from here?

Awakening is not the end of the path; it is the beginning of embodiment. Now that you've reclaimed your truth, it's time to live it. To align your reality with your energetic self. This is where the abstract becomes actual. Where the invisible becomes structural.

Part Three is where we move from awakening to alignment. This is where you begin to discover your original blueprint: your vision, values, purpose, and life on your highest timeline. It's where the energy you've remembered becomes the life you live, not in theory, but in action.

You didn't come here to escape life. You came to align with it and lead from the Life Intelligence itself.

You've awakened. Now it's time to align.

PART THREE:

ALIGN
ALIGN
ALIGN
ALIGN

Integration

Chapter 16:
Embodiment

The Work Of Alignment

Awakening is not the end of the path. It is the beginning of alignment and embodiment.

Alignment is the moment when awakening turns into a way of life. It is the point where your inner truth begins to shape your outer world.

You have undressed the roles that were never yours. You have awakened to the self beneath the layers. Now the question is: how will you live from this place? How will you align your life with the truth you have remembered?

Alignment means congruence. It means that who you are inside matches how you show up outside. It is the marriage of your deep intrinsic nature and structure, of vision and practice, of deep inner knowing and outer action.

Embodiment is the process that makes alignment real. To embody is to let your truth take form through your choices, habits, relationships, health, and work. Embodiment is how the Source moves through you in your daily life.

This part of the book will guide you through the alignment process. You will uncover your purpose, create a map for your life, design a sacred strategy, and choose aligned action every day. You will also meet the honest challenges of embodiment, including the watch-outs that can pull you off course, before seeing what it looks like to live undressed in every corner of your life.

Alignment is not about perfection. It is about congruence. It is the bridge between awakening and living, between clarity and congruence, between the self you have remembered and the life you are here to create.

What Alignment Is

Alignment is the point at which awakening stops being an idea and starts becoming a way of life. It is what happens when your inner truth begins to shape your outer world. Alignment is congruence. It is the place where what you believe, what you value, and who you know yourself to be are reflected in how you live.

You have already undressed the roles that were never yours. You have awakened to the deeper self beneath the layers. Now comes the question that will define the rest of your journey: how will you live this truth?

Alignment is not abstract. It is practical. It reveals itself in how you eat and rest, how you show up in your relationships, how you use your voice, how you work and create, how you handle money, and how you choose to spend your time. Every choice either reflects alignment or pulls you back into misalignment.

Why Alignment Matters

Without alignment, awakening will always feel incomplete. You can see clearly and still live in conflict with what you see. You can know the truth and still avoid embodying it. You can hold awareness and still repeat the same old patterns.

Many people reach awakening and assume they have arrived. They experience clarity and mistake it for completion. But insight alone does not transform a life. Alignment is what closes the gap between remembering your truth and living it.

In my own journey, I began to notice how often people get stuck here. Once you have awakened, you cannot go back to your old life. You cannot slip comfortably into performance, into the corporate treadmill, or into the systems you once inhabited. You see through it all, and you cannot unsee it. Yet what often follows is not purpose, but drift.

I have watched people reach awakening and then float. They step out of their old identities, but without a new framework, they are left in limbo. They live very much in the moment, which sounds noble, but often it is not sustainable. Many become unanchored, financially unstable, or disconnected from the greater purpose that their essential self longs to express.

This is where I believe many spiritual teachings stop short. They take you as far as awakening and then leave you there, wide-eyed but unequipped. They tell you presence is enough, but they do not help you rebuild your life around the truth you have seen. And that can be dangerous. Without direction, awakening can become another form of escape. Without structure, the desire to change your whole life after awakening can lead to collapse.

This is why alignment matters. Alignment is what takes awakening out of the void and sets you back on a path. It gives you a framework for your new life. It gives structure to your vision, purpose to your daily choices, and clarity to your next steps. It ensures that awakening is not just an inner shift, but the beginning of an outer transformation.

Alignment matters because it is the integration of awakening. It is the stage where vision becomes structure, where purpose becomes practice, where the life intelligence is expressed through you in the way you live each day. Without alignment, awakening remains a moment. With alignment, it becomes a way of being.

The Cost of Misalignment

If you stop short of alignment, the life you live will not match the truth you carry. You will know who you are, but still act against it. You will feel the friction of clarity without congruence. This gap creates exhaustion, disconnection, and frustration.

Misalignment shows up in many forms. It shows up as staying in relationships that drain you, even though you know your worth. It shows up as forcing your body through cycles of depletion, even though you know it needs care. It shows up as building a career that looks successful but feels empty inside. Misalignment is the feeling of betraying yourself while fully aware that you are doing it.

The cost of misalignment ripples outward into your health, your purpose, your relationships, and your contribution. When you live against your truth, the people around you feel the dissonance. The life you are building on the outside becomes hollow because it is not aligned with the truth on the inside.

The Promise of Embodiment

Embodiment is the way through. To embody is to let your truth take form. It is how alignment moves from concept to reality. Embodiment makes awakening sustainable by rooting awareness in the body, in practice, and in action.

Embodiment is not about perfection. It is about congruence. It is about choosing, again and again, to let the life you live match the truth you know. It is not a one-time event but a rhythm you cultivate. Some days you will feel fully aligned, other days you will notice yourself slipping out of it. The promise of embodiment is that you can always return. Alignment is never lost. It is only remembered and practiced.

When you live embodied, you discover a new kind of freedom. You no longer need to hold awareness tightly, because it naturally moves with you. You no longer need to force purpose, because it expresses itself through your choices. You no longer live in conflict with yourself because your inner and outer lives are speaking the same language.

Embodiment is the real work of alignment. It is the bridge between awakening and transformation, between clarity and congruence. It is what allows life intelligence to move through you, as you, in the world. For an alignment check, go to the Undressed playbook. https://www.gemdentith.com/playbook

Chapter 17:

Purpose

Remembering Why You're Here, and What Truly Matters

"In the quantum field, every possibility exists in a state of potential, waiting to be observed and brought into reality. By tapping into the original blueprint of your soul, you align with the purest form of this potential, allowing you to manifest a life that resonates with the highest frequencies of the universe."

— Dr. Amit Goswami, Quantum Physicist and Author

Your original blueprint refers to the divine, perfect template or design of your unique expression, encoded with your highest potential, purpose, and unique gifts.

This is the manifestation of Life Intelligence manifesting through you. It's such an important energy to explore, I wanted to dedicate an entire chapter to it.

Over the course of this lifetime and others, and through various experiences, this original life plan, encoded in Life Intelligence, is what I'm calling a blueprint. The journey of activating your original blueprint is about reconnecting with this divine template, bringing it to the forefront of your mind so that you can realign yourself with your divine function.

To activate your original blueprint, the key lies in aligning your consciousness with life intelligence (Universal Intelligence), the same intelligence that holds the blueprint for all living creations, including your own.

As you attune more fully, you surrender to the energies of source to flow through you as a pure expression of universal creation. You become a vessel through which the supreme energy manifests, functioning as an integral part of the universal mind. In this state, you are not merely a passive observer of life but an active participant in the divine process of creation.

In this chapter, we'll use practices to first attune you to the flow of life and then tap into life intelligence so you can create a clear, actionable, and transformative plan for living your best life aligned with your true nature's original blueprint.

Why You Shouldn't Miss This Step

Developing a strong connection to life intelligence provides you with your original blueprint (a realized intrinsic purpose) that serves as an internal compass, guiding your decisions and actions. This connection is not only about aligning with a higher purpose but also about unlocking your full potential, allowing every aspect of your life to evolve and expand in harmony with the universe's natural tendency toward growth.

In the previous activation, we focused on surrendering to inner guidance, listening to the subtle stirrings of inherent qualities, passions, and aligned desires within you (signs that life intelligence is guiding you toward your true purpose). Now, we will deepen this communication with Universal Intelligence, enabling you to see your divine blueprint with renewed clarity. This chapter is about envisioning and manifesting the two-point-zero version of yourself, your higher ideal, true self, in every area of your life.

Aligning with The Universe

Alignment serves as a shorthand for aligning with universal life intelligence. The deeper intelligence of all life, and the code keeper that holds the key to your life's purpose, giving it meaning and a function to fulfill in this lifetime.

Before you can activate your original blueprint (the unique life path or purpose encoded within your intrinsic nature), you must first align your awareness with the energy of the universe. This has been the book's objective to date.

This alignment is crucial because it opens channels of communication with Life Intelligence, enabling you to receive the insights, guidance, and "downloads" necessary to know, understand, and live your highest purpose. This alignment is essential for unlocking and activating your unique, original life plan, the one that resonates with the highest vibrations and the most grounded, honest, ideal version of you.

Alignment serves as the foundation for activation. It involves attuning the body, mind, and spirit to the higher frequencies of the universe, thereby making you receptive to the subtle, yet powerful, signals from Life Intelligence. Without this alignment, it would be difficult, if not impossible, to access the deeper layers of your life's blueprint and the specific guidance needed to manifest it in the physical world.

As you align with the universe and the essential oneness of all existence, your body-mind system becomes a finely tuned instrument, emitting a frequency that resonates with the universe. In this state of attunement, you become receptive to the subtle vibrations of Life Intelligence (much like a radio receiver tuning into a specific station).

You might have heard people talk about being "open to receive." If you want to know what your life plan should be, it's not about using your analytical mind to think through the myriad of options; it's about being open enough to truly commune with the universe, making you more sensitive to the guidance and insights it offers.

Likewise, to manifest anything in your life, it's not just about telling yourself or the universe that you're ready. It's about showing it by attuning your body and mind to the universe's frequency.

What's clear to me is that you first need to align with the universe by realizing with the three universal energies, which naturally shift your awareness to a state beyond personal thought (a state of surrender and flow where interfering thoughts are absent). Adding practices such as breathwork, meditation, and moments of silence to this practice further enhances clarity. Just as water becomes clear when it is still, so too does your mind. In this stillness, your mind is primed for clearer vision as you move towards activating the original blueprint. Breathwork, coupled with submitting to the universal energies and spending time in silence, tunes your body and mind to be fully receptive to the insights and realizations that arise.

Only when you are in this state of receptivity can you receive downloads from life intelligence and access your soul's innate records (an ethereal library of all your energetic self's experiences and knowledge).

I'd like to invite you to undergo an alignment session with me now. Find a comfortable place to begin this alignment, and we'll begin.

Using Breathwork and Silence to Attune with the Universe

One of the simplest ways to align with the deeper intelligence and realize your original blueprint is to use the breath as a tool to get into your body and the present moment, and then as a gateway back to alignment.

If you find that your system is in overdrive and you have lost connection with your true, original self, it indicates that your thoughts are obscuring your true nature and purpose, much like how clouds obscure the sun on a cloudy day. However, your original nature, like the sun, is always present (it is just temporarily obscured). It is that simple. So, when you feel overwhelmed by "cloudy weather," when your mind is overactive, just use this practice as a gateway back to your original self.

I have recorded a Breath Awareness Inner Exercise: The Gateway to Alignment Practice. I suggest you do this now before reading on. Visit: https://www.gemdentith.com/playbook This practice plays a crucial role in regulating your body's nervous system, bringing it back into balance and into alignment.

Now that you are primed and aligned with the universe, you are ready to communicate with it, to receive your original blueprint, and to come to know your life plan.

Communing with Universal Intelligence

Unlike human communication, which primarily relies on words, communication with Life Intelligence occurs through vibration rather than language.

Think about the last time you walked into a room and immediately sensed a shift in energy. You didn't need anyone to tell you what was happening (you felt it). This is because the universe communicates in vibrations, and so do you, whether you realize it or not.

When you operate from a higher plane, such as interpersonal

or transpersonal awareness, you naturally transcend the lower planes of being and the lower emotions associated with the physical and mental planes of reality (emotions like fear, anger, and frustration). Instead, you align with the higher frequency vibrations that Life Intelligence resonates with.

Operating from a state of Transpersonal Awareness automatically tunes you into the inherent high-frequency emotions of joy, contentment, gratitude, and appreciation. These emotions are not just feelings; they are vibrational states that align you with the frequency of the universe.

Just as a radio dial tunes into different frequencies to pick up various stations, your state of awareness and emotional frequency determine the "station" of your life experience. When you elevate your frequency, you're essentially tuning into the higher vibrations of Life Intelligence, opening the channels for clear communication and guidance.

This vibrational communication is how you connect with your divine blueprint and purpose. By raising your vibration and aligning with these higher frequencies, you attune yourself to the messages and insights that Life Intelligence continually broadcasts. These insights are subtle but powerful, guiding you toward your true path and helping you fulfill your highest potential.

Now, to commune with the universe, I'm going to ask you to repeat The Gateway to Alignment Practice, and then I invite you to ask for guidance by listening to the Visualization Exercise: Exploring Your Authentic Life Purpose. For the recording of this, visit https://www.gemdentith.com/playbook

How do I know if I'm aligned?

Apart from feeling in a state of flow and joy, when you are aligned with Life Intelligence, you will start noticing things you hadn't noticed before. Doors that were previously closed will begin to open, and people around you may start treating you differently. You will find yourself aligning with the natural flow of life, blocking out distractions with laser focus on what needs to be done. While alignment doesn't eradicate challenges, it changes how you approach them. Instead of reacting, you respond from a higher perspective, with more wisdom and grace.

Remember, this is not a one-time exercise. To keep your connection with Life Intelligence strong and to stay aligned with your divine blueprint, create a sacred space or ritual for this practice. Whether it's lighting a candle, sitting in a specific spot, or beginning with a few deep breaths, this daily ritual will anchor you in your practice and deepen your connection over time. Make this practice a part of your daily routine for the next thirty days until your purpose is clear. As you practice daily, affirm: 'I am aligned with my highest purpose. I trust the universe to guide me on my path.' These affirmations will strengthen your connection to your divine purpose. Consistency with this purpose-alignment practice will deepen your connection with the universe, making it easier to receive guidance and live in accordance with your highest plan.

As you conclude this session, take a moment to thank the universe for the guidance received. Close with a deep breath, feeling gratitude for the clarity and connection that is growing within you. Before you go on with the rest of this chapter, you might need to put the book down for a day or two to allow the images, messages, and visions to marinate. Just like a good marinade enhances the flavor of food over time, letting these insights sit and absorb will deepen their impact, allowing them to fully infuse your understanding.

Declare Your Life Assignment

Your life's purpose is a powerful declaration of your core assignment and the unique contribution you are meant to actualize in this lifetime. It serves as your guiding star, helping you stay aligned, focused, and fulfilled. Building on what you've realized from previous chapters, your new beliefs, values, your original self and its inherent qualities, characteristics, and traits, you'll want to move you from understanding who you are at your core to why you are here. Your why! Why you exist, what you'll do in this lifetime, your purpose, and whom you'll serve,

In the last exercise, where you asked for guidance on your life purpose, you might have clarity on what this is for you. Now we want to craft your insights into a statement, which will become your life purpose statement.

"The purpose of my original true self is to [create/bring/offer/contribute] [specific impact or change] by [how you will do it through your unique gifts, talents, or actions], guided by [your core values that drive this mission]."

I have created a worksheet in your Playbook for this exercise. Head to: https://www.gemdentith.com/playbook to record your life purpose.

Now that you have some clarity on your life purpose and how life intelligence is to manifest through you. Next, I'll guide you through your inner values.

Your Intrinsic Values: The Compass That Guides You

If a purpose serves as your guiding light, intrinsic values act as the compass that helps to shape your decisions and actions. They serve as guiding principles that inform your choice, playing a crucial role in keeping you focused on the life you are to create. Values provide a framework for aligning your behaviors with what truly matters to you and help you navigate through various life situations and challenges without getting too distracted.

In this section, I will guide you through an activation exercise to help you understand your values. With your original nature and its purpose at the forefront of your mind, it is time to explore how the universal intelligence seeks to express itself through you, shaping your new value system.

When your values align with your life purpose, they guide you toward your authentic self and aspirations. Your core values serve as the compass that guides your life, shaping your beliefs, attitudes, and motivations. They help you on a more superficial level to prioritize what is important to you and make choices that are in alignment with your true nature.

To activate your values, go to the worksheet in your Playbook for this exercise, head to https://www.gemdentith.com/playbook

Now that you know who you are, your life assignment, and your core values, we can move to the next stage: creating your life plan.

Essential Insights

In this chapter, you've reconnected with the key energetic building blocks for the blueprint of your higher self (your true design, your true function). You've aligned with the frequencies of life intelligence, opened to your life purpose, and received insight into the deeper "why" behind your existence. You've explored what it means to surrender your analytical mind and instead attune to the guidance flowing from the deeper wisdom of innate intelligence.

You've also clarified your intrinsic values (the compass that keeps you rooted in who you truly are). These values are not abstract ideas. They shape your path, your relationships, your voice, and your way of moving through the world.

You now carry a clearer sense of what wants to be birthed through you (and what your life is meant to serve).

Key Takeaways

- Your original life blueprint holds the memory of your life purpose and assignment. It is always there, even when obscured by the noise of life.

- True alignment begins not with effort, but with attunement (allowing yourself to commune with Life Intelligence beyond language).

- Emotions like joy, gratitude, and devotion raise your frequency and deepen your receptivity to life's guidance.

- Your life purpose and core values provide a North Star. When followed, they help you make decisions that honor your true self.

- Breathwork, stillness, and daily energy rituals can act as gateways to remembering and embodying your highest truth.

Journal Prompts

- What message did I receive from Life Intelligence about my life assignment?

- What values emerged that feel non-negotiable to who I truly am?

- In what ways have I been living out of alignment with my original blueprint?

- What does it feel like in my body to be fully aligned

with my life purpose?

Action Plan

- Write your life purpose statement and place it somewhere visible.

- Create a sacred space for daily attunement (a corner, a candle, an altar, a breath ritual).

- Begin each morning with the affirmation: "I am aligned with my highest path. I receive with ease and act with clarity."

- Read your values aloud at the start or end of each day to anchor into them.

Final Thought

You now know who you are, why you are here, and what truly matters to you.

You are no longer chasing purpose (you are remembering it, living it, becoming it).

Now that your blueprint has been activated, the next step is to give it structure (to shape the vision you've seen into a life that reflects it in every dimension). In the next chapter, we'll begin that sacred process of translating your true purpose into structure. You'll create your own map (a living guide for designing a life in full alignment with your highest truth).

Let's build the bridge between your inner awakening and your outer reality.

Chapter 18:

The Map

Bringing Your Soul Assignment to Life, One Dimension at a Time

Just like a well-run business has a business plan, a clear vision, and defined milestones, your life needs a structure to hold your energetic expansion. Without a conscious framework, it's all too easy to drift, struggle to sustain what you are building, feel pulled in a hundred directions, or pour your energy into the wrong places.

You might have the best intentions. You might even know exactly why you're here. But without the scaffolding to hold that purpose: the habits, the structures, the grounded actions that bring it to life, things start to slip through the cracks. Even the brightest inspiration fades without a container to sustain it. When it does, discipline dissolves. The vision that once burned fiercely begins to blur. You show up in one area and fall behind in another, pulled between your soul's rhythm and the world's noise. Over time, that gap between who you are and how you're living stretches into exhaustion, confusion, and quiet misalignment. You feel inspired but inconsistent. Awake but unanchored. I know this because I've lived it.

Alignment doesn't happen by happy accident. It's by conscious design.

The most fulfilled, vibrant, magnetic people I've ever met didn't just "follow their intuition" (they built a life around it). They structured their days, energy, priorities, and environment to support the energy required to actualize their life's purpose.

That's what this chapter is about.

It's not about falling back into control and micromanaging every corner of your life. It's more about coming into coherence so you can stay on course. It's about creating a deeply congruent, fully integrated map that guides every dimension of your being: your work, your relationships, your health, your environment, your finances, your growth, and your purpose.

This isn't a rigid checklist. It's not some productivity hack or goal-setting worksheet. It's a living document that reflects your life purpose, with the flexibility to evolve as you do.

In the next few pages, you'll be guided through a process that brings structure to your life vision. You'll assess where you are now, define where you want to be, and begin mapping out how to close the gap across Nine Dimensions of Alignment.

You're not just designing your goals. You're co-creating with the deep intelligence within, so you can start the process of living in true alignment.

Nine Dimensions of Alignment

Your life is never just about one or two areas, such as work and family. To be truly fulfilled, you need to address all aspects that contribute to a balanced and harmonious life. Having been a coach for over two decades, I've realized that the happiest and most successful people I've encountered are those who are balanced and aligned across nine core dimensions. These dimensions, which I categorize as alignment with self, others, and things, are as follows:

Alignment with Self: Source, Self, Sustenance, and Skills

Alignment with Others: Service, Social

Alignment with Things: Security, Scene, Safaris

These aspects of alignment with self, others, and things serve as a foundation for understanding and shaping your authentic path. By exploring these dimensions, you can gain a clearer sense of your passions, values, and goals, enabling you to craft a life vision that encompasses your authentic self and aligns with your true nature. Below, these dimensions are listed and described in detail. As you read through each description, you will score each one in terms of how abundant and how fully expressed and aligned your purpose and values are within these dimensions.

Exercise: How Aligned Are You: 9Ss' of Alignment Score Card

How to Score Each Dimension: First, you score one to five, where one equals not very aligned, five equals most aligned. You will add your current score and your ideal score, then note what you can do to move it closer to your ideal score. After this exercise, we will deepen this into your subconscious with a life plan activation.

The First Dimension: Source Alignment

At the foundational level, when you align with the deeper intelligence of life (life intelligence), you gain clarity about who you are, how the world works, and your place within it. From this awareness, you understand your purpose and see how life itself is guiding you. You start to notice when you are connected and when you are not, and how to return to alignment. From this place, you harness a deeper intelligence in all that you do, confident that life is always opening new doors and moving you toward something better. Connection with this intelligence unlocks your creativity, resourcefulness, and unique genius. And when you live from that connection, you experience a steady flow of peace, knowing life is always working for your growth.

Score where you are today: Today's score:

Now score where you'd like to be: Ideal score:

What can you do today to move into greater alignment?

The Second Dimension: Soul Self Alignment

This dimension focuses on the authentic alignment of your original self with the clarity you need to serve at the next level of being, as a human in service to universal intelligence. When you gain full self-alignment, you have a clear vision in your mind's eye of how you need to show up, including your physical appearance, as well as the visual, verbal, and emotional expressions of your original self. With full self-alignment, you are not only clear about your true values, but you also behave in accordance with them at all times. You realize that your authentic self is your most expressive self, like your most expressive three-year-old version of you. It is the self that is a creator, not a consumer, one that can only give value as its inherent nature is to be of service to others. One that needs to be known and heard so that it can share its gifts with others at a level of magnitude only the universe can know. In this dimension, you have full integrity; your inner values, characteristics, and intentions align with your external expression. There is total congruence between who you say you are and how others experience you. In other words, you 'walk the talk.' As a result, your confidence is magnified, and you become a role model for others. By creating full alignment in this dimension, you are honest with yourself, you know how your essential self inherently feels, and you feel into this now, not later. You don't bluff alignment. You have a level of self-awareness that you know you can move into greater alignment by making small changes now, raising your presence, influence, and credibility in the most authentic way possible, just by being more of the real you.

Score where you are today: Today's score:

Now score where you'd like to be: Ideal score:

What can you do today to move into greater alignment?

The Third Dimension: Service Alignment

This dimension encompasses how you serve humanity and contribute to the planet's health through your work, whether you run your own company or work within a professional setup. Being in full-service alignment means you know who you serve and the value you provide, and you are clear on where you need to take your career or business to make the greatest positive impact on people and the planet, while also making a profit. When fully in service alignment, you live by the triple bottom line, where profit is important, but so is social impact and the planet's health. You have inspired goals and objectives, and clear results and targets. You are clear on who your mentors are or need to be, and you have a path to realize your service. You know how you are programmed for service; this gives you purpose now, and you feel into this now, not later. You know you need inner alignment first before you can go out into the world and make it happen.

Score where you are today: Today's score:

Now score where you'd like to be: Ideal score:

What can you do today to move into greater alignment?

The Fourth Dimension: Skill Alignment

This dimension is about ensuring you have the required capabilities needed to realize your life purpose. When you are in full skill alignment, it means you are taking full responsibility for your own learning curriculum. This dimension requires you to conduct an honest skills and competency audit of where you are now versus the skills you might require to fulfill your life's purpose. It's one thing to know your purpose, and another to realize you don't yet have the knowledge or skill capability to realize it. You don't need to be the finished garment yet, but for full skill alignment, you need a plan to fill in your skill gaps. Before jumping straight into action mode, first, visualize yourself competently doing what you see yourself doing. And then get radically honest with yourself about which skills you need to hone to realize your visualized potential. It's all too common that people get stuck in indecision, without the necessary tools or experience to move forward. Having been a change consultant for over a decade, I know there are steps you need to go through to successfully change. Skill-building is one of them. The most successful people I know are lifelong learners. They have clear goals and a clear learning curriculum for the skills they need to learn to fulfill their life's purpose. They also carve out time every day to learn those skills. They know they are built to learn, and that knowing gives them confidence. Growth no longer feels like pressure; it feels like possibility. They trust their capacity to evolve, to absorb, to adapt.

Score where you are today: Today's score:

Now score where you'd like to be: Ideal score:

What can you do today to move into greater alignment?

The Fifth Dimension: Sustenance Alignment

The fifth dimension refers to sustenance alignment. Sustenance is considered the key to priming and fueling your mind and body, so they can fulfill their duty on your journey to fulfill your life purpose. This dimension considers your health: physical, mental, and emotional. It's crucial to prime the mind and body to perform any task you need it to perform. For example, if your purpose is to lead people on expeditions and you're significantly overweight and smoke heavily, you're not in alignment. It is as simple as that. To be fully aligned with the sustenance dimension, you have a plan to fuel your body-mind system with the nourishment and routine that support its aim. When you are in sustenance alignment, have a clear vision of what your exercise routine, nutrition, sleep schedule, and nervous system regulation practices need to be to ensure that your body-mind vessel is attuned and aligned to ensure it keeps in steady communication with universal intelligence and also keeps its hormones and emotions in balance. With sustenance alignment, you'll have clear objectives, key results, and a plan that supports your purpose. You'll also know that you have access to abundant health now, and you feel into this now, not later. You know that to attune with universal intelligence, you'll need to keep your body vessel free of chemicals and toxins so that the energy can flow through you more easily.

Score where you are today: Today's score:

Now score where you'd like to be: Ideal score:

What can you do today to move into greater alignment?

The Sixth Dimension: Social Alignment

Social alignment is about the relationships in your life and re-envisioning which presences in your circle keep you aligned with your purpose. Your circle includes intimate partners, friends, family, peers, mentors, and community. In this area, you'll assess your relationships to see which ones support your purpose and which ones drain or distract from it.

Here you'll also begin to envision your ideal aligned relationships, set clear goals, and invest time in nurturing them in balanced, sustainable ways. People who score highly in this dimension feel abundant in their relationships now, rather than chasing fulfillment somewhere in the future. They're nourished by the connection that already exists. They feel full, present, grateful, trusting, fully supported, expressed, and open with others. They know that everyone is a reflection of life intelligence energy, and that everyone is in their life for a deeper purpose: to learn a life lesson by fully embodying one of life's incumbent qualities. They accept everyone as they are and understand the power of possibilities of every connection.

Score where you are today: Today's score:

Now score where you'd like to be: Ideal score:

What can you do today to move into greater alignment?

The Seventh Dimension: Scene Alignment

This dimension relates to your environment (your physical space and surroundings) and whether they are attuned to your life's purpose. By envisioning the kind of environment that supports you, and creating a clear plan to bring elements of that vision into your present reality, you increase your sense of alignment.

Being aligned with your surroundings doesn't always mean moving house or making dramatic changes. For some, it does, but for many, it's about inviting in what you need to bring your current environment into harmony with your inner vision. It could be as simple as rearranging your bedroom to catch the morning light, decluttering a space, or making room for objects that uplift you.

People who thrive in this dimension also tend to feel called toward nature (whether it's walking by water, being in a forest, or simply tending their own garden). They connect with their immediate environment in the present moment, not postponing it for later. They care for their space intentionally, recognizing that how they treat their environment reflects how they treat themselves.

Even small, mindful changes can shift this alignment. When you take care of your surroundings, they, in turn, take care of you.

Even making tiny changes now can increase your scene alignment score.

Score where you are today: Today's score:

Now score where you'd like to be: Ideal score:

What can you do today to move into greater alignment?

The Eighth Dimension: Safari Alignment

This dimension is about immersing yourself in the experiences that will deepen your aliveness and knowledge. When your experiences align with your purpose, you expand your spirit and align yourself with it. It's like a perpetual cycle. To obtain greater safari alignment, you want to experience places and go on adventures that open you up from the inside out. Often, before you even consider experiences as a key dimension to fulfilling your overall life purpose, you might be someone who, every year, goes to the same holiday destination and each time, says that next year we'll do something different, more fulfilling, but you often don't follow through, as it can take planning or just choosing differently. To get into alignment, envision all the wonderful places on your bucket list and give yourself permission to go and do them, as it will further deepen your growth. You'll want to set dates and keep your commitments to align your adventures with your purpose. You will see how being in greater safari alignment can also enhance the social dimension, where you'll naturally circulate with others walking a similar path as you.

Score where you are today: Today's score:

Now score where you'd like to be: Ideal score:

What can you do today to move into greater alignment:

The Ninth Dimension: Stability Alignment

The security dimension refers to your finances and investments. Financial literacy is critical. Paying attention to your financial needs in the short, medium, and long term, and then building the financially stable foundation you need to fulfill your purpose, is essential to scoring highly in the stability dimension. Too often, people who experience a spiritual awakening neglect their financial needs because they haven't found a way to live in the modern world after realizing their spiritual self. However, unless you want to be begging on the streets or bartering your way through life, you need to be mindful about putting in place the financial framework that aligns with the authentic life you are building. Getting fully aligned in the financial dimension is about securing your future as an independent person. This means investing in your future, investing in others, and investing in the now. Being in full alignment means you have a financial plan that supports the life you are building. Often, you might need to look at your beliefs around money and start by reframing money as pure energy. It's an energy exchange for the value you provide. Like energy, money is abundant; you just need to know the principles of wealth creation to create more of it. Like you need to understand the principles of energy to produce higher-quality energy, see money as a pure energy exchange, and make small changes or plans now, will put you into more secure alignment.

Score where you are today: Today's score:

Now score where you'd like to be: Ideal score:

What can you do today to move into greater alignment?

If you can see it and feel it, you are experiencing it, you are living it. This is what I strongly believe, when you truly embody what you deeply desire at a deep level, not because it is something you need, but what wants to come though as it's the nature of who you are and is your divine destiny, then all you need to do is move the old self and all the old resistance that's getting in the way, out of the way, then the real you will naturally want to pour through you, it's inevitable. Then you can embody your true self and upgrade your identity.

Activate the Vision for Your Life Plan

With the messages and insights from the wisdom carried in deeper intelligence and knowledge about the nine key dimensions of a holistically aligned life geared to enable you to fulfill your life's purpose, we will expand this further with an activation exercise designed to tap into your creative imagination and bring forth a vivid image of all nine dimensions.

As you visualize each dimension, see your original, confident, and competent original self, fully immersed in the experience. Engage your senses and emotions to create a vivid image of your destined reality, the reality that is happening now. By engaging your senses and emotions, you can paint a detailed picture of what your most powerful you looks and feels like, the strategy for this area, and a high-level plan.

Repeat this exercise as many times as you feel you need more clarity. When I was pulling down my blueprint, I would repeat this exercise daily to see how much more information and clarity would come through.

As you complete this journey of activating your original blueprint, remember that this process is ongoing. Just as the universe is in constant flux, so too is your path to alignment and fulfillment. The practices and exercises in this chapter are tools you can return to whenever you need to realign with your divine purpose or gain more clarity on your purpose.

Your original blueprint is a living, breathing template of your highest potential, and it will continue to unfold as you deepen your connection with Universal Intelligence. By staying attuned to life intelligence itself and consistently applying the principles of alignment, you empower yourself to live authentically, with purpose, and profound impact.

Take with you the understanding that alignment is not a destination but a way of living. As you move forward, carry your life purpose statement close to your heart, and let your values guide you. Trust in the process, knowing that every step you take brings you closer to embodying your highest self and fulfilling your life's divine purpose.

Be patient with yourself and allow the insights and visions to integrate fully. The universe has a way of revealing the path at the right time, and your continued practice will ensure that you remain open to receiving this guidance.

To begin this activation, "Activate the Vision for Your Life Plan," head to https://www.gemdentith.com/playbook

Essential Insights

This chapter gave you the structure your life purpose needs to materialize in the world.

By working through the nine Dimensions of Alignment, you created a map (The Living Blueprint) that reflects your truth across every area of your life: from your body to your bank account, your purpose to your people, your inner clarity to your outer environments.

Alignment isn't about perfection. It's about coherence. And coherence comes when your thoughts, values, and actions flow in the same direction.

Now that you've activated your original blueprint, this chapter gave you the tools to live it (with clarity, focus, and depth). As you begin to walk this path, your life will begin to mirror the frequency of your in-built design. You'll feel it in your energy. You'll see it in your relationships. You'll know it in your results.

This is the sacred return to self. A life no longer designed by old patterns or external pressures, but a life authored by life intelligence, expressed through your limitless life force.

Chapter 19:
Living Document

Building the Bridge from Vision to Reality

By now, you've remembered who you really are. You've explored the deeper dimensions of your life's purpose, mapped that across the 9 dimensions of alignment, and felt into what alignment actually looks and feels like across each one.

But here's where most people get stuck. They have the vision. It's anchored and it's activated. But they never give it form. It stays in their head, never translating what they've seen, felt, or heard into something they can actually build their life around. And so the wisdom drifts away, forgotten in the noise of the everyday.

This is where structure becomes sacred. You need somewhere to put the insight. You need something that holds the frequency of your in-built energetic design so you can return to it again and again. You need a container that supports the vision (not suffocates it). Something that doesn't box you in, but keeps you tethered to your truth when the winds of life try to pull you off course.

That's what this chapter is about. The Living Blueprint isn't just a worksheet or a one-off exercise. It's a life-aligned design system. A way to take your purpose, your values, and your vision, and everything you've discovered through the last chapter, and shape it into something real. Something balanced, coherent, and visual. Because your energy wants to be lived.

In this chapter, I'll show you how to work with the blueprint in a way that's intuitive, empowering, and grounded in reality. Not only will it help you stay aligned, it will become your compass in times of confusion. Your touchstone when you feel you need a bit more anchoring. It's a structure for embodying your insights, and for sustaining presence when distractions come your way.

Why You Need Structure When You're Aligning

One thing I've noticed (both in myself and with the people I work with) is that during a period of spiritual awakening, we can easily fall into the idea that we only need to surrender and "let life lead you." We hear messages like "trust the process" or "follow the flow," and while those sound beautiful and, at a fundamental level, suggest that everything is always working out for you, because you're always learning valuable lessons from every experience you encounter, these statements can sometimes be misleading. Or at the very least, incomplete.

Because if you're anything like me, when you're highly attuned or deeply open, you're also more energetically porous. Your system can become sensitive, and our focus can become fragmented. And unless there's a conscious anchor in place, a reference point for where your energy is destined to go, you can get pulled into too many different projects, and your life force energy can start to feel scattered.

This is why I created the Living Blueprint. Not just to know your truth, but to stay aligned with it enough so that you start to live it out, so that it materializes into lived experience rather than pure fantasy.

I've found that without a clear, coherent container to hold your vision, your attention will drift. It happens to almost everybody. In the beginning, more so, because only you know your truth, because you may not have said it out loud, and because you're not living it yet. Therefore, in the early stages of realignment, your old life will most probably still have a tiny pull on you. Or at least someone in your life will still get you doing things you know deep down you don't want to be doing anymore. So, you'll end up saying yes to things that don't serve you. You'll take on energy that isn't yours, and you'll forget the very thing you remembered so clearly only days (or even hours) ago.

For me, even to this day, the blueprint has become something I return to whenever I feel I'm being pulled off track. It's not just a visual tool; it's an energetic one. It keeps my consciousness on track. It keeps me from leaking my energy into things that dilute or distort who I truly am. It reminds me what matters, what I'm building, and where I'm meant to direct my energy next.

It's about staying clear. Because clarity is power, and your purpose can't manifest if you're not focused.

Introducing the Living Document

The Living Document is a sacred structure, a deeply rooted framework that gives form to everything you've uncovered on this journey so far. Your purpose, your life assignment, your values, the qualities you are embodying, and your vision across the 9 dimensions of alignment. Everything is held here. This is where your inner clarity becomes outer direction, where you move from the inner knowing of what you deeply desire to embody it.

I call it a Living Document because that's exactly what it is: alive. Flexible. Evolving as you evolve. It's not about creating a perfect plan; it's about giving your newfound clarity a home outside your head, like a mirror, a map, and a rhythm that keeps you aligned.

Here's the essence of how it works:

- At the top, you anchor your life purpose statement, vision, values, and core jewels (the qualities of your most authentic self that you are working to align with more).

- Then, you explore what alignment looks like across the nine dimensions of your life.

- You get radically honest about your current reality, name the gap, and begin to see the stepping stones that will carry you forward.

- From there, you create seasonal strategies (clear, life-aligned focus areas for the next chapter)

That's the practice, not perfection, but presence. Not rigid plans, but living alignment.

This is one of the most powerful embodiment tools I can share with you. It's where the insights you've gained so far turn into a structure you can actually live by.

To make it simple for you, I've created a Living Document template in your Undressed Playbook. Go to https://www.gemdentith.com/playbook where you'll find step-by-step guidance and space to create your own document.

This is how your Living Document becomes real. The template is not something you fill out once and file away. It's a living conversation between you and Life Intelligence. And it's the foundation for everything that comes next. I tweak mine monthly or whenever more clarity appears within me. It's the bridge between awakening and alignment, it's the moment your inner truth takes shape as a lived reality.

After you complete this exercise, you'll take action by creating your quarterly seasonal strategy to set clear, actionable intentions so you can start living as your most aligned magnetic self.

Chapter 20:

Aligned Action

Life Intelligence Is Always Talking To You

"Manifestation is not about making things happen. It's about aligning with what is already happening and taking inspired action to bring it into reality."

— Abraham Hicks

In this chapter, we explore the importance of taking courageous, aligned, and inspired action to manifest your life plan. The quote from Abraham Hicks reminds us that your life plan already exists as your original blueprint. You're not creating it from scratch; instead, you're aligning with what already exists, what's already encoded within Life Intelligence, allowing it to naturally come into being. Aligned action is about tuning into universal intelligence, recognizing your purpose, and following the guidance that's presented to you.

In this chapter, you'll learn to align with what already exists within your life blueprint and take inspired, aligned actions from that awareness.

Alignment comes from being in tune with universal life intelligence and truly owning and having certainty that it always knows what's best for you. When you know something as your truth, it takes on a certain je ne sais quoi. Inspiration happens within you when you experience a moment of undeniable clarity (an energy that naturally moves you into action).

Whether you see aligned action as pulling your truth to you or as aligning yourself with it, until what you have written in your living document is fully realized, there is a skill that you will need to acquire, which is to stay anchored in the present while you take action. I call this having present-forward momentum (present enough in reality, and forward-moving enough to co-create your destiny in line with the universe's original plan for you).

In this chapter, I share more personal stories, and we'll explore a few practical techniques to help you take aligned, inspired action and maintain that delicate balance so you continue your journey with grace.

The Power of the Present Moment: The Universe is Always Talking To You

Anchoring into the present moment is not just "new age woo-woo" (it is essential). Being fully present allows you to tap into universal life intelligence, access solutions to your challenges, and align with your original blueprint. Only in the present can you reach your full potential, commune with the universe, and activate that deep wisdom within you. When you are grounded in the now, you open up a well of wisdom and infinite possibilities that guide you forward with clarity. This present awareness enables you to intentionally shape your life with each action and decision.

When you're fully present, aligned with life intelligence, in "present-forward mode", you are engaging with life while staying grounded in the present. On the other hand, the "happiness-whore" state is one in which you're constantly chasing external validation or fulfillment, striving for something outside yourself rather than recognizing what's already available to you now.

Now you see why there is so much emphasis on being present (not as a passive state, but with a bias toward forward movement).

When you stay in a present-forward mode, you're always progressing on a path that aligns with your life's purpose. In contrast, falling back into old patterns and happiness-seeking habits only recreates more of the same past results.

Many people are not anchored in the now (they are so busy that they miss the subtle but powerful things in life, including the people and opportunities life sends their way).

One of the most powerful realizations I've had is that when we are truly present, life is constantly communicating with us. This might be through people, signs, or unexpected events. When you're in a present-forward mode, you're more open to these signals. Let me share a few personal stories that demonstrate how being fully present allowed life intelligence to guide me in unexpected ways.

Personal Stories

1. An Unexpected Gift Through a Friend

One day, I was stuck on a piece of writing for this book. Rather than forcing it, I paused, trusting that something would eventually come to me. Now, often we expect inspiration to come from within, believing we'll be the ones who have the insight or idea. However, when you're present and open, the universe may deliver the answers in unexpected ways.

That's exactly what happened when one of my good friends, someone I usually discuss corporate matters with, sent me an article out of the blue. It was a bit strange because our conversations rarely strayed from work or business topics. Still, I clicked on the link she sent (mostly out of politeness) and read through it. The article mentioned a particular institute, and when I clicked through to their website, I found exactly what I needed to move forward with the section of my book that had been stalling me.

If I had been operating from a place of impatience or preoccupation or if I had been in a rush or forced myself to push through, I might have missed the solution altogether. I would have dismissed the article, thinking I didn't have time to engage with something unrelated. But because I was present and open, I received what I needed from an unexpected source. This moment was a reminder that when we stay open and present, the universe delivers what we need at the right time, often from the most unexpected sources.

2. The Surprise of Small Talk

Another example of how being present allows the life intelligence to guide you happened during a workshop. We were asked to pair up with someone we hadn't spoken to before and engage in some small talk. Now, I'm not one for idle chatter, especially in a forced setting. And to be honest, I had no interest in the person I was partnered with. I assumed we had nothing in common and was already preparing myself to simply go through the motions.

But I chose to be fully present, rather than listen to the judgmental thoughts running through my mind at the time. I listened, I engaged, and to my surprise, the woman I was speaking with shared the exact solution I needed to an issue I had been struggling with in my coaching practice for months. I had hit an impasse and couldn't find a way through it, but here, in the most unexpected moment, she provided the key to unlocking my problem.

The lesson here is that letting go of judgment and being

fully engaged, even in seemingly insignificant situations, can yield key insights and solutions. Being present allows you to receive what you need, even from unlikely places.

Had I stayed in my judgmental mindset, I would have dismissed the conversation before it even began. But by being present, I received the exact information I needed. It was yet another reminder that the universe communicates through people, and everyone we meet may have something to offer us. This taught me the value of staying fully present and open, even in situations that don't seem important at first. And that the universe is always ready to guide us if only we're open to receiving it and (if we're willing to listen).

Because in reality, everyone you interact with is a mirror.

3. The Gym Encounter

As I neared the end of writing this book, I experienced yet another example of the universe communicating through an unlikely source. I was at the gym, where I've been a regular for over a decade. There are people I chat with casually, but I've never really thought too much about them outside of that environment. One day, a man who was using all the weights I needed caught my attention. I politely asked him if he was going to be much longer, and to my surprise, he was incredibly helpful, even going out of his way to find a bar for me.

We struck up a conversation, and I casually mentioned that I'd been busy writing. It turned out he was working on a presentation on change management in his business, and he had recently been on a personal transformation journey, including losing weight and spending time at a Buddhist monastery. As we talked, I realized that his journey mirrored much of what I had been writing about in my book. It was as if the universe had orchestrated this encounter to show me that the ideas I was sharing were resonating with people in real life.

By the end of our conversation, he was interested in buying my book and continuing his personal transformation. If I had dismissed him based on my initial assumptions, I would have missed out on this profound connection. Again, the universe was communicating through a simple encounter, reminding me that we are all connected and that every interaction has the potential for growth and learning.

These experiences have taught me the value of being present and open to the universe's guidance. When you live in a present-forward mode, you stop missing the signals life constantly offers. You begin to see that every person, every encounter, every moment holds something valuable (if only you stay present and receptive). Everyone is in your life for a reason, and when you stop judging or shutting yourself off, you open yourself up to the infinite ways the universe is communicating with you.

So, next time you find yourself frustrated or stuck, remember that the answers may not always come from you. They may come from someone you least expect, from a conversation, a stranger, or a sign. Stay present, stay open, and let the universe speak.

Expanding the Present Moment

Even small changes every day can have a compounding effect. Have you ever felt time open up? This sense of spaciousness enables you to respond thoughtfully, generate fresh ideas, and deeply experience joy and connection.

Let me illustrate this with a personal story.

Personal Story

Seeing Through the Eyes of the Divine: A Story of Conflict and Connection

During my eldest daughter's tricky teenage years, our family home often felt like a war zone. The atmosphere was tense, the kind of environment many families with teenagers can relate to. My daughter was exhibiting typical hormonal teenage behavior. She wasn't doing anything extreme like drinking or taking drugs, but the emotional charge in the house was palpable. My husband at the time, her stepfather, was very much driven by his survival self. He tried to parent by control, believing he could resolve her rebelliousness by enforcing rules, which only led to more friction.

This home conflict happened just before COVID hit, so it was already a period of upheaval for everyone. And the emotional conflict between her and my husband escalated. Every disagreement felt like a battle, and my role as mother became the protector and mediator.

So how did I handle it? This is where seeing through the eyes of pure loving awareness made all the difference.

Rather than engaging in the emotional wrestling match that was playing out before me (becoming enmeshed in the arguments or adding to the tension). I chose a different approach. When tension played out, instead of reacting or trying to wrestle mentally or emotionally, I decided to simply observe. By choosing to observe, I detached myself from others' heightened emotions in the moment. This gave me the mental and emotional clarity I needed to remain grounded and anchored in the present.

Seeing through the eyes of Pure Awareness is not about physical detachment but rather about creating a mental space (a gap between the situation and my own reactions), allowing me to connect to more of the qualities I needed to respond to the situation. In those moments of clarity, I wasn't thinking about myself. Instead, I was fully focused on my daughter, seeing her as more than just a hormonal teenager but as someone struggling with emotions and changes she couldn't yet comprehend.

Through this lens, I was able to understand at a heart level and with deep intuition what was needed. It wasn't to create more conflict or attempts to control her behavior. The solution, in that moment, was simple: let her be. Let the situation settle. And then, I would go to her, hug her, and tell her that she was safe, that she was loved. I reassured her that the confusion and changes she was feeling were part of growing up, but that no matter what, she was safe.

This hug, this moment of deep connection, would bring her back online, so to speak. The tension would dissolve, and she would feel a sense of safety, knowing at least one person in the house had her back. She was still a child, after all, and we, as the adults, had to be the ones to lead with calmness and compassion.

What I learned from seeing Sienna through pure awareness eyes was the gift of deep listening (truly seeing my daughter in that moment). This perspective allowed me to understand what she needed without forcing my own emotions into the situation. Each time it may be different, but that is the beauty of this way of seeing.

Anchor Before you Serve

I have "serve the moment" tattooed on my thigh as a reminder to be fully engaged and anchored in whatever activity I am performing in that moment.

This means giving the person or the activity my full attention.

By living authentically in the now, you become a conscious co-creator of your reality, shaping your experiences with clarity, intention, and purpose. You embody the essence of your true nature, radiating a sense of peace, joy, and fulfillment that inspires and uplifts both yourself and those around you.

My invitation to you is to embrace the power of the moment as you continue your journey towards living truly aligned and authentically, and let the moment of now be the foundation for how you show up and respond to what life is presenting to you.

Presence exercises

One of the most powerful shifts you can make at this stage is learning how to anchor yourself in the present moment. Because truth only lives here (in the now).

For me, presence is the bridge between awakening and embodiment. It's not enough to "get" an insight. You have to practice staying awake to it in real time. Otherwise, the old self slips the clothes back on without you even noticing.

I use two anchors more than any others: deep belly breathing and anchoring questions. Both are simple, but potent.

Deep belly breathing brings you out of your head and into your body. It shifts your nervous system, grounds you in the moment, and reopens the gate to life intelligence and your true self.

Anchoring questions are like truth tests. They help you pause before acting and ask: Which self is running this show (the old survival self, or the true self aligned with essence)?

These two practices have become my stabilizers. They keep me from spinning back into performance or distraction, and they help me live more of what I've remembered.

I've written out the full step-by-step instructions for both of these exercises in your Undressed Playbook, along with other presence practices you can experiment with (including "Presence in Action," which helps you carry presence into the most ordinary moments of daily life). Go to: https://www.gemdentith.com/playbook

For now, what matters is that you know: presence isn't abstract. It can be practiced. It can be anchored. And the more you do, the more natural it becomes to live from the truth of who you are.

By bringing mindfulness into your daily activities, you infuse each moment with purpose, presence, and authenticity. You become a conscious co-creator of your reality, shaping your experiences with clarity and intention. As you become more present, you naturally open yourself up to opportunities and support from the universe. This state of alignment allows you to move beyond passive living and into a space of Divine, Aligned Co-Creation, where your thoughts, emotions, and energy align with the flow of the universe's life intelligence, attracting what is in harmony with your true self.

Divine, Aligned Co-Creation

You are always creating and manifesting, whether consciously or unconsciously. Whatever you think about most of the time often manifests in your life, following the natural flow of cause and effect. You think it, feel it, generate energy around it, and act on it. Whether you create chaos or a masterpiece, your inner reality acts like a magnet, attracting what aligns with your energy.

Divine, Aligned Co-Creation is different (it is the process of aligning with universal energies and realizing that you are a vessel for divine life intelligence to express itself through you, manifesting in the physical realm). By connecting to the divine within and surrendering to its subtle guidance, you open yourself to infinite possibilities. This process goes beyond personal will and taps into the universal flow of creation, allowing miracles and synchronicities to unfold. It is a dance between your intentions, life intelligence, and the greater unfolding of your true self. Through Divine, Aligned Co-Creation, you can align your desires with the highest good and experience the magic of co-creating a reality that reflects your true self's purpose.

As you embark on the journey of co-creating your life with life intelligence awareness, here are some reminders to assist you along the way:

As you set out on the journey of co-creating your life with life intelligence, there are some useful reminders that will assist you along the way:

You Co-create with Universal Energies

As you immerse yourself in the process of manifesting your goals and intentions, it is crucial to acknowledge that the manifestation is not solely dependent on your personal energy. Instead, your body and mind act as channels through which divine energies flow. When you align heightened emotions with the things you desire, the universal energies work in harmony with you, allowing your plans to materialize faster. By releasing your fictitious personality and surrendering to the co-creative process with the universe, you invite the possibility of profound and transformative manifestations.

Be a Magnet for Success

To attract success and abundance into your life, it is essential to cultivate a state of being that magnetizes positive outcomes. This means keeping your egoic Happiness Whore desires in check while you observe the natural flow of the universe. Instead of forcefully pushing for what you want, allow yourself to be in a state of receptive flow, aligning your thoughts, emotions, and actions with the desired manifestations of your true self. In this state, you become a powerful force, like a magnet, pulling things toward you that are in alignment with your highest good while naturally repelling what is not meant for you.

Finding the Balance: Push vs Pull

Divine, aligned co-creation is a balance between taking inspired action and surrendering to the flow of the universe. It's about finding that delicate line between effort and ease. While it is important to take proactive steps towards the goals you set, it is equally vital to trust the process and surrender the outcome to the higher intelligence at work. What is even more important is that you stay anchored and grounded in presence, even if you cannot quite see the fruits of your efforts. Remember, a rose seed germinates in the soil for approximately six weeks before you start to see the emergence of the seedling and its leaves. Therefore, surrendering to the process is just as important as the daily action you take.

Become a Magnet and a Container for Your True Desires

To manifest your deepest, most authentic desires, it is crucial to not only be in alignment with your true nature but also to be in alignment with what you wish to attract. This requires clarity of intention, the ability to receive and hold the energy of what you desire, and alignment with the frequency of those desires.

Being a magnet for your desires means cultivating the energy, emotions, and mindset that draw your desires toward you effortlessly. But attracting them is only half of the equation. To truly manifest what you want, you must also become a container (a vessel capable of holding and nurturing the energy of those desires once they arrive). This means expanding your capacity to receive, grow, and sustain the abundance, love, success, or other desires that you are calling in.

Often, we attract what we are energetically aligned with, but if we haven't prepared ourselves to hold onto or manage those manifestations, they can slip away or create imbalance. For example, you may attract new opportunities or relationships, but without the internal structure and emotional resilience to support them, they may not be sustainable. This is where the container aspect comes in (you must expand your inner capacity to hold, nurture, and grow the manifestations that enter your life).

By aligning with your true self, serving the present moment as conscious awareness, and embodying the qualities and values of what you wish to manifest, you become a powerful attractor for the life you envision. But equally important, by cultivating emotional resilience, self-awareness, and inner strength, you can hold, sustain, and amplify the energy of those manifestations, ensuring they fully integrate into your life.

Being both the magnet and the container is a dynamic process (it's about constantly expanding your capacity for abundance and fulfillment, while staying grounded in your true self). As you align with your highest purpose, the universe flows through you, allowing you to not only attract your real, innate desires but also sustain them as they flourish in your life.

The Importance of Focus

Focused intention and attention are such critical practices or ways of being. Focus is not just a tool for productivity (it's a powerful practice for aligning with your highest timeline and living an authentic life).

If there's one thing that will deter you from realizing your original blueprint, it's distractions. Distractions are your number one enemy on the path to living authentically and in alignment with your higher self. What are distractions? They're everything that's fighting for your attention (whether it's the constant pings and notifications on your phone, the stream of social media, or the background noise of modern-day life).

Distractions pull you away from your highest timeline, your true path. Think of distractions as toxins for the mind, blocking your ability to remain aligned. There's a great saying: Where your attention goes, your energy flows. This couldn't be more accurate. If you're constantly giving your attention to low-vibrational distractions, your energy will naturally be pulled away from your highest potential.

Focus is about choosing to engage with what truly supports your evolution, allowing you to stay connected to your authentic self. It's about tuning out the distractions and tuning into your purpose.

Staying on Your Highest Timeline

We've touched on the concept of timelines earlier. Imagine that every decision you make, every moment of focus or distraction, nudges you towards or away from a different version of your life.

I was sitting with my eighteen-year-old daughter just before she left home for university, and we were discussing the meaning of timelines. What she said was so profound that I've included her quote here:

"Mum, there are countless timelines, countless potential paths, and with each choice, you either move closer to actualizing your highest self or you step back toward an old path. The more you stay

on your highest timeline, the more you become your highest self."

— Sienna Skye Osman

Well, from this wise eighteen-year-old, I learned something I hadn't fully grasped until my thirties: the significance of your highest timeline. It was one of those moments where I became the student and she became the teacher.

To further elaborate, by staying focused, you remain aligned with your highest timeline (the one that aligns with your true potential, your original blueprint). But when distractions consume your time and energy, you risk branching off into lower timelines, where your growth and evolution are stunted, and where you fall back into old habits and patterns.

Your highest timeline represents your fully actualized self (the version of you that is living in alignment with your life purpose). To stay on this path, you must prioritize focus and discipline, keeping distractions at bay. When you are aligned with this timeline, everything flows (opportunities, relationships, and synchronicities all seem to fall into place). But the moment you allow distractions to dominate, you risk branching off into a lower timeline that pulls you further from your true self.

Go on a Detox from Distractions

One of the best ways to maintain focus and stay on your highest timeline is to go on a detox from distractions. I'm not just talking about detoxing from social media or cutting out Netflix binges (though that's a great place to start). I'm talking about eliminating anything that takes you away from your truth (whether it's negative people, endless news cycles, or internal mental chatter that keeps you stuck in self-doubt).

When I experienced my first spiritual awakening, one of the first things I did was stop consuming the news and media.

At the time, I had been working as a consultant for the UK Cabinet Office and a global media organization, yet the constant news stories and political noise no longer interested me. I was seeking clarity and truth, and all those distractions felt like static. I didn't want to fill my mind with other people's agendas or societal noise. I wanted to tune into my own truth.

This is what I encourage you to do as well. Look at your life and ask yourself: Where am I being distracted? It could be by social media, negative relationships, or even your own mental patterns. Begin to disconnect from the noise and reconnect with your inner guidance.

Time is Precious

Now, if you're struggling to stay focused, allow me to give you some tough love. Consider this: How many weeks do you have left on this planet? If you're forty-two years old, like me at the time of writing this, and the average life expectancy is around eighty years, that means I have roughly thirty-eight years left. That's just under two thousand weeks!

Calculating how many weeks you may have left is a sobering yet powerful reminder that time is finite. When you break it down into weeks, it becomes startlingly clear just how precious each moment is. It's a call to use your time wisely, to focus on what truly matters, and to align yourself with your highest timeline so you can live a life of purpose, authenticity, and fulfillment. Time is slipping by whether we acknowledge it or not, and the choice to stay focused or get distracted will determine the trajectory of your journey.

Each week, each day, each moment, is an opportunity to stay aligned with your highest timeline. When you waste time on distractions, you're not just wasting time (you're stepping away from the version of you that is fully realized, aligned, and in tune with your divine purpose).

My Final Thoughts on Staying Focused

Every decision you make either moves you closer to or further from your true self. By staying focused, you ensure that you remain on the timeline that reflects your highest potential. The more distractions you eliminate, the more clarity you'll have to follow the path that is meant for you.

Remember: staying on your highest timeline isn't just about what you do; it's about what you don't do. It's about the boundaries you set, the distractions you cut, and the attention you give to what really matters.

Final Thoughts: Taking Inspired Action Now

Aligned action is about stepping into your anatomical destiny with confidence and trust. By combining deep presence, intentional steps, and inspired action, you can manifest your authentic life.

Whether through deep belly breathing, anchoring questions, or mindful actions, the tools in this chapter help you stay grounded as you move forward. As you practice these techniques, they become second nature, guiding you to live fully in alignment with your original life plan.

The Time Is Now!

If there's one core lesson from this book, it's this: you cannot manage time, but you can manage what actions you fill your present moment with. Time will continue passing whether you choose to engage with it fully or not. Many people try to control time, but it's simply a series of "nows." Picture time as a string of moments, each representing a present "now." These moments link together, forming the timeline we experience as life.

When you delay action, you're postponing it to a future "now" that hasn't yet arrived. But when that moment comes, you might not feel ready, and you'll push it off again. The truth is, the future is nothing more than a series of present moments. There is no separate "future" (just actions you defer to later). So ask yourself: If you don't act now, when will you?

Whatever you've been postponing, this message is for you. What is the first small step you can take today to align yourself more closely with your purpose?

Take that step now, with love, with intention, and with trust in your ability to create the life you desire. Remember, the power to shape your future lies in what you choose to do in this very moment. Now is the time to act.

Essential Insights

Chapter 20, Aligned Action, focused on the importance of aligning with universal energy and taking inspired, intentional steps toward your life's purpose. The concept of aligned action is introduced: you don't force outcomes; instead, move with the natural flow of the universal life intelligence. This chapter emphasizes that your life blueprint already exists (your task is to align with it and take actions that resonate deeply with your life purpose).

Aligned action comes from tuning into the present moment and tapping into universal intelligence. When you are truly aligned, you begin to recognize opportunities that were always present, but previously unseen. This state of being fully present, described as present-forward momentum, allows you to act in the moment while remaining open to the future unfolding naturally. The key takeaway is that when you act from a place of alignment, everything flows with more ease, and the energy of the universe supports your every step.

Journal Prompts

- How often do I feel truly aligned with my actions? Reflect on the times when your actions flowed naturally, and you felt connected to a deeper purpose.

- What daily practices help me tune into universal intelligence and stay present? Consider what activities or habits bring you into alignment and how you can integrate them more consistently.

- How can I embrace "present-forward momentum" in my life right now? Think about how you can balance being present with taking action that is aligned with your future goals.

Action Plan

Anchor in the Present: Spend a few minutes each day practicing stillness and mindfulness. Use this time to tune into your breath and the present moment, allowing universal intelligence to guide you.

Take Inspired Action: Once aligned, choose one small action that feels inspired and aligned with your higher purpose. Trust that even small steps can lead to significant changes when you act from a place of true presence.

Stay Open to Universal Guidance: Be conscious of the subtle signs, synchronicities, or inspirations that come your way. Stay flexible and let the universe guide you, rather than trying to control every detail.

Chapter 21:

Living Undressed

Untouched. Turned on. Undeniably real.

There comes a moment when the cage that you once thought you were in breaks open. Not because you forced it open, but because you finally realized it was never locked.

The life intelligence that moves you was never created to keep you on the sidelines of life. It was meant to move through you and walk with you quietly as you step fully back in.

Living undressed is what happens when you stop standing at the edge, observing and hesitating, and instead fully and unapologetically collapse into the stream of your own life. It is the point at which life intelligence relaxes into the background and you give yourself permission to laugh again, to love again, to play again, to live again.

This is where clarity and aliveness meet. It is where wisdom and wildness join hands. The highest form of spirituality is not detachment from life. It is engagement with it. You are life, now live it.

What Living Undressed Looks Like

Living undressed is about presence that does not need proof.

When you live undressed, you walk into the room as you are, and that is enough. Your truth becomes visible without explanation.

It is about standing in your wholeness and loving all parts of you because you are sacred. It is about the quiet strength of knowing you belong because you are made from life intelligence.

Living undressed looks like unforced laughter. It looks like comfortable silence rather than awkward. It looks like loving fully without bargaining for safety. It looks like moving through life with a steadiness that comes from the inside rather than from approval outside.

To live undressed is to embody the freedom you once thought you had to chase. It is to carry the stillness of presence and the aliveness of engagement together in the same breath. It is to live awake and alive at once.

Relationships Reclaimed

One of the first places you feel the shift into living undressed is in your relationships. When you are caught in the observer trap, people sense the distance. Your children feel you are distracted. Your partner feels you are half-present. Friends notice that something is missing in your energy, even if they cannot name it. You are in the room, but not entirely with them.

Living undressed restores that missing presence. When you return to life as both awake and alive, the people you love feel the difference immediately. Children who once pulled at your sleeve for attention suddenly receive the full weight of your gaze, and with it, the reassurance that you are here. Partners who once felt you hovering on the edge of intimacy now feel you drop fully into connection. Friends who had grown used to the version of you that was always analyzing now rediscover your warmth and playfulness.

To live undressed in a relationship is not about showing up as the perfect parent, partner, or friend. It is about showing up whole and alive. It is the willingness to be seen in your truth, even when that truth is messy or imperfect. It is the courage to laugh, to cry, to love, and to be vulnerable without needing to control how you are perceived.

When you stop hiding behind the observer and allow yourself to collapse back into presence, relationships are no longer performances. They become living, breathing exchanges of truth. You do not just offer wisdom or guidance. You offer yourself. And that offering is what rekindles intimacy.

Health and Vitality

Living undressed also transforms the way you relate to your body. For much of life, health is treated as a problem to fix or a system to control. You force your body to perform, you punish it when it does not, and you measure it against standards that were never yours to begin with. In survival mode, the body becomes a machine you drive until it breaks down.

When you begin to live undressed, that relationship changes. Your body is no longer a burden or a battlefield. It becomes a sacred vessel. You start treating it not as an enemy to discipline but as an ally to listen to. Instead of pushing through exhaustion, you rest. Instead of numbing your stress with habits that deplete you, you choose what nourishes you. Food becomes fuel and pleasure rather than a source of guilt. Movement becomes joy rather than punishment.

Health, in this way, is no longer about control. It is about congruence. It is about letting the way you care for your body reflect the truth you have remembered inside. When you stop performing for approval, you stop performing with your health as well. You no longer chase quick fixes or punish yourself for imperfection. You live in a way that sustains you, not drains you.

The irony is that when you stop forcing health from fear, vitality begins to return on its own. Energy rises not because you pushed harder, but because you became aligned. Sleep deepens because your mind is not at war with itself. Your immune system strengthens because your body is not constantly bracing against stress. Wholeness is not something you achieve. It is the natural state that emerges when you live congruently.

To live undressed in health is to honor your body as the ground of your presence. It is important to remember that you cannot embody your truth if you are disconnected from the vessel that carries it. Health is not separate from spirituality. It is spirituality made physical. When you live in alignment with life intelligence, your vitality becomes the evidence of your embodiment.

Work and Contribution

Living undressed also reshapes how you show up in your work and contribution. In the survival self, work often becomes performance. You strive to achieve, to prove, to climb higher in order to feel enough. Even when success comes, it rarely brings the peace you were chasing. The cost is often exhaustion, disconnection, or a constant sense that you must do more to justify your place.

When you begin to live undressed, the performance drops away. Work is no longer about proving your value. It becomes the channel through which your truth and your presence are expressed. You do not enter a meeting to impress. You enter it to contribute. You do not build a business to prove you are capable. You build it as an extension of your purpose. Success is no longer measured only in money or recognition, but in congruence.

Living undressed at work means you bring your whole self to the table. You speak when truth calls you to speak, not because you are performing for approval. You listen deeply rather than calculating your next move. You no longer hide behind strategies alone. Your energy and presence become part of your professional currency. People remember not just what you said but how they felt in your presence.

Contribution, in this sense, expands beyond career. It is the way you move through the world. Every action becomes an offering. Every conversation becomes an exchange of truth. The legacy you leave is not only in what you build, but in the alignment you embodied while building it.

To live undressed in your work is to serve from authenticity. It is to let your purpose flow through the roles you play without becoming trapped in them. It is to let your contribution arise not from striving but from alignment. And when that happens, you discover that the most powerful work is not what you achieve, but who you become in the process.

Everyday Embodiment

Living undressed is not only revealed in big choices or dramatic transformations. It is woven into the ordinary rhythms of daily life. The test of alignment is not how awakened you feel in meditation or how inspired you sound on stage. The test is how congruent you feel in the quiet spaces no one else sees.

Everyday embodiment looks like waking up without immediately rushing into performance mode. It is taking a breath before you check your phone, and choosing to ground yourself before the world makes its demands on you. It is preparing food not as a task to be rushed through, but as an act of nourishment and care. It is walking outside and noticing the color of the sky, the sound of birdsong, and the feel of the ground beneath your feet.

Living undressed in the everyday means you allow presence to infuse the small moments. You listen attentively when your child tells you about their day. You feel the warmth of your partner's hand without needing to analyze it. You savor the first sip of your morning tea as though it were a gift. These may sound like simple acts, but they are evidence of embodiment. They are the places where truth shows itself in form.

Congruence is not measured in your grand visions or long-term strategies. It is measured in how you move through your days. Do your choices honor your body? Do your words match your heart? Do your actions reflect the truth you have remembered? When the answer is yes, even the most ordinary moment becomes sacred.

To live undressed is to stop waiting for life to begin and to recognize that life is always here, in this breath, in this step, in this very moment. Every day is no longer background noise. It becomes the ground where alignment takes root and grows.

The Call to the Reader

You have walked the path of this book. You have undressed the layers that once defined you. You have awakened to the truth of who you are beneath them. And now, you are invited to live in alignment (not as a concept or theory, but as a daily reality).

Living undressed is not about becoming someone new. It is about allowing yourself to be fully who you are. It is about letting the truth you have remembered move into every part of your life: your health, your work, your relationships, your purpose, and the way you inhabit the ordinary moments of your day.

The real transformation does not happen in these pages. It happens when you close this book and step back into your world. It happens in the way you choose to speak with the people you love, the way you care for your body, the way you show up to your work, and the way you honor the whispers of the intelligence of life that wants to live through you. The journey is not abstract. It is lived.

Do not wait for the perfect conditions. Do not wait to feel ready. Begin where you are. Choose one place in your life to live undressed today, and let it expand from there. Congruence is built moment by moment, choice by choice. Each step you take in truth plants a seed that grows into a life that matches your soul.

A Closing Declaration to Self

I will carry truth like perfume into every room I enter.

I will sustain my alignment, letting my body be my guide, my breath my anchor, my presence my power.

I will let my work shine with authenticity, never performance.

I will give my relationships the rare gift of my naked, undivided attention.

I will make the ordinary moments (the coffee, the laughter, the quiet, the sex) fully embodied experiences.

And above all, I will never again forget the original shine of who I am beneath the layers.

I will live awake.

I will live alive.

I will live utterly, deliciously, unapologetically undressed.

Chapter 22:
2:50 A.M.

The moment you were born. The moment you remembered.

It's 2:50 a.m. again. But this time the cries are not from a delivery ward. They're quieter, deeper, the sound of your soul exhaling. No swaddle, no blankets, no bright hospital lights.

You've just stepped out of one of those nights that live in your cells forever (a themed A-Fest party in Ibiza, drenched in music, movement, and Tantra-soaked sensuality). Hours of dancing, bodies painted, hearts unarmored, souls turned inside out. And then, when the music finally faded, we walked together toward the sea. Bare feet on warm stone. Salt air on our skin. Stars scattered like a thousand eyes watching us remember who we are.

We stood there in the hush after the ecstasy, looking out over the water, looking up at the endless dark sky, and I felt it (that quiet, holy fuck realization). Lucky. Alive. Completely at home within myself.

This is not the rebirth that comes in sterile sheets. This is the rebirth that comes from living so fully you almost can't hold it. Dancing until your legs ache. Laughing until you cry. Spilling truths and spilling everything you once thought kept you safe. And then collapsing into the kind of stillness that strips you all the way back to the original.

This is what it means to live. Fully undressed. Naked. In your power. In your safety. In your worth.

You're not home to a shinier, polished version of yourself to impress the world. You're home to the raw, the real, the one who was always underneath.

And it's 2:50 a.m. again. As an adult, this is the ultimate mirror moment, the place where your nervous system finally exhales, because life is so imperfectly perfect.

What began in that hospital room, wrapped in newness and awe, has led you here. Not an arrival in achievement, but an arrival in truth. Not becoming someone new, but remembering the self that was always waiting. Somebody true.

And maybe you were right all along. Maybe the greatest love story of your life isn't about someone else or something else at all. Maybe it was always about meeting the one, your deepest nature.

And it all began here, when you finally undressed. This journey has been a striptease. Not for the world. Not for a lover. But for your soul.

It's 2:50 a.m. again. And this time, you're awake. You're alive. You're living undressed.

Undressed Summary

You have been reading "Undressed", a book about liberating yourself from the Happiness Whore habit. It has been a journey to the center of your being to discover your true, authentic, unapologetic, sensual, most powerful self, while shedding the layer of your old fictitious personality. Essentially, it has been a book about awakening. Awakening to your true essential self and realizing the nature of your true divine essence. Not everyone has the opportunity to awaken in this lifetime. Many people do not even know what it means to truly awaken to their true self, but you have taken this courageous journey, and for that, you should be proud. Liberating yourself from the Happiness Whore habit and embracing your sensual inner self is a powerful act of self-love and self-empowerment.

As you move forward on your path, remember that the journey of self-discovery is ongoing. Embrace each moment with an open heart and a curious mind. Keep shedding the layers that no longer serve you, and welcome the blossoming of your true, authentic self.

And if you feel called to take your journey even deeper, join us for The Undressed Experience, a three-day immersion into your naked truth, your inner power, and your deepest purpose. Go to www.gemdentith.com to discover live events and retreats.

For now, may you continue to shine brightly as the divine essence that you are, and may your journey be filled with love, joy, and profound self-realization. You have all the tools and wisdom within you to navigate this beautiful journey of awakening.

Thank you for walking this path, for daring to undress what was never truly you. The world needs more awakened souls like you.

With love, always undressing alongside you,

Gem

Gem Dentith Aka Retired Happiness Whore

Share Your Story & Inspire Others!

As you step into a higher level of being, you'll begin to notice something incredible (the patterns in others' lives, the ways they unknowingly create chaos or cling to old fears, outdated beliefs, and attachments).

You'll see how people hold on to false identities, stuck in facades that no longer serve them. It can be tempting to help them see what you've discovered on your journey to awakening, right?

When you first reconnect with your authentic self, it feels like you've uncovered a hidden treasure. The transformation is so powerful, you'll want to shout it from the rooftops and share it with everyone you know! But here's the thing: while your heart is in the right place, it's essential to remember that everyone's path is unique, and they'll awaken at their own pace.

Instead of pushing your insights onto others, let them be drawn to the changes they see in you. When they notice your newfound peace, joy, and unshakable inner strength, they'll naturally want to know what's behind your transformation. That's your moment to share your story (not with pressure or judgment) but from a place of authenticity. Remember, real transformation is magnetic when it's lived and not forced!

From my own journey, I've learned that everyone is doing the best they can with the awareness they have. When you embrace this, it brings deep compassion, patience, and freedom. You no longer feel the need to change others (you simply radiate the authentic self you've uncovered, and others will be drawn to your light when they're ready). I love hearing stories of personal transformation and growth! If you'd like to share yours, please get in touch via DM https://www.instagram.com/iamgemdentith/. I can't wait to hear your story!

Join a Like-Minded Tribe

One of the most exciting parts of your journey is finding a community of people who are on the same path. Imagine surrounding yourself with others who get it, who understand your experiences, and support your transformation. It's a powerful thing to be seen, heard, and celebrated for the growth you're going through!

Inspire others simply by being yourself (let them be curious about your change instead of trying to force your story on them, like the time your mum tried to make you eat cold, cooked carrots). We've all been there, right? She had the best intentions, but we've learned there's a better way to share the good stuff!

That's why I hold space for an incredible community. If you're looking for a deeper connection, you don't have to go it alone. We're all walking this path together, and we'd love to have you join us!

Retreats

If you're ready to take your growth to the next level, I also offer immersive retreat experiences that are designed to supercharge your connection to yourself and others. Think of it as a deep dive into your inner world, surrounded by supportive, like-minded people!

Retreats provide a unique opportunity to deepen your connection with the process and immerse yourself in a like-minded community. Being part of a loving community that supports and uplifts one another is essential for your personal growth. The magic of being seen, heard, held, and supported by others can be truly transformative.

In the book "Undressed," you have learned to liberate yourself from the Happiness Whore habit and embrace your true self. If you have enjoyed this journey, consider taking it further by attending one of our retreats. Visit www.gemdentith.com to discover the latest retreats.

About the Author

Hello, my name is Gem Dentith. I was the ultimate Happiness Whore, the ultimate desire seeker, and overachiever. My journey on this quest for unconditional happiness started as a result of trying to heal a broken head following a teen eating disorder.

I was only fourteen when I first started to question things, when my rosy childlike glasses started to crack, and when I first realized that life wasn't as it was painted out in the movies. As a child, I was the go-getter, the happy-go-lucky child, always smiling, always shining, singing, and dancing. It wasn't until I developed my overthinking habit at age fourteen that the feelings I felt in my body changed from feelings of love and connection to feelings of separation and desperation. By the time I was thirty-two, I'd tried out about twenty different careers (and partners, if I'm honest!). I moved around a lot, and in the end, I started working as a consultant managing change, because I thought it was a sign that I was particularly good at it. I was forever chasing happiness, and in the pursuit of it, I'd gained quite a lot of worldly experience and career successes. See formal bio for corporate success: https://www.linkedin.com/in/gemmadentith.

The search for happiness through achievement and others continued until the day I blacked out on a train while carrying my six-month, unborn child. It was also the day before my thirty-second birthday. Neither age nor the fact that I was pregnant slowed me down. This was five years ago. It was the turning point from the external quest to an internal one.

However, the Happiness Whore habit didn't subside just because my drive was internal. Two years from my first realization, then thirty-four, the search was greater. It just looked different from the outside because now I was also a qualified executive and personal coach and a yoga teacher. And once again, I was doing all the right things. Every morning, I would get up, meditate, practice my yoga, journal, and then do my daily visualizations and affirmations. Throughout the day, I would read spiritual texts, and once or twice a week, I would have a call with the coach, but again, I was slowly burning out. I was exhausted by all this personal development activity. I didn't see it at the time, but it was still survival self-desire for spiritual attainment; it was just disguised. I was still attributing my happiness to a future destination, to a practice, and to a guru. So I gave in to the universe. I stopped doing everything. I packed away my books and audio devices and unsubscribed from all my daily newsletters. I surrendered.

One day, as I was just going about my life, I found myself in a busy cocktail bar in St Albans, celebrating a girlfriend's birthday. We were just sitting around the table, and one of the louder girls who was at our party waved a couple of guys over to join the party of women. One of them squeezed in between me and another girl, facing the birthday girl. We did the pleasantries and said hello. I said my name, and then he asked what I did for a living. For a moment, I paused, wondering what to say as I'd just packed away all my coaching and personal development things and was feeling a little bit uncomfortable about having to lie about loving what I did, especially if he then asked how much of it I actually practice myself. I thought to myself, I just need to be honest, so then, above the loud music in the bar, I blurted out, 'I'm a performance coach using a scientific brain-based neuroscience approach to create change, and I teach yoga and also work for the government in a change program. However, I'm not satisfied with how I'm coaching people as I'm feeling a little exhausted by all the things I need to do in a day to feel okay.' Going on to say, 'It takes me two hours in the morning and an hour in the evening to maintain a good state of mental health, but it's not sustainable, so I don't know what I will be doing in the near future.' Anyway, this chap's jaw dropped, and then he asked if I'd ever come across an understanding called the Three Principles discovered by Sydney Banks. At this point, I thought this guy, whose name is Alex (and is happy to mention our story), was either a little bit intoxicated or a little bit simple. As it turns out, he was and still is a very successful entrepreneur in London. Who has since bought the bar where we first had this conversation.

This little nudge from the universe has since turned my world inside out. Now I have new eyes in which to see the foundations of our human and spiritual existence. With success, I use this understanding to coach senior leaders, entrepreneurs, women, and children, and show up like a beacon of light wherever I go. This new connection to life intelligence, or universal sacred-self or inner-self, as I call it, has become my new guidance system. It has different rules from the ones I habitually grew up with, so it's been a process of readjustment. In doing so, I've learnt some basic, fundamental principles that keep me aligned, connected, and operating from a place of love rather than survival self.

undressed

This is the work that makes it all work but it must be embodied. Scan the QR code and download the companion Playbook & guided meditations for free.

Printed in Poland
by Amazon Fulfillment
Poland Sp. z o.o., Wrocław
13 January 2026

dead3f03-5a90-4050-8086-67ca0e552faeR01